Contents

Illustrations

About the Author

Col Mike Worden

Prior to his assignment as director of the chief of staff's staff group at Headquarters United States Air Force in April 1997, Col R. Michael Worden was commander of the 354th Operations Group at Eielson Air Force Base (AFB), Alaska. The 354th Group oversees a squadron of night vision goggle-equipped A/OA-10s, and a squadron of LANTIRN-equipped F-16s and Pacific Air Forces Cope Thunder large forces employment exercises. This squadron provides air forces trained and equipped for close air support, air interdiction, and offensive counterair.

Colonel Worden is a distinguished graduate of the United States Air Force Academy, Colorado Springs, Colorado, receiving a bachelor's degree there in 1976. He was also named an outstanding graduate after completing pilot training at Reese AFB, Texas, in 1977. Colonel Worden graduated from the Squadron Officer School, Maxwell AFB, Alabama, in 1983 and Maxwell's Air Command and Staff College in 1988. Duke University conferred upon him a master's degree in military history in 1986 and a doctor of philosophy degree in the same area in 1993. Earlier, in 1991, he participated in Operations Desert Storm and Provide Comfort, the allied effort to establish no-fly zones over Kurdish refugees in Northern Iraq.

He is married to the former Lori E. Dickinson of Bellevue, Washington. They have three daughters, Erin, Leslie, and Renee.

Preface

If many people understand the services and why they behave the way they do, then the collective institutional behavior will change if only to preserve self esteem. Pretensions or facades, once pierced and widely discussed, are likely to be dropped. Foibles or follies, once discovered and publicly analyzed, are likely to be avoided.

—Military analyst Carl H. Builder
The Masks of War

Numerous studies have focused on American airpower, particularly since it became a dominant force in modern warfare. Yet, only a handful of these studies have offered a critical evaluation of air leadership, and even fewer have shown a concern for the institutional dynamics that shape air leadership. Therefore, at least one study needs to ask, "Who are the air leaders and where have they come from?"

This analysis focuses on the career specialty of Air Force general officers who served between 1953 and 1973. It indicates the clear dominance by rated or flying officers (mainly pilots and a few navigators) within Air Force leadership.

The issue here is not whether pilots should dominate the Air Force—the fact is they do. Rather, a more interesting phenomenon is that persons who sit on top of the world's most powerful air force are almost exclusively fighter pilots; yet, their institution and its doctrine were created before World War II by bomber pilots.

This reality has caused some recent concern within the Air Force. Many nonfighter pilots seem concerned about their prospects for success within the institution. In August 1991 a popular underground "brown paper," titled "TAC-umcizing the Air Force: The Emerging Vision of the Future," was circulated around the air staff and the Air Force.[1] This satirical essay about the dominant fighter culture concluded that "first, manly men [fighter pilots] must dominate Headquarters USAF.

Second, they must command all Air Force major commands. Last, USAF must have a wing structure [favoring fighter units] which will grow and nurture the future leaders of the Air Force." The brown paper's popularity sparked a sequel by the same anonymous author in August 1992, titled "ACC [Air Combat Command] Back to the Future: The Second Coming of the Manly Man."[2] In sum, the literature in Air Force newspapers and journals indicates this cultural issue still concerns many within the institution.[3]

In this study I describe when, how, and why this remarkable shift in leadership from bomber generals to fighter generals occurred. In that sense, the study is also a brief history of Air Force thinking. It provides the first detailed evaluation of rival groups as they cope with change and vie for influence within institutions like the Air Force. The methodology and message used in this study enhance our appreciation of today's Air Force and have major implications for understanding leadership and change in other organizations.

I address both internal institutional dynamics and external influences on the institution and its selection of senior leaders. I believe the careers, attitudes, and actions of generals illuminate Air Force perspectives and policies. Therefore, I use a detailed spreadsheet to trace the careers of all four-star generals, to show a clear dominance of bomber generals in the early years, and to illustrate how they created a revolution in leadership between 1965 and 1982, the time the Vietnam War played a central role.[4] The data uncovered trends in the grooming, promoting, and assigning of Air Force leaders over time. A survey of institutional statistics helped to explain further the nature and extent of this change in leadership. This study terminates in 1982, when the leadership change culminated with the selection of the first in a continuous string of generals with fighter backgrounds as Air Force chiefs of staff.

To demonstrate attitude formation of the generals better, I canvassed the literature on military sociology and ideology. Additionally, extensive research and use of Air Force oral histories and personal interviews enhanced the human and attitudinal dimensions of this study. The evidence indicates that differences in World War II and Korean War formative experiences of the Vietnam era and post-Vietnam era generals led to a difference in perspectives as senior leaders.[5] To analyze more closely generation differences of Air Force four-star generals, I divided them into generations based on markedly different formative experiences, all of which is explained in detail in chapters 1 and 2. I utilized oral history, personal interviews, military and social history, statistics, computerized data analysis, and sociological findings to gain insights into the remarkable shift in Air Force leadership and ultimately completed the manuscript in December 1992.

Notes

1. "TAC" is an acronym for Tactical Air Command—the organization of predominantly fighter pilots.

2. ACC is an abbreviation for Air Combat Command, an allegedly fighter-dominated organization that is composed of both the assets of former Tactical Air Command (fighters) and Strategic Air Command (bombers).

3. See, for example, Julie Bird, "Fighter Mafia Taking Over," *Air Force Times*, 1 February 1993, 12–13. Bird cites that 7 percent of all officers are fighter pilots, yet more than 70 percent of all major commands are commanded by fighter pilots. Similarly, all Air Force four-star generals are fighter pilots and more than 50 percent of those with more than two stars are also; 85 percent of three- and four-stars are rated.

4. The Air Force public affairs department publishes standardized biographies of all Air Force generals which include their assignment history.

5. Other authors have come to the same conclusion. See Carl H. Builder, *The Masks of War: American Military Styles in Strategy and Analysis* (Baltimore: Johns Hopkins University Press, 1989), 6–8: "Like all individuals and durable groups, the military services have acquired personalities of their own that are shaped by their experiences and that, in turn, shape their behavior. And like individuals, the service personalities are likely to be significantly marked by the circumstances attending their early formation and their most recent traumas."

Acknowledgments

I would like to thank Doctors Bill Scott and Tim Loperis from Duke University as well as Dr. Richard Kohn from the University of North Carolina for their patience and good counsel in reviewing and improving this work. I am especially indebted to Doctors I. B. Holley and Alex Roland also of Duke University for their close mentoring of and their eternal patience with my schedule and my work—every inch along the way. Besides these generous principals of my dissertation review board, I extend heart-felt thanks to Dr. David MacIssac and Gen John Shaud, USAF, Retired, for reviewing and commenting on the manuscript "free of charge." In addition to thanking the many retired Air Force general officers who so honestly provided insights during interviews, I am grateful to the Department of History at the Air Force Academy for providing a few months of free time after service in Southwest Asia to begin work on this effort before attending Army War College.

But most of all, I am again indebted to my wife Lori and my three daughters, Erin, Leslie, and Renee. Like so many other military families, they have faithfully endured the challenges of assignments all over the world, and the extensive time spent on this dissertation came largely at their expense. I dedicate the book to them.

Chapter 1

Formative Years in Total War

All advocates of every theory of American security turn back to the experiences of World War II for historical examples—for illustrations—to prove the soundness of their own arguments.

—House Armed Services Committee Report, 1950

Formative experiences condition leaders and enable them to grow. These experiences apply especially to a person's most impressionable years—young adulthood. The emotional intensity of combat, especially during these formative years, amplifies the imprint on the memory and behavior of the future military leader. In the case of this study, the generals who would rule America's Air Force for its first three decades developed some lasting perspectives on warfare, airpower, and leadership early in their careers. Their pioneering experience in aerial warfare centered around the airplane and its attempt to return decisiveness to wars of the mid-twentieth century. What promise the new medium held for speedy decision quickly faded in bitter combat, and the harsh realities of the fighting scratched an indelible mark on the minds and souls of these future four-star generals. The consequences of this profound experience help to explain, in part, the conduct of this generation as senior leaders during the Vietnam War era.[1]

From 1941 to 1977 these officers rose to positions of command in the United States Air Force. Although the last one retired in 1981, this "World War II generation" dominated senior Air Force leadership positions until 1978. Still, World War II made noticeably different impressions on those who commanded in that supreme effort and on those under them who fought it. Therefore, the section below defines two World War II generations.

First, the "senior World War II generation" was comprised of those four-star Air Force generals who were commissioned between 1926 and 1932. They were largely professionals—82 percent of them West Point graduates—who entered the

1

shrunken Army during lean years of the Great Depression. Finding life in the US Army little better than civilian life during the depression, this daring group turned its interest skyward (94 percent of them became pilots), where the hazards of flying flimsy airplanes increased fatalities and fostered cohesion. This coterie of aviators viewed themselves as an elite group, a privileged few who had entered a realm of great future potential. They entered the newly established Air Corps (1926) as pioneer aviators in time to see and hear the legendary, outspoken, and recently court-martialed Billy Mitchell, air enthusiast and prophet. Relative to society, this well-educated lot numbered 94 percent college graduates, and 59 percent of them participated in the debate and ultimate canonization of airpower theories by attending the Air Corps Tactical School (ACTS) before World War II. There the gospel professed the efficacy of strategic bombing, which promised a decisive alternative in warfare to the slaughter of World War I. Bomber pilots comprised 69 percent of this generation, and 86 percent of those attending the ACTS before World War II were bomber pilots and commanders in that war.[2] In addition, 88 percent of the pilots in this group would command a squadron or wing in combat in the Second World War. With few exceptions, most of them departed World War II as wing commanders and air division commanders, preoccupied with the operational employment of forces in total war, while glancing only occasionally into the world of strategy and higher policy. The most remarkable characteristic of this group was their age. Explosive mobilization for war and wartime attrition had catapulted 90 percent of them to flag officer rank and responsibilities by war's end—the vast majority would finish the war while in their thirties. Such youth would enable those who remained in the Air Force to dominate increasingly its senior leadership positions through 1965.

Second, the "junior World War II generation" of generals received their commission between 1932 and 1945. Rapid expansion and bloody attrition also boosted members of this group who were commissioned before Pearl Harbor to the rank of colonel by war's end. The junior generation of future four-star generals reflected a different demography, one more reflective of the draft and society at large. Only 41 percent of them had graduated from West Point, and more than one-third of the group was comprised of "aviation cadets" who held no college degrees. Only 29 percent had experienced the opportunity to go to the Air Command and Staff College (ACSC) (which had replaced the ACTS in1946), and they went only after the war. All were flyers, mostly in bombers (60 percent). This drafted generation of predominantly pilots and flight leaders did most of the fighting in World War II. Only 43 percent of them became combat squadron commanders, and 7 percent occupied combat wing commander positions in that war. They held less education and were further removed from command, policy making, and the vigorous fight for service autonomy (though not unaffected) than were the senior generation. All were younger than 35 by war's end, and they would dominate senior leadership positions in the Air Force from mid-1965 to 1977, with the last retiring in 1981.

Air Force officers at the rank of major and below in the Korean War would become the senior leaders in the "post-Vietnam era."[3] The "Korean War generation" received their commissions too late to participate in World War II but in time for combat in the limited war in Korea. Regarding demographics, they were much like the junior cohort of World War II—50 percent West Point graduates and 27 percent aviation cadets. This reflection illuminated the draft and call up of reservists for the Korean War. The Korean War generation were better educated by the time they became four-star generals (91 percent had received bachelor's degrees, 73 percent master's degrees, and 14 percent doctorates) than the World War II generation (84 percent of whom had bachelor's degrees, 14 percent master's degrees, and 2 percent doctorates). Additionally, they had received more extensive service schooling: 59 percent had graduated from ACSS, while 86 percent had graduated from a war college. Compare this statistic to the 38 percent and 59 percent respectively from the Second World War generation. In contrast to the latter, 60 percent of the Korean War generation flyers were fighter pilots, and these future leaders would take a broader career path to the top than their predecessors. This generation would dominate four-star general billets from 1978 to 1987.

To understand better how these future leaders would approach the challenges of the Vietnam and post-Vietnam eras, one must further dissect their early formative experiences. Who were these young Americans who wished to become military pilots in the decade surrounding what would become (unbeknowns to them) history's most destructive war?

Air Corps recruiting in the United States during World War II was quite effective. "HERE'S ACTION, BUDDY . . . AVIATION CADET TRAINING IS THE KEY TO A BRILLIANT FUTURE,"[4] stated a handsome young fighter pilot with a smile and twinkle in his eye after swooping past a downed enemy fighter. These and other announcement logos posted nationwide attracted tens of thousands of recruits. While Army psychologists cautioned that "the urge to fly is felt as an impulse and is not subjected to introspection or analysis," they admitted that it attracted "action-oriented" young men who desired to master the air with "this supertoy, this powerful, snorting, impatient but submissive machine [that] enables the man to escape the usual limitations of time and space."[5]

But practical matters also caused those 18- to 27-year-old recruits to fly for the Air Corps. Increased pay, the prestige of becoming part of a technical elite, extensive technical training, the promise of faster promotion, and a distinct edge for postwar employment impacted recruits' desire to avoid the dreadful draft as "doughboys."

This effective recruiting program attracted many of the best young men from West Point and from society. Henry H. "Hap" Arnold, commanding general of the Army Air Forces (AAF), cautioned that an "athletic, serious-minded, industrious boy who is given to the pursuits of games and who follows vigorous athletic schedules is generally more successful than the bookworm type."[6] Tens of thousands of adventuresome young men applied, especially when the draft began.

To stem the flood of recruits, the Air Corps instituted rigorous entrance requirements for pilot training. Pilot applicants had to volunteer for combat duty at the outset. Until 1941 they had to have at least two years of college; thereafter, they had only to pass a standardized three-hour academic examination for initial screening (only 53 percent of them passed in 1942). They then had to endure a rigorous physical examination and comprehensive interview by the flight surgeon. Extensive psychological screening attempted to select those who would be able to learn how to fly with the least difficulty, and psychiatric screening sought to determine those best suited to withstand the emotional stresses of combat flying.[7] A series of further academic and psychomotor tests that screened and classified candidates followed. Academic testing valued math, mechanics, and English scores most; humanities, social sciences, and vocational skills mattered least—though academic achievement did not "materially increase an individual's score on the pilot's portion of the tests or improve his chances of finishing training."[8] Psychomotor testing evaluated finger dexterity, speed and distance judgment, coordination, aiming skills, steadiness under pressure, balance, speed and accuracy of perception and reaction, and ability to divide attention and assimilate stimuli under conditions of confusion. The student was then awarded a score or "stanine" on a scale ranging from one to nine. Generally, the highest scorers overall were to become pilots, followed by navigators and bombardiers. The needs of the service would determine what the minimum acceptable scores might be at any given time. Approximately 25 percent failed these tests between 1943 and 1945.[9]

The survivors were younger, healthier, and drawn from a higher educational base than other soldiers. The Air Corps received the "cream of the crop"; it enlisted 41 percent of the top two brackets of the Army General Classification Test. After passing the bewildering series of tests and examinations, the apprehensive applicants ripened into cocksure elitists. As a research group noted, "They were very much aware of the fact that they represented a highly selected superior group of soldiers."[10]

Those selected from outside West Point then entered the indoctrination phase of training—aviation cadet "preflight school."[11] Preflight schools had originated in World War I to socialize and discipline raw recruits and to condition them to accept the goals and purposes of the Army Air Service, now the Army Air Corps. The six-month program was modeled on the harsh discipline and regimentation of West Point and would last until 1964, with a peak production of 114,000 officer-aviators each year during World War II.[12] The objective focused on loyalty, hardiness, obedience, zeal, and, most of all, cohesion. It solicited active heroic skills and perseverance, as opposed to managerial talents and reflectiveness. The once haughty recruits endured the relentless pressure of military, academic, and physical training.

The aviation cadet schools had little time to perform the miracle of instant officership. The school sought to destroy and to create. The staff sought to weed out those who couldn't function under mental and physical stress and to strip the selfish individuality of the student. In its place the school fostered teamwork, honor, cohesion, competitiveness, and a "fighter spirit." Practicality and action overshadowed discussion and theory. Though the school employed such harsh methods as hazing, sleep deprivation, harassment at meals, endless physical and mental stress—and though it sometimes produced exaggerated forms of behavior—it did yield, at least temporarily, a disciplined and regimented cadet, eager for the challenge and relief of pilot training.[13]

Upon completion of extensive testing, evaluation, and military training, the young pilot candidates traveled to the numerous new pilot training bases that were springing up in the South and Southwest, where the climate offered the best conditions for flying. From nine bases where three hundred pilots received training each year before 1939, the pilot training system grew to 84 bases that produced 30,000 pilots annually some few years later.[14]

The initial flying experience was profound. Psychologists noted the following:

> Nothing is so powerful and yet so responsive to delicate touch as a modern aircraft. Flying a plane requires skill, strength and fine control, which is demonstrable at every turn and each landing. The mastery of the power in the machine is a challenge which gives a justified sense of accomplishment when it has been successfully met. Furthermore, the flier increases his sense of power by identifying himself with his plane, which he feels as an extension of his own body. He thereby achieves a feeling of aggressive potency bordering on the unchallenged strength of a superman. This is well illustrated in Colonel Robert Scott's book, "God Is My Co-pilot," where, in an account of his flight over Mount Everest in a little P-43, the author

describes how he felt that he had humbled this highest mountain and then patronizingly saluted his fallen opponent.[15]

The initial glamour, excitement, and pleasure of flying soon matured into a passion for mastery and competence, as student pilots competed for choice of aircraft after their first 20 weeks of "primary" and "basic" flying training. Pilots learned mechanical skills through repetition, procedures through rote memory, and flying skills through natural or disciplined psychomotor routines. Psychologists found the new flying activity quickly became a student's obsession, and the focus on technique and machinery created a mental approach that attempted "to avoid ambiguities" and that kept thought on a "concrete, organized, and rational level." Interestingly, pilots scored relatively low on intellectual skills.[16]

At the end of basic flight training, students received notice that they would enter single-engine or multiengine advanced training.[17] Psychologists had tried to construct testing to discriminate between fighter and bomber pilots. Bomber pilots needed to be more deliberate and orderly in their thinking, with slower, but dependable decisions and actions. Also, they were expected to be more mature team players. On the other hand, the air arm wanted fighter pilots to show more alertness, respond quicker, and display higher motivation and controlled aggressiveness than other single-engine and multiengine pilots. While psychologists never developed such classification testing satisfactorily, instructor pilots made their judgments along similar lines—could the student handle an aircraft alone with self-reliant judgment and skill? Could he lead a crew in a complex and expensive aircraft? Ultimately, the decision was based upon (1) flying aptitude, (2) individual preference, and (3) aircraft availability.[18] By and large those with the best pure flying skills progressed to advanced single-engine training, unless they desired to fly bombers.[19]

At advanced single-engine school, instruction stressed acrobatics and combat maneuvers to prepare General Arnold's "individualists . . . with quick agility and facility" to fly his fighters.[20] The school stressed "the handling of maneuverable, speedy training planes and the development of instantaneous control reactions in students."[21] Only the most promising students in the advanced single-engine school went on to gunnery training and fighter-transition training; the remainder flew noncombat single-engine planes or transferred to bomber school.[22]

General Arnold's "more stolid, plugging type" progressed to multiengine advanced training.[23] Bombers required maturity, crew leadership, cooperation, and disciplined procedural compliance.

Psychologists noted that flying fighters and bombers

> requires a different sort of person to fly each type successfully. Or rather, the pilot tends to develop a different flying and combat personality when he is exposed to one type of plane or to another. In general, the flying characteristics of heavy, four engine or two engine bomber type aircraft are those of steadiness, lack of maneuverability, reliability and great power over a long distance. Combat missions consume many hours and require considerable persistence and endurance. The fliers in such groups, especially the pilots, tend to fit in with these characteristics. They are usually older, more mature, steadier, and less willing to take risks and indulge in flashy maneuvers than fighter pilots.[24]

Indeed, both skills focused on machinery and technique, and both found their flying environment reinforced behavioral patterns.

By late 1943 growing numbers of pilot-training graduates entered combat units remarkably experienced. They had more than three times as many training hours in flight as their German counterparts and had survived a program that suffered more attrition than combat would demand.[25]

But they did not know that. New Army Air Forces (established as AAF in 1941) pilots had all volunteered for combat and accepted their role as officer-warriors. They ran higher risks than did other combat officers. They were more likely to be killed, wounded, captured, or missing in action.[26] Twice as many air officers died in combat as compared to ground forces, despite their much smaller numbers. Air officers also died in higher percentages in noncombat accidents.[27] This development led them to develop condescending views of "paddle-feet" or "ground-hounds," those earth-bound or noncombat officers.[28]

In return for such sacrifice, the Army Air Forces rewarded its flyers. For aircrews combat was only episodic, and numerous researchers related that "between missions aircrews usually had more physical comforts and far more opportunity for relaxation, recreation, and amusements than did combat personnel in Ground Force units." The AAF created overseas vacation centers and redistribution centers at Atlantic City and Miami Beach. Its leaders gave aircrews time off between missions and frequent leaves or passes to cope with the stress of combat. Aircrews received superior medical support too.[29] Most important, unlike ground soldiers, aircrews could come home after they had flown a certain number of sorties or combat hours, usually 25 to 35 heavy bomber missions, 50 missions for medium and light bombers, and three hundred combat hours for fighters—all varied slightly depending on the time of the war.[30]

As a result, the Army Air Forces enjoyed significantly higher morale and quality of life than the ground forces. Extensive surveys, analyses, and questionnaires revealed young airmen enjoyed faster promotions, greater job satisfaction, preferential treatment, more pride in their organization, a greater willingness for combat, and many more awards and decorations than their peers in any other branch of the Army. Additionally, aircrews were perceived as part of the most respected and desired branch of the Army and part of the arm that contributed most to the war effort and produced the most likely recipients of postwar civilian employment.[31] But these rewards and accomplishments were necessary to address the heavy toll of combat on the Army Air Forces.

Fighter and bomber pilots were exposed comparably to combat. They had roughly the same number of crews and aircraft on hand overseas.[32] Fighters flew more than twice the sorties and more combat hours than heavy bombers but fewer hours in the dangerous skies over Germany. This scenario was particularly evident when, in one six-month period, heavy bomber crews sustained 40 percent more casualties than fighters and 60 percent more than medium bombers in the European theater.[33] Although bombers may not have lost as many pilots as fighters, the total number of casualties coupled with the sense of helplessness weighed heavily on their morale.[34] Bombers were relatively slow and predictable and could seldom achieve surprise. For mutual protection, they had to fly rigid formations and couldn't maneuver well, even if they tried. And bombers were the prize of enemy fighters and flak.[35] Immobility, long periods of cold and cramped inactivity, and unbearable postures created incessant muscular tension. Claustrophobia and numbing dangers from frostbite and hypoxia lengthened their every mission. Prolonged anticipation of the sudden fury of attack increased anxiety. The sense of utter despair and helplessness upon missing the target or losing an aircraft deepened the disposition of bombers crews.[36]

Survival depended on teamwork and machinery. The lack of either increased anxiety. Crew members unable to function under stress as they'd been trained reduced the chances of mission success and survival. The complicated air machine on which they depended and with which they interacted was either their coffin or their deliverance. For the survivors, anxiety over the airplane's performance, in time, grew to reliance and trust in it as an effective means of war and vessel to safety. The machines became friends and possessions, and aircrews gave them personal names, usually feminine, thankfully kissed and patted them, and cared for them like the cavalrymen's horses of old. The marriage of man and machine in the test of combat would have tremendous implications for the attitudes of surviving future generals. Like the cavalryman, the World War II flyer grew subjective and immodest about his steed.[37]

The growing affection between man and machine was exceeded only by the crew's bonds to each other. Psychologists remarked that "the impersonal threat of injury from the enemy, affecting all alike, produces a high degree of cohesion so that personal attachments throughout the unit became intensified. Friendships are easily made by those who might never have been compatible at home and are cemented under fire."[38]

Aircrews huddled together on American bases throughout the world. Aircraft commanders were responsible for the conduct of their crews; each crew member, in turn, possessed a specialty upon which the entire crew depended. In the face of such danger, crews clung together both on and off duty, usually under the close supervision of each other or of others in their unit. Close supervision and interdependence in the air and on the ground coupled with relatively short tours of duty evoked a high sense of conformity, discipline, obligation, and regimentation.[39] Innovation and initiative were more the concern of field commanders, whose tour of duty generally exceeded that of the crews.

This sense of cohesion was essential for morale. Medical statisticians at Eighth Air Force examined 2,051 aircrews who began their 25-mission requirement during the bombing of Germany. Only 26 percent of them finished their missions, and on average 4 percent were lost for each mission. The mean number of missions completed was 14.72.[40] Mere survival in the Army Air Forces meant success, particularly when bombing results were so uncertain. Crews counted their missions, not the number of targets destroyed. Remarkably low sick-call rates until the final mission ended reflected the strong cohesion and commitment between crew members. By mid-1944 it was common for bomber groups to award unofficial "lucky bastard" certificates to those who had survived their required number of missions.[41]

To lead men through this ordeal provided a great challenge for young commanders.[42] Army psychologists analyzed combat leadership and found that air commanders at the squadron and group level had to be technically proficient, strong in character, and decisive. They had to be courageous and sometimes had to share the risk. Effective leaders were demanding, yet they respected the limits of the men. They fought hard to make their men feel special by securing passes and fighting for creature comforts. Balancing the relentless demands of the mission against the fragile morale of his boyish airmen was not the young commander's only problem. He was overwhelmed also with operational matters. As one senior World War II generation bomber commander related: "The only thing I was thinking about was living for the next twenty-four hours and . . . trying to keep my outfit alive and the airplanes flying. . . . We weren't thinking about strategy at the time. . . . We had to have an air force before we could do anything."[43]

Bomber commanders showed resolve, steadfastness, and determination. Sortie production, tonnage dropped, and bombs on target were their concept of strategy; strict flight discipline, perseverance, and growing numbers their methods.

Though the fact was not widely publicized, the Army Air Forces lost more fighter pilots than it did bomber pilots.[44] Yet, surveys indicated that morale within the Army Air Forces was inversely related to the size of the unit aircraft. Fighter units enjoyed higher morale and motivation. Partially because they had to be self-reliant, fighter commanders closely monitored their airmen for any signs of "anxiety reaction" or "slight physical impairment." They immediately removed from flying status airmen who were slipping. On some occasions, they transferred disqualified pilots to another combat assignment as bomber pilots.[45]

The fighter commanders benefited from the filtering process of pilot training and the affirmative action above, but they faced some different leadership challenges. Like their multiengine cousins, fighter pilots relied on and trusted their machinery for safe passage and mission accomplishment. Similarly, their goals were an obligated three hundred combat hours, with as much enemy equipment destroyed in the air and on the ground as practical. But in contrast to bomber pilots, fighter pilots generally flew shorter missions, were kept busy with the activity of flying their machines in a more dynamic environment, and could usually maneuver to avoid enemy threats. They also normally flew in less restrained formations where mates could lend assistance. So the fighter pilot often was too busy, too briefly exposed, and too independent to experience the degree of anxiety and tension of the bomber pilot and his crew.

One psychologist spent months with a fighter squadron in combat and noticed how the squadron had its own value system that represented "the total social, economic, political, and educational world for the individual member. . . . [Its] status system pervades everything he does, as there is no way to get away from it." He further observed that fighter pilots were cliquish combat elites, self-reliant and aggressive, who valued technical knowledge over education. He viewed the qualities of the leader as "dependability, standard quick judgment, a 'cool head,' aggressiveness in the air, and usually superior flying ability. . . . [These] personal qualities of

12

leadership became the criteria for judging men."[46] The Army Air Forces encouraged fighter pilots to stick with their leader and to employ teamwork; it forbade abandoning wingmen and openly criticizing elders. It encouraged initiative, flexibility, and cooperation with bombers, ground forces, and allies. The result, as with bomber pilots, was a cohesive community whose first loyalty resided within that community.

Inducing cohesion was not the only profound effect that World War II had on its junior generation. The vast majority functioned in some leadership role at wing level or below. They were intimately familiar with the demands and realities of combat. They invested in machinery and believed in airpower, and the survivors proudly felt it justified. They took pride in being men of action and of decision—men who valued experience over education.[47] They also appreciated the value of training and the supreme importance of air and numerical superiority. They saw themselves as highly skilled elites; as such, they entered the theater with a cohesion that was intensified in the dangers of war and would endure long afterwards. They had finite goals—to perfect technique as they fulfilled their combat contracts or to motivate others to do so.

But perhaps not enough of them, to include the senior generation, recognized the true limits of their wartime experience. The explosive expansion in the Army Air Corps from 20,196 personnel in 1938 to the Army Air Forces numbering 2,372,293 by June 1944 had rocketed this small cadre of young regular officers into combat unit leadership positions. At that level their responsibility was simply to put bombs on target as quickly and as efficiently as possible. Their challenges were largely tactical and operational, not strategic. They were concerned with how best to execute the mission, as opposed to what mission to execute. As one historian puts it, they had "to fashion the machinery of war, not to worry about its purposes."[48] Their major problems concerned adverse weather, bombing inaccuracy, maintenance and supply problems, crew morale, and enemy resilience, not strategic issues.

The senior Air Corps generals of World War II were air strategists. They had a new technology, a new frontier for prosecuting war, and a new theory of daylight precision

13

strategic bombing against military/economic targets to prove. Theirs was the realm of strategy and politics, which proved to be more than they could handle without assistance. And so their visionary high priest, General Arnold, hired civilian analysts to help convert nonbelievers to the gospel of strategic bombing by refining the text.[49] In October 1942 Arnold authorized the establishment of operations analysis sections throughout the AAF.[50] Their first responsibility was to help make strategic bombing work, an accomplishment that senior leaders felt would guarantee service independence after the war. Operations analysts helped to determine enemy bombing vulnerabilities, critical target systems, bomb and fuse selections, bombing and gunnery techniques, and battle damage and loss implications; they also provided general mission analysis and strategic advice. Arnold dispatched these civilian missionaries from his "Vatican" in Washington to "prepare to solve problems on the spot in combat theatres."[51] He also brought other civilians in to help with military analysis, code breaking, and intelligence.

Realistically, the high command could do little more than to improvise. The Air War Plans Division-1 (AWPD-1) had projected that the full weight of the bomber buildup could not be exercised until 1944. However, in 1942 the political necessity of doing something quickly, while the Army trained and the Navy reconstituted itself from Pearl Harbor, produced a piecemeal implementation of strategic bombing that yielded marginal results. This undersized beginning had the unfortunate side effect of refining and increasing German defensive measures and preparations.

Exigencies of the moment inevitably undermined the air campaign. In late 1942, as US and British air forces began to build for the massive strategic onslaught of "Fortress Europe," they were diverted to North Africa. At the Casablanca Conference in early 1943, heavy Allied shipping losses and German air superiority over the continent induced political leaders to change bombing priorities to submarine pens and the German aircraft industry. In March of 1944 Gen Dwight D. "Ike" Eisenhower assumed control of the bomber force to prepare for the Allied invasion at Normandy. Only in September of 1944 did the Army Air Forces regain full control over its strategic forces to prosecute the targeting plan in Europe.

To confound things further, airpower proved difficult to assess. Aerial reports, even photographs, could be deceptive and often arrived late. Certainly, damage was being done, but officials always did not know to what extent.[52] Because of the lack of criteria and capability to judge the effectiveness of daylight precision bombing, the strategy of the faithful became one of hope.[53] Without being able to agree where to place emphasis, the effort increased in size and scope with a determination that the enemy would collapse under the sheer weight of the assault. When the enemy refused to buckle under, as had been prophesied, measures of success defaulted to sorties flown, tonnage dropped, and targets "hit."[54] Strategy was reduced to a targeting exercise, and the only recourse was to escalate, even to include urban areas.[55]

A related problem arose because it was hard to prove how destruction would bring victory or break the will of the enemy. It also was difficult to determine just how airpower could best influence surface warfare, since few unbiased progress reports existed. Convincing judgment awaited after-action reports. And so, with few means for testing ends, emphasis turned to means. Hence, the AAF channeled its energies into the refinement of technique.[56]

Confusion at headquarters meant confusion in the field. Commanders from squadron to wing level mistook means for ends, tactics for strategy, and the latter for sorties, tonnage, and simple targeting.[57] In June 1945, when General Arnold asked Maj Gen Curtis E. LeMay when the war against Japan would end, LeMay, soon-to-be commander of Twentieth Air Force, replied that he'd "been so busy fighting it I haven't figured out a date. . . . Give me thirty minutes, and I will give you a date." Then LeMay got with his staff and reviewed the targets yet to be hit. They estimated that by 1 September (or 1 October—accounts vary), those targets would have been hit, and "if there is no industry left up there, there can't be much war left going on."[58]

In sum, World War II had a profound effect on the operationally oriented World War II generation. The high price of admission granted them elitism; the high cost of attrition created an unbreakable cohesion. The latter cast an emotional veneer, as most intense combat tends to, over their forming attitudes on technology, leadership, airpower, and warfare.[59] The World War II generation had employed trustworthy machines in increasing numbers and, they perceived, with increasing effectiveness. Even at their level, they believed their single-minded perseverance towards total victory was an essential ingredient in the triumph. The World War II generation valued experience over education and discipline over critical analysis. They were doers, not thinkers—though many thought their operational experience created sufficient strategic background.[60] They were proud of their independent contribution, a role they felt was worthy of service independence.

Both World War II generations were too consumed with the activity of war to comprehend their contribution to victory. They had to wait until the war ended, and the postwar analysts began to understand the extent of their contributions. Yet senior leaders in the AAF, who were exposed to the frustrations of subordination to the Army longer, had been actively preparing for service independence since at least late 1943.[61] Army Air Forces commanders were planning to use the findings of the highly acclaimed and impartial *United States Strategic Bombing Survey* to justify their prewar doctrinal proclamations and to assure independence, even before results were complete.[62] If results weren't favorable, some air officers were prepared to debate and refute them.[63] Senior leaders of the AAF remained convinced that only "independent airmen" could plan and employ airpower to its full potential, and they had earned that right in World War II. Since they viewed their independent employment of strategic bombing as a potential means of victory itself, a concept wedded to service autonomy, naturally they held great interest in the results of the bombing survey.

The *United States Strategic Bombing Survey* reinforced the preconceived notions held by most readers. To strategic bombing enthusiasts, ample evidence indicated "Allied air power" in Western Europe was *decisive in and of itself,* and the survey implied the same in its summary of the Pacific. It surmised that strategic bombing would have halted

Germany's armament production by May 1945 and resulted in the collapse of resistance a few months later. Similarly, it suggested that by the end of 1945, Japan would have surrendered without atomic bombs, Russian intervention, or land invasion.[64] The bombing survey suggested that "even a first-class military power—rugged and resilient as Germany was—cannot live long under full-scale and free exploitation of air weapons over the heart of its territory."[65] The summary report for the Pacific stated the same was true for Japan, and it went on to say that "for the future it is important to fully grasp the fact that enemy planes enjoying control of the sky over one's head can be as disastrous to one's country as its occupation by physical invasion."[66] Satisfied with the survey's assessment and confident in the efficacy of strategic bombing, bomber commander lieutenant general James H. "Jimmy" Doolittle reflected the Army Air Forces' view when he stated in late 1945 that "the Navy had the transport to make the invasion of Japan possible; the Ground Forces had the power to make it successful; and the B-29 made it unnecessary."[67]

Though results of the *United States Strategic Bombing Survey* satisfied the dominant bomber pilots of the World War II generation, as well as those who had fought for air supremacy, other airmen had a different perspective.[68] Interestingly, there was no "tactical bombing survey" nor was there a comprehensive analysis of how all elements of airpower interacted to achieve victory. The vagueness of the strategic bombing survey left many uncommitted observers unconvinced of the decisiveness of strategic bombing. To them the survey's "Allied air power" was more than "American strategic bombing," *decisive* remained undefined, and Japan did not necessarily mean Germany.[69] World War II generation fighter generals who spent most of their early years in support of armies and Allies through interdiction and close air support were more inclined to think of airpower as a *decisive element* complementary to land power.

The bombing survey meant something else to many people outside the AAF. Historian Walter Millis argues that tactical aviation was most significant,[70] as does civilian theorist Bernard Brodie.[71] General Eisenhower, supreme commander of the Allied forces, acknowledged that the ability of tactical airpower "to intervene in the land battle" enabled the successful invasion at Normandy; without it, the invasion would have been "criminal."[72]

In this latter instance tactical airpower made its greatest, though most indirect, contribution to service independence. The fighter pilots—who had driven the enemy fighter-bombers away and had then strafed, bombed, and scouted in close coordination with the advancing American armies—had won the admiration and respect of the ground forces. If these airmen wanted service independence, the trusting ground force commanders were more inclined to oblige. In fact, in January 1946 Eisenhower made Gen Carl A. Spaatz, former bomber commander and the first chief of staff of the Air Force, promise to sustain a strong tactical air capability before Eisenhower would agree to service independence.[73]

In the immediate aftermath of the war, top AAF leaders were careful to acknowledge publicly that victory had been a "triphibious" effort, a victory of combined arms.[74] But the loaded question they posed to governmental leaders and to the public was, "What sort of force structure is best for the future?"

Notes

1. For alignment purposes, this generational study of Air Force leadership defines the Vietnam era as the period from 1961 (first occasion for US Air Force involvement) to 1977 (when World War II generation generals become a minority of Air Force four-star generals).

2. For purposes of this study, I have categorized the backgrounds of generals as bomber, fighter, generalist, or engineer and based my categorization on the preponderance of experience within that specialty in the formative years (first 15 years of service). If I could discern no solid foundation, I then labeled the generals generalists.

3. Again for purposes of generational analysis, this study defines the post-Vietnam era as the period from 1978 (when Korean War generation generals began to dominate four-star positions) to 1982 (when the selection of the first in a continuous string of fighter generals as chief of staff of the Air Force capped the ascension of fighter generals).

4. US Army, "Army Life and United States Army Recruiting News" (Governors Island, N.Y.: Recruiting Publicity Bureau, US Army, December 1943), 19.

5. Roy R. Grinker Sr. and John P. Spiegel, *Men Under Stress* (Philadelphia: The Blakiston Company, 1945), 5–6. Army psychologists

conducted this study of men in training, in combat overseas, and in several thousand convalescent hospitals.

6. Henry H. Arnold and Ira C. Eaker, *Winged Warfare* (New York: Harper and Brothers, 1941), 30–31.

7. Grinker and Spiegel, 9.

8. Vance O. Mitchell, "The First Generation: A Policy History of the Air Force Officer Corps, 1944–1973" (unpublished manuscript, Office of Air Force History (OAFH), Washington, D.C., May 1991), 718; and Wesley Frank Craven and James Lea Cate, eds., *The Army Air Forces in World War II*, vol. 6, *Men and Planes* (1955; new imprint, Washington, D.C.: Office of Air Force History, 1983), 553.

9. Joseph F. Dorfler, "The Branch Point Study: Specialized Undergraduate Pilot Training" (ARI Report no. AU-ARI-86-5, Maxwell AFB, Ala.: Air University Press, June 1986), 4–5; Mitchell, 719; Craven and Cate, 546, 551; and Mark K. Wells, "Aviators and Air Combat" (PhD diss., King's College, London, 1992), 19, 24. Sometimes height and weight standards, quotas, and instructor preferences were factored into selection of aircraft.

10. Samuel A. Stouffer et al., *Studies in Social Psychology in World War II*; vol. 2, *The American Soldier: Combat and its Aftermath* (Princeton, N.J.: Princeton University Press, 1949), 340–42. More than one hundred research experts who studied soldier attitudes for the four years of the war obtained their data through these extensive surveys, questionnaires, interviews, and sociological and psychological studies. See also Craven and Cate, xxvi.

11. Author spreadsheet. Eighteen percent of the senior World War II generation, 59 percent of the junior World War II generation, and 50 percent of the Korean generation went through some sort of preflight school.

12. Gary L. Wamsley, "Contrasting Institutions of Air Force Socialization: Happenstance or Bellwether?" *American Journal of Sociology* 78, no. 2 (September 1972): 402; and Mitchell, 10. Approximately 600,000 aviation cadets entered for World War II, and 300,000 graduated by early 1945.

13. Craven and Cate, 559; and Wamsley, 401–16.

14. Alfred Goldberg, ed., *A History of the United States Air Force, 1907–1957* (Princeton, N.J.: D. Van Nostrand, 1957), 50–51. Author spreadsheet. Ninety-four percent of the senior generation, 98 percent of the junior generation, and 95 percent of Korean generation were pilots.

15. Grinker and Spiegel, 5–6.

16. Paul M. Fine and Bryce O. Hartman, "Psychiatric Strengths and Weaknesses of Typical Air Force Pilots" (Brooks AFB, Tex.: USAF School of Aerospace Medicine, 1968), 35. The authors provide an extensive analysis of a cross section of 50 pilots and a less detailed survey of 240 other rated pilots and navigators.

17. Author spreadsheet. Sixty-nine percent of the senior and 60 percent of the junior World War II generation became bomber pilots; 60 percent of the Korean generation became fighter pilots.

18. Craven and Cate, 553, 572; and Dorfler, 5. The factors involved in selecting follow-on aircraft have remained the same through 1971, and from 1978 on. Sometimes preferences for fighters exceeded demand; and other times, not enough men of the required physical qualifications desired bombers. Aircraft availability and physique determined assignments when there were too few men.

19. Dewan D. Madden, "Tactical Fighter Pilot Selection Considerations" (Air Command and Staff College Report, Maxwell AFB, Ala.: Air University, 1973), 37. Madden calculates that 32 percent of the pilot training graduates through 1973 have become fighters.

20. Arnold and Eaker, 31, 36.

21. Craven and Cate, 572.

22. Ibid.

23. Arnold and Eaker, 31.

24. Grinker and Spiegel, 27.

25. Goldberg, 95; and Craven and Cate, 577–78. Between July 1939 and August 1945 advanced flying schools graduated 193,440, while 124,000 failed training or became casualties. Headquarters Army Air Forces, *U.S. Army Air Forces Statistical Digest: World War II* (Washington, D.C.: Office of Statistical Control, December 1945), 49, 67. Pages 78–79 show that between December 1942 and August 1945, 36,700 fighter pilots were trained and 367,600 bomber crewmen were trained.

26. Wells, 99; and Mark Clodfelter, *The Limits of Air Power: The American Bombing of North Vietnam* (New York: Free Press, 1989), 10. Clodfelter cites that 63,000 Americans were downed in World War II.

27. Wells, chap. 7, passim; and Michael S. Sherry, *The Rise of American Air Power: The Creation of Armageddon* (New Haven, Conn.: Yale University Press, 1987), 205. Sherry writes about the deaths of 35,946 airmen in noncombat situations.

28. Robert C. Stone, "Status and Leadership in a Combat Fighter Squadron," *American Journal of Sociology* 51 (March 1946): 394. Psychologist Stone, who spent several months with combat units, stated further that civilians were considered "the lowest of the low," and that "group pride . . . strengthens the view that all members have a special status, while everyone else is an outsider."

29. Stouffer, 352–57.

30. Ibid., 325, 359, 386.

31. Ibid., 326–28, 348; and Samuel A. Stouffer et al., *Studies in Social Psychology in World War II*, vol. 1, *The American Soldier: Adjustment During Army Life* (Princeton, N.J.: Princeton University Press, 1949), 272, 288, 299, 301, 306.

32. See *Statistical Digest, World War II*, 84–85, for aircrews on hand overseas. See page 127 for aircraft on hand, 221 for sorties flown, and 275 for hours flown. See also Goldberg for aircraft on hand (p. 92).

33. Stouffer, vol. 2, 407. Stouffer cites the following casualties per 1,000 per six months in the European theater for January to June 1944: 350 medium bombers, 523 fighters, and 887 heavy bombers (10-man crews).

34. Headquarters, European Theater of Operations, "Survey of Fighter Pilots in the Eighth Air Force, A Comparison with Heavy Bomber Pilots," 7 August 1944, Air Force Historical Research Agency (cited hereafter as AFHRA), Maxwell AFB, Ala., July–August 1944. Forty-three percent of the fighter pilots survived a three-hundred mission tour; 58.9 percent of the bomber pilots survived their 25-mission tour.

35. Stouffer, vol. 2, 408. "In interviews, men who flew in heavy bombers often asserted that they sweated out antiaircraft attacks on almost every one of their missions; they sometimes explicitly stated that they felt extremely tense when their ship was exposed to flak while flying in formation because they realized that nothing could be done about it."

36. Ibid., 408–9; Grinker and Spiegel, 29–30; and Wells, 86. Bombers "practiced very limited evasion action within the confining constraints of their formations. . . . Of questionable value . . . it nevertheless boosted aircrew morale."

37. Perry McCoy Smith, *The Air Force Plans for Peace, 1943–1945* (Baltimore: Johns Hopkins University Press, 1970), 18.

38. Grinker and Spiegel, 21–22. The authors also noted that "although the combat crews are thrown together only by chance, they rapidly become united to each other by the strongest bonds while in combat."

39. Wells, 130. Breaking formation integrity was a court-martial offense in some units; aircrews never were to abandon the lead group, even if it were off course.

40. Mae Mills Link and Hubert A. Coleman, *Medical Support of the Army Air Forces in World War II* (Washington, D.C.: Office of the Surgeon General, 1955), 704–5; and Richard H. Kohn and Joseph Harahan, eds., *Air Interdiction in World War II, Korea, and Vietnam: An Interview with Earle E. Partridge, Jacob E. Smart, and John Vogt Jr.* (Washington, D.C.: OAFH, 1986), 39. "The bloody 100th" Bomb Group was assigned 40 B-17 bombers and 1,700 men in June of 1943. By May of 1945 they had lost 180 bombers and 1,751 airmen.

41. Stouffer, vol. 2, 383.

42. Author spreadsheet. The senior World War II generation had reached their thirties during the war; 38 percent commanded a bomber squadron and 44 percent a bomber wing in the war. The junior World War II generation were all less than 35 years old; 31 percent commanded a bomber squadron and 13 percent a bomber wing; but most were combat pilots. See also Mitchell, 23. The average age of the Army Air Forces' officers in 1945 was 25.

43. Interview with Curtis E. LeMay, cited in Sherry, 179.

44. For example, the 406th Fighter-Bomber Group, in five days of close air support during the Battle of the Bulge, had 57 of its 60 aircraft damaged or destroyed in combat. See Stouffer, vol. 2, 408.

45. Ibid., 400, 408; and Wells, 132. Seventy percent of fighter pilots expressed a desire to undertake another combat tour; 25 percent of bomber pilots were willing to return.

46. Stone, 389–94; and author spreadsheet. Six percent of the senior generation were fighter squadron commanders, and 6 percent were fighter wing commanders in World War II; 12 percent of the junior generation were fighter squadron commanders, and 5 percent were fighter wing commanders in World War II.

47. Col Noel F. Parrish, "New Responsibilities of Air Force Officers," *Air University Quarterly Review* 1, no. 1 (Spring 1947): 29–42. Parrish, one of the leading early Air Force writers, acknowledged "air activities have most often attracted men of active rather than literary leanings." Smith, 12, 113–16. Smith argues that there were no academics in the Army Air Forces, that only the advice of civilian scholars in the physical sciences was appreciated, and that postwar planning suffered from this absence.

48. Sherry, 179.

49. Wesley Frank Craven and James Lea Cate, *The Army Air Forces in World War II*, vol. 1, *Air Plans and Early Operations* (Washington, D.C.: OAFH, 1955), 67. The authors state that bomber advocates have dominated the Air Force since 1935. Claire Lee Chennault, *Way of a Fighter: The Memoirs of Claire Lee Chennault*, ed. Robert B. Hotz (New York: G. Putnam Sons, 1949), 20. Chennault, an outspoken fighter general, was initially "disqualified" from the Air Corps in 1937 for being "hard of hearing." He wrote, "The bomber generals had an inflexible orthodoxy all their own and were just as ruthless and unforgiving in squelching opposition within the Air Corps as the Army and Navy were in attempting to smother the development of airpower."

50. Robert Frank Futrell, *Ideas, Concepts, Doctrine: Basic Thinking in the United States Air Force, 1907–1960*, vol. 1 (Maxwell AFB, Ala.: Air University Press, December 1989), 142–43. These mostly civilian analysts and scientists would number more than 400 by war's end.

51. Ibid.

52. Diane T. Putney, ed., *ULTRA and the Army Air Forces in World War II: An Interview with Associate Justice of the U.S. Supreme Court Lewis F. Powell Jr.* (Washington, D.C.: OAFH, 1987), 41. Powell claimed there was a good program for gaining battle damage assessment from photo reconnaissance when weather cooperated, sorties were available, and radio intercepted. (But on the distant strategic targets, eye witness accounts from the bombers and their cameras usually were all the air planners had to work with for some time.)

53. Thomas H. Greer, *The Development of Air Doctrine in the Army Air Arm, 1917–1941* (Washington, D.C: OAFH, 1985), 60. Greer records that even Maj Gen Haywood S. Hansell Jr., an architect of the air plans to defeat the Axis powers, admitted that strategic bombing was "based on hope more than fact." See also Caroline Ziemke, "In the Shadow of the Giant: USAF

Tactical Air Command in the Era of Strategic Bombing, 1945–1955" (PhD diss., Ohio State University, 1989), 4.

54. Clodfelter, 10. Clodfelter's analysis of World War II asserts that unconditional surrender encouraged the strategic bombing campaign that was characterized more in terms of size of effort than in precision bombing. "The bludgeon rather than the rapier meshed with the purpose of obliterating the political as well as the military foundations of the Axis nations." See also R. J. Overy, *The Air War: 1939–1945* (New York: Stein and Day, 1980), 108–15. The limits of technology and intelligence significantly undermined targeting and precision bombing.

55. Sherry, 233. Dr. Edward L. Bowles, former professor at Massachusetts Institute of Technology and Arnold's head of systems analysis program, lamented over "the insidious practice in the Air Forces of measuring air activity in terms of bombs dropped" instead of "targets damaged or obliterated."

56. Ibid., 182. In November 1944 a colonel on Arnold's staff complained, "We have placed a premium on the operator rather than the theorist," and Arnold himself regretted "that we have probably lost a certain degree of initiative and imagination, and that all of us are, perhaps, war-weary."

57. Haywood S. Hansell Jr., *Strategic Air War Against Japan* (Maxwell AFB, Ala.: Air War College, Airpower Research Institute, 1980), xiii. Hansell, a strategic bombing commander in the Pacific, a contemporary of the senior World War II generation, and a drafter of the air plan to defeat the Axis, proudly cited pioneering air theorist Giulio Douhet in his memoirs: "The choice of enemy targets . . . is the most delicate operation of air warfare. . . . It is precisely in this field that the commanders of future Air Forces will be able to give proof of their ability." Hansell also noted how Arnold was inclined "to measure strategic air attack in terms of tonnage and sorties" (p. 48).

58. Richard H. Kohn and Joseph Harahan, eds., *Strategic Air Warfare: An Interview with Curtis E. LeMay, Leon W. Johnson, David A. Burchinal, and Jack J. Catton* (Washington, D.C.: OAFH, 1988), 64; Thomas M. Coffey, *Iron Eagle: The Turbulent Life of General Curtis LeMay* (New York: Crown Publishers, 1986), 174; Curtis E. LeMay with MacKinlay Kantor, *Mission with LeMay: My Story* (Garden City, N.Y.: Doubleday, 1965), 381; and Sherry, 300.

59. David MacIsaac, "Voices From the Central Blue: The Air Power Theorists," in *Makers of Modern Strategy: From Machiavelli to the Nuclear Age*, ed. Peter Paret (Princeton, N.J.: Princeton University Press, 1986), 636. MacIsaac notes this is not unlike the observation of eminent World War II air historian Noble Frankland that "people have preferred to feel rather than to know about strategic bombing."

60. Sherry, 180. Sherry notes in an interview with Curtis E. LeMay how LeMay lamented not having a formal education to debate strategy and politics, but in World War II the "main thing was to have enough energy to get off your a— and do something."

61. Herman S. Wolk, *Planning and Organizing the Postwar Air Force, 1943–1947* (Washington, D.C.: OAFH, 1984), 31; and Herman S. Wolk, "Planning and Organizing the Air Force," *Aerospace Historian* 34, no. 3 (Fall/September 1987): 168. Arnold and Gen George Marshall, Army chief of staff, had agreed early in the war to postpone the question of Air Force independence until after the war. See also James Parton, "The Thirty-One Year Gestation of the Independent USAF," *Aerospace Historian* 34, no. 3 (Fall/September 1987): 154.

62. The survey was headed by civilians and included 300 civilians, 350 officers, and 500 enlisted men, who scoured records, visited targets, and conducted extensive interviews with enemy leaders.

63. David MacIsaac, *Strategic Bombing in World War II: The Story of the United States Strategic Bombing Survey* (New York: Garland Publishing, 1976), 119–35; and Joseph W. Caddell, "Orphan of Unification: The Development of United States Air Force Tactical Air Power Doctrine, 1945–1950" (PhD diss., Duke University, 1984), 123.

64. David MacIsaac, ed., *The United States Strategic Bombing Survey* (hereafter *USSBS*), 10 vols. (New York: Garland Publishing, 1976), 1:38; 7:26.

65. Ibid., 1:39; and *United States Strategic Bombing Survey Summary Report (European War)* no. 1 (Washington, D.C.: Government Printing Office [GPO], 30 September 1945): 16.

66. *USSBS*, 7:27; and *United States Strategic Bombing Survey Summary Report (Pacific War)* no. 1 (Washington, D.C.: GPO, 1 July 1946): 28.

67. Pegasus (pseud.), "The Forty-Year Split. The Second Twenty Years: 1940–1960," *Army* 15 (August 1965): 59; and Futrell, 170. Even before the end of the war, air enthusiasts, especially in the Pacific, were making confident predictions: "On 8 August 1945 Marshall admonished Spaatz and LeMay for the 'incalculable harm' they'd done to the Army by stating that 'our present Army is not necessary for the further prosecution of the War in the Pacific,' and that 'invasion will be unnecessary and that the future of the Armies has been decidedly curtailed.'" The Army Air Forces also ensured that 426 B-29s overflew the Japanese surrender ceremony on board the Missouri.

68. *USSBS*, 6:1. "The significance of full domination of the air over the enemy—both over its armed forces and over its sustaining economy—must be emphasized. That domination of the air was essential. Without it, attacks on the basic economy of the enemy could not have been delivered in sufficient force and with sufficient freedom to bring effective and lasting results."

69. David MacIsaac, "The Evolution of Air Power Since 1945: The American Experience," in *War in the Third Dimension: Essays in Contemporary Air Power*, ed. R. A. Mason (London: Brassey's Defence Publishers, 1986), 13.

70. Walter Millis, *Arms and Men: A Study in American Military History* (New York: Putnam, 1956), 291. "The combination of the tank and the tactical airplane continued to dominate most theatres down to the end."

71. Bernard Brodie, *Strategy in the Missile Age* (Princeton, N.J.: Princeton University Press, 1959), 107. "It was in tactical employment that success was most spectacular and that the air forces won the unqualified respect and admiration of the older services. By contrast, the purely strategic successes, however far-reaching in particular instances, were never completely convincing to uncommitted observers. Against Germany they came too late to have a clearly decisive effect; against Japan they were imposed on an enemy already prostrated by other forms of war." See also MacIsaac, "Air Power Theorists," 636. Bomber lieutenant general Ira C. Eaker, former commander of the Eighth Air Force in World War II and a committed observer, commented that this observation was a "slanted, prejudiced view wholly unrelated to the facts."

72. Futrell, 173.

73. Lt Gen Elwood "Pete" Quesada, transcript of oral history interview by Lt Col Steven W. Long Jr., USAF, and Lt Col Ralph W. Stephenson, USAF, 12–13 May 1975, AFHRA, Maxwell AFB, Ala.; and Ziemke, 27. Ziemke documents the instrumental role Quesada played in convincing Eisenhower and Bradley to support Air Force independence. See also Richard H. Kohn and Joseph Harahan, eds., *Air Superiority in World War II and Korea: An Interview with Gen James Ferguson, Gen Robert M. Lee, Gen William Momyer, and Lt Gen Elwood R. Quesada* (Washington, D.C.: OAFH, 1983), 65; and Wolk, "Planning," 170.

74. Gen Henry H. Arnold, "Report of the Army, H. H. Arnold, Commanding General, Army Air Forces, Air Power and the Future, 1945," ed. Walter Millis, *American Military Thought* (New York: Bobbs-Merrill Company, 1966), 457. See also Gen Carl A. Spaatz, "Strategic Air Power: Fulfillment of a Concept," *Foreign Affairs* 24 (April 1946): 385–96.

Chapter 2

Marketing A Vision
(1945–53)

The basic planning, development, organization, and training of the Air Force must be well rounded, covering every modern means of waging war. . . . The Air Force doctrine likewise must be flexible at all times and entirely uninhibited by tradition.

—Gen Henry H. "Hap" Arnold

The theory of strategic deterrence that formed the heart of subsequent Air Force strategic doctrine coalesced in 1945–1946 and was well developed by early 1947, far in advance of the war plans, aircraft, or supply of atomic weapons to implement such a concept.

—Air Force historian John T. Greenwood

Contextual factors after World War II would influence strongly how the government and public responded to the airmen's offer to provide future security. Perceptions of the threat to national security and economic concerns dominated the debate. President Harry S. Truman, a former Senate Appropriations Committee member, was determined to control inflation and put the United States back on a sound economic footing. He felt a strong economy would enhance national security through military and economic aid programs in support of the Marshall Plan, the Truman Doctrine, and his Fair Deal. Secretary of State George C. Marshall and George Kennan of the State Department Policy Planning Staff influenced Truman's assessment that the Soviets were in no condition at that time to challenge the United States and its atomic arsenal. Consequently, Truman reduced defense spending from 40 percent of the gross national product in 1944 to 4 percent by 1948.[1]

Across the river, in the newly built Pentagon, the services expressed concern about how they were to measure up to newfound "superpower" obligations. Budget cuts and rapid postwar demobilization created chaos within the military. Under pressure to integrate, economize, and demobilize within shrunken budgets, the services scrambled for bureaucratic survival and a role in the postwar defense establishment. For the Army Air Forces, the new environment compelled a unity of voice and purpose. It would strive first for independence and second for preeminence, with airpower as the foundation of national security.[2]

On the heels of the *United States Strategic Bombing Survey* results, Army Air Forces leaders argued that strategic bombing was the most economical, cost-effective, and sensible way to provide security to a war-weary nation and its weak, distant allies. The availability of very long range bombers (including the newly developed B-36) and atomic weapons rekindled public faith in the efficacy of strategic bombing.[3] Even Bernard Brodie eventually would attest to the revival of Giulio Douhet's theories.[4] In the eyes of many in the Army Air Forces, a sufficient number of atomic bombs would return decisiveness to war. An expert on the period noted the following:

> The air leaders stressed the preeminence of air power as the primary rationale for independence. The advent of the atomic weapon and the achievements of air power during the war meant that [importance] of the ground and naval forces had diminished. The Air Force was now the "first line of defense." The oceans no longer insulated America from the rude shocks of war. . . . Now even a few bombers penetrating enemy territory could leave tremendous destruction. It could be argued that the atomic bomb had resurrected Giulio Douhet. War had become total. There would no longer be sufficient time to mobilize.[5]

The external unity of voice and purpose the Army Air Forces conveyed during the critical struggle for postwar roles reflected the preeminence of service independence within the Army Air Forces. As one analyst pointed out, "All energies were focused on this fight for autonomy, and fighter doctrine—which challenged the omnipotence of bombers—was suppressed in favor of proving the decisive role of bombers."[6] It fostered, as bureaucratic analyst Philip Selznick recalled, an excessive value on strategic versus tactical forces "particularly in an early period of intense struggle for an assured status. An emphasis on strategic competence . . . is congenial in the struggle for autonomy and prestige."[7] It was not unusual for the institution to focus where its contribution might be most relevant and exclusive. The budget cuts compelled even more unanimity in support of autonomy by way of the strategic mission. By October 1945 General Spaatz succinctly stated, "We have only one real defense: a planned and ready air offensive."[8]

The implosion of postwar demobilization and reorganization distorted planning and hindered doctrinal review. From a peak of 2.4 million personnel in March 1944, AAF fell to 300,000 by May 1947. Bewildering challenges from new technologies of jet engines, atomic weapons, long-range ballistic rockets, and air refueling paled in comparison to mounting world crises— communist advances in east Europe; threats to Greece, Turkey, and Iran; the fall of Czechoslovakia and eventually China; the Berlin blockade; and the Soviet atomic bomb. Postwar base closures, celebrations, air shows, and state fairs further distracted the AAF and later the Air Force.[9] In this climate, officials neglected doctrinal review, including real problems of bombing accuracy, targeting, effective interdiction, communications, and integrated analyses of tactical and strategic airpower. Junior fighter cohort general William W. Momyer recalled, "Our preoccupation with the strategic concept of war did more [than anything else] to frustrate any thinking on the employment of other aspects."[10]

According to retired fighter major general Perry McCoy Smith's analysis, "Bombardment and autonomy were natural partners, but fighters were antithetical to both."[11] To support a fighter-oriented doctrine was to point out weaknesses in strategic bombing and hurt the case for autonomy. Appeased by the role of long-range escort, most of the fighter community willingly conceded doctrinal preeminence to the bomber enthusiasts in the interests of autonomy. The achievement of autonomy, however, came too late to arrest the trend towards strategic tunnel vision and dogmatic doctrine. The postwar doctrine differed from prewar doctrine in little more than incorporation of long-range escorts.[12]

In the first major postwar reorganization of the AAF in March 1946, the Army chief of staff, General Eisenhower, supported an independent Air Force contingent upon a capable Tactical Air Command (TAC). This ensured TAC's existence as an independent command and a haven for fighter and transport pilots. However, TAC's commander was Elwood R. "Pete" Quesada, a fighter commander with extensive combat experience in the European theater but only a major general. The Strategic Air Command (SAC), also known as the bomber command, was commanded by George C. Kenney, a four-star general with extensive combat experience in the Pacific theater. In addition, only one of the eight Army Air Forces generals with three or more stars was a true fighter general. One observer noted how officials placed the fighter generals into "military Siberias far from where the press or Congress could hear the questions they raised."[13]

The Army Air Forces' proposal for a postwar force structure was a strategic-oriented, 70-group force-in-being. On the eve of independence, the Air Force was clearly committed to autonomy by way of strategic bombing in its rank and force structure, organization and planning, and doctrine. General Spaatz gave priority to "the backbone of our Air Force—the long-range bomber groups and their protective long-range fighter groups organized in our Strategic Air Force."[14]

In the immediate postwar years, the Army Air Forces attempted to keep its "unity of voice" measured and restrained. Too much acrimony would alienate the other services; too much restraint would sacrifice the visibility their hard-fought cause needed for recognition and independence. But the former was more natural for the aggressive and confident air veterans, especially the dominant bomber advocates. Arnold wrote to Spaatz less than two weeks after the first atomic bombing at Hiroshima. He expressed concern regarding how distractions from strategic bombing clouded public opinion as to strategic airpower's true decisiveness:

> We were never able to launch the full power of our bombing attack. . . . The power of those attacks would certainly have convinced any doubting Thomases as to the capabilities of a modern Air Force. I am afraid that from now on there will be certain people who will forget the part we played.[15]

It didn't take long for the air enthusiasts to respond. Then a reservist, bomber general James H. "Jimmy" Doolittle stated publicly that airpower would limit the future wartime role of the Navy to ferrying supplies and would use the Army only to occupy the homeland of an enemy it already had crushed.[16] General Kenney agreed with Doolittle that aircraft carriers were obsolete and that all airpower should fall under the Air Force.[17] Army Undersecretary for Air W. Stuart Symington commented in December 1946: "To ever relegate strategic air again to a secondary position under the Army would be to ensure the failure of adequate national defense." This conclusion was evident, he said, to "anyone who has no axe to grind."[18] Though a few bursts of arrogance escaped, the Army Air Forces was careful to restrain its active duty members from provocative remarks. The more daring remarks were left to civilian friends and retired or reserve officers of the Army Air Corps.[19]

With Army and political backing, the AAF became a separate service in September 1947. This reorganization left generals experienced in managing bombers in command of all operational commands save TAC. Symington, the new secretary of the Department of the Air Force, and his self-avowed "tight-knit group of activists" and "revolutionaries" were not satisfied with administrative independence. At the first annual convention of the Air Force Association on 15 September 1947, he made the following statement:

> No Air Force can be created by legislative action alone. All the National Security Act of 1947 has done is to give us the green light. It must be considered an opportunity and not an accomplishment. . . . We certainly cannot rest on our laurels.[20]

Symington went on to admit his determination to get "as much of the pie as I could for the Air Force" and his activist group was also "determined. It was a hard fight and it was a good fight. We survived."[21] The National Security Act did not confer instant parity on the Air Force; it would not be self-supporting for another two years and more than two hundred agreements later.

Shortly after independence, the president's Air Policy Commission, charged to investigate the integration of national aviation policies, recommended the United States needed "an adequate Navy and Ground Force . . . but [the military establishment] must be built around the air arm. . . . Our military security must be based on air power."[22] Three months later, a congressional investigative team, the Joint

31

Congressional Aviation Policy Board, also endorsed the air offensive strategic striking force.[23]

Entering bitter budget battles with the growing confidence of heading an independent service, Symington and the air advocates grew increasingly outspoken and radical. On 10 January 1948 Symington told a New York audience, "We feel, with deep conviction, that the destiny of the United States rests on the continued development of our Air Force. The question of whether we shall have adequate American air power may be, in short, the question of survival."[24] Many in the other services favored a traditional "balanced force concept" which divided the defense budget more equitably among the services. Six months later Symington, in a "gloves-off" talk in Los Angeles, criticized the balanced force concept of American defense and those "axe-grinders dedicated to obsolete methods" of warfare who contended that Air Force appropriations might unbalance the three armed services.[25] One month later General Kenney (SAC) made the following claim:

> The Air Force that is superior in its capability of destruction plays the dominant role and has the power of decision. The inferior air force has no role. Before it can be built up the war will be over. The advantage accruing to the aggressor who makes such a surprise attack has become so great that it can almost be considered decisive.[26]

The new Air Force's professional journal, the *Air University Quarterly Review*, began cataloguing a flurry of confident assertions. Alexander de Seversky, a Russian émigré, aircraft manufacturer, engineer, author, and air enthusiast, claimed airpower alone could have won World War II: "We could have bombed them to a pulp destroying the last vestige of their industrial civilization and leaving them to dig out of the debris for the next two or three generations."[27] Lt Col Joseph L. Dickman claimed the atomic bomb validated Douhet's theories, and in a pinch, tactical aviation should be sacrificed for the development of strategic aviation.[28] Lt Col Frank R. Pancake argued for a "Pax Americana" by way of strategic airpower, and Lt Col John P. Healey believed the proper deterrent use of atomic weapons was sufficient to meet our expanding foreign policy aims.[29]

Outside observers noted an increase in "romantic" views of the new Air Force. One observer wrote the following:

Air power romanticism was a natural successor to the naval romanticism which had sprung up a half-century or so earlier; its advocates were in the direct line of the Mahanist proponents of the beginning of the first decade of the century. A preponderant Strategic Air Command—like the Great White Fleet—appeared a device for performing as a world power without getting too deeply enmeshed in the complex, dangerous, interior affairs of Eurasia.[30]

Those advocating the expansion of airpower and its potential, especially with atomic weapons, found a receptive Congress and public. America was not comfortable making great economic sacrifices in peacetime, and universal military training (Truman and Marshall's preference) was intrinsically unpopular, especially in the shadow of a great war with its substantial human and material costs. Reliance on airpower fit the nation's industrial, technological, and progressive style; a long-range strategic striking force appealed to residual isolationist sentiments as well.[31] Like the Great White Fleet, a strategic air force would be an emblem of a great power, would deter war, and would be used effectively as a diplomatic tool. Though comprehended by few at the time, the endless capabilities of the Air Force were based on its enduring doctrinal trinity of globalism, indivisibility, and decisiveness.

Globalism was predicated on the centralized management of airpower. From early in World War II, General Arnold labored to centralize airpower. In November 1942 he explained his concept in a letter to General Spaatz, then commander of the Eighth Air Force in England:

> Air operations in Europe must be controlled and planned by one man. . . . Unless we are careful, we will find our air effort in Europe dispersed the same way we are now dispersed all around the world. We will find as many different bases of operations operating under as many different commanders as there are land commanders. This must be prevented. We should take advantage of the ring of air bases with which we are surrounding Germany so as to secure maximum striking power. This, of course, takes into consideration the question of weather, the question of location of targets, and the question of priority of targets. Quite obviously, with one man in command of all the air, he can move the mass of his air where it will be most effectively employed and use the rest of it to support the ground arm.[32]

After disastrous results with parceling out tactical airpower early in the North African campaign, the Army Air Corps secured approval for centralized control of theater tactical airpower under the new field service regulation Field Manual (FM) 100-20, *Command and Employment of Air Power*, on 21 July 1943.[33] Six months later, at the Sextant Conference in Cairo, Arnold was able to establish Spaatz as commander of United States Strategic Air Forces in Europe (USSTAF) directing both the Eighth Air Force in England and the Fifteenth Air Force in the Mediterranean.[34]

Nevertheless, the centralization of regional airpower had to take a further step to become global. Arnold turned to the Twentieth Air Force in the Pacific to develop and conceptually validate the roots of globalism.[35] The strategic bombers of the Twentieth Air Force became in Arnold's words, a "global weapon the organizational and operational concept of which is unique among the Armed Forces of the United States" in that it answered only to the joint chiefs (with Arnold as executor) and cut across theaters and traditional chains of command.[36]

To many, Arnold's "global" experiment of the highly centralized and tightly supervised Twentieth Air Force defeated Japan through strategic bombing. With atomic-capable intercontinental bombers on the horizon, the Air Force could patrol the globe at the pleasure of the joint chiefs and independent of the Army or Navy. The Army Air Forces' position became national defense policy on 12 December 1946 with the publication of Joint Chiefs of Staff (JCS) 1259/27. It stated that "the 'air atomic' strategic air force should only come under the orders of the JCS because of the overriding importance of its strategic mission to national security."[37] After the war, General Spaatz, who had witnessed the activities of the Twentieth Air Force, routinely emphasized the global striking force capable of "launching . . . heavy blows from any point on the globe against any other point."[38] Strategic Air Command was to become the agent of American global striking power and the nation's first line of defense.[39] The young Air Force took this calling seriously and invested heavily in building a bomber force capable of striking anywhere in the world at any time with overwhelming force on a moment's notice.[40]

Theoretically, indivisibility referred to airpower's employment as a single entity, something to be managed flexibly by airmen across the strategic and tactical spectrum to accomplish the mission. In the 1943 FM 100-20, versatility of air forces was policy: "The aim of the strategic air force is the defeat of the enemy nation"; these forces could "be joined with the tactical air force and assigned tactical air force missions" when the "action is vital and decisive."[41] Strategic forces, indeed, had performed many tactical missions in World War II, notably in Italy and at Normandy. Air Forces thus were responsive, flexible, effective, and indivisible—if centrally controlled by "independent airmen."

Finally, Air Force enthusiasts professed a *decisive* capability. The bombing survey gave believers sufficient evidence that, had airpower been massed and applied relentlessly by airmen against appropriate industrial vital centers without recurring tactical and peripheral diversions, airpower would have shortened the war and won it with fewer American casualties. Airpower clearly would have been the decisive arm; at least no one would have been able to prove otherwise. Now, given the experience of World War II, the advocates of airpower could employ better technologies and additional destructive weapons more effectively to render a quick decision with less cost to America. This decisiveness, brought about by massive destruction of enemy vital centers, favored using extreme means in war to gain a decisive end—"no substitute for total victory"—a condition that times and circumstances would challenge.

The air arm's unity of voice, vision, and faith convinced those who wanted to believe it, or who thought it could be achieved soon. But, in reality, the rhetoric exceeded the reach of airpower.[42] SAC was far from global, with significant shortfalls in bomber range, atomic weapons, and global communications systems.[43] Indivisibility existed only on paper, as SAC would become increasingly ill equipped for conventional operations and TAC was rapidly disintegrating, with little cooperation between the two. And decisiveness was difficult with such small numbers of planes and atomic bombs, not to mention poorly trained crews. As before the war, airpower advocates oversold service capabilities. Even though they had achieved service independence, the fervor of their radical beliefs demanded service preeminence. As one analyst remarked, "Ideology . . . remained more extreme than interests required. . . . The Air Force overemphasized the efficacy of airpower in the quest for service independence, and this radicalism outlived the incentives that spawned it."[44] The romantics assumed the omnipotence of airpower, and competition for small defense budgets promoted extremism. Perhaps unwittingly, the Air Force entrenched itself in a narrow and increasingly dogmatic doctrine—strategic bombing.

Technology functioned both as an instigator and a messiah to the air advocate. Married to machines, the World War II generation generals understood how numbers and technology altered the calculus of battle. If numbers were unaffordable, then, preferably bigger, higher-flying, faster and longer-range strategic bombers would make up the difference. In short, an institutional technological zeal would make doctrinal dreams seem real.[45] This goal would remain the Air Force's primary solution to doctrinal shortfalls.

To institutionalize this chronic craving for technologies, General Arnold had appointed Dr. Theodore von Kármán in the fall of 1942 as head of a new scientific advisory group and had in 1944 directed him to look into the technological future to guide Air Force programs for the next 10 to 20 years. After a year's study, the group produced in December 1945 a 33-volume report entitled *Toward New Horizons*. It concluded that atomic-equipped transoceanic rockets were possible and that weapons destructiveness would increase, as would the speed and range of aircraft. In the short term, manned bombers would be the most decisive instruments of warfare. Kármán's new horizons held promise, but budget limitations forced the abandonment of many of these strategic programs and held implications for tactical and transport aviation. Most money went "to support the [strategic] Air Force in being."[46]Additionally, the allocation of funds to the bomber advocates biased future research and development programs away from other promising fields. Maj Gen Donald L. Putt, director of Air Force Research and Development, complained in 1949:

> There are those in high positions in the Air Force today who hold that research and development must be kept under rigid control by

"requirements" and "military characteristics" promulgated by operational personnel who can only look into the past and ask for bigger and better weapons of World War II vintage. . . . They have not yet established that partnership between the strategist and the scientist which is mandatory to insure that superior strategy and technology which is essential to future success against our potential enemies.[47]

As a result, the Air Force funneled most of its research and development funds towards making bigger airplanes fly faster, higher, and farther at a time many in the Army and a few in the Air Force were calling for alternative technologies as well as smaller airplanes that flew slower, lower, and closer.[48]

The latter concern became most publicly apparent when the Navy, concerned about its institutional future and the soundness of strategic bombing as America's first line of defense, drew Congress into the debate through the "B-36 investigation," held between May and October 1949. Bitter over the cancellation of its supercarrier by the Truman administration and challenged by the new Air Force in the Navy's traditional role as America's first line of defense, the Navy publicly criticized the preeminence of the Air Force's doctrine of strategic bombing and specifically its new centerpiece—the B-36 intercontinental bomber. While promoting its own capabilities, the sea service questioned the B-36's capabilities, the efficacy and morality of atomic strategic bombing, and Air Force neglect of tactical aviation. Though they had many good points, Navy spokesmen seriously undermined their own position by their own methods, contradictions, and indiscriminate allegations. Fabricating reports, personalizing attacks, and damning atomic bombing—while claiming to be better able to do it—did little for their cause. The politically adept new Air Force chief of staff, Hoyt S. Vandenberg, calmly refuted the assaults by citing Air Force efforts to support existing JCS war plans.[49] He provided assurances that the indivisibility of airpower and the versatility of aircraft would enable adequate support of armies. Jets and bombers, Vandenberg argued, could meet the needs of the Army.[50] In the hearings, the Army backed Air Force efforts to attend to Army needs of air support.[51]

These often acrimonious hearings convinced the Air Force even more so that it had a public mandate for strategic bombing. The tone of the debate embarrassed Secretary of Defense Louis Johnson and resulted in the promulgation of his Consolidation Directive 1, which stated that all information emanating from the Pentagon would be reviewed by censors not only for security but for policy and propriety.[52] Concern over interception of its bomber fleet by fighters, a point raised in the hearings, influenced the Air Force decision to develop and procure the big, high, fast, and long-range B-52. The B-36 hearings ultimately compelled the Air Force to give even greater impetus to strengthening its strategic capabilities at the expense of those tactical capabilities.

But this development was not new to the Tactical Air Command. Chaotic demobilization in the postwar Air Force was magnified in TAC. Numerous aircraft ferrying requirements, endless air shows (159 in 1946 alone), an inability to retain maintenance technicians, excessive tactical airlift requests, an increasing demand for escort fighters and interceptors, challenges of jet, radar, and communication technologies—all served to complicate TAC's nearly stillborn establishment in 1946; it was a command without sufficient money or priority to meet its demands.[53] The TAC commander, General Quesada, was well respected by the Army, which his IX Tactical Air Command had supported well in the European war. As a symbolic commitment to them, Quesada moved TAC headquarters to Langley Field, Virginia, to be close to Army Ground Forces (later Army Field Forces) headquarters at Fort Monroe, Virginia. While Quesada believed in the preeminence of strategic bombing, he worked hard with minimal funding and only a small staff to appease the Army while defending the needs of the Air Force. He was aware both of Spaatz's commitment to Eisenhower and the Key West agreement which pledged that "the tactical mission was not subordinate to the strategic mission and the latter must not be pursued at the expense of the former."[54] Outnumbered and outvoted in the Air Force hierarchy, Quesada could do little as a fighter general.

By late 1948 the new commander of SAC, senior bomber cohort lieutenant general Curtis E. LeMay, convinced senior Air Force leaders to endorse strategic bombing as the young Air Force's "primary mission." Furthermore, the new

Continental Air Command (CONAC) absorbed and subordinated Air Defense Command (ADC) and TAC. The emerging cold war paradigm favored ADC, and CONAC relabeled Air Defense Command regulations as its own while attempting to collocate its headquarters with ADC's. TAC was neglected, with no aircraft assigned and a planning staff of only 66.[55] Though this consolidation officially sought to streamline, cut costs, and address needs of air defense and reserves, Quesada felt it had the "sinister motives" of a shuffle in general officer positions. He fought it, refused command, resigned his assignment, and retired a few years later.[56] But even CONAC, which commanded two-thirds of the Air Force mission, garnered only 20 percent of its budget.[57]

By 1949 TAC was truly a pawn in a game of chess between the Army and the Air Force. Continued budget limitations threatened TAC's existence. Some in Air Force headquarters wanted to give TAC to the Army.[58] Others saw TAC as a luxury whose budget should be trimmed to free more money for SAC.[59] Fighter lieutenant general Otto P. "Opie" Weyland recounted that SAC should have priority, yet "SAC wasn't satisfied with most of the chips . . . they wanted them all." The tactical community, Weyland argued, had to fight "just to preserve a force structure."[60] Furthermore, CONAC stated TAC's primary mission was "to support operations of SAC and Military Air Transport Service (MATS) as directed by CONAC."[61] But General Vandenberg did not want to lose the tactical mission.

TAC had labored hard to appease growing Army concerns over close air support. Both services conducted several joint exercises, but haggling over who was to control CAS and how it was to be conducted proved an early obstacle. TAC clung to FM 100-20 as its Tactical Air Force doctrine. This manual assigned top priority to air superiority, secondary importance to air interdiction, and tertiary priority to close air support. It also enabled airmen to retain centralized control over tactical air forces. The Army was unhappy with bottom priority, particularly if the situation desperately called for CAS. A SAC-dominated Air Force that was building jet fighters to fly higher and faster to escort and intercept critical bombers was not building technologies conducive to close air support. TAC felt jets were more survivable, but its attempt to modify the F-80 jet for CAS was aborted for lack of money.[62] Funding limits rationalized lack of doctrinal scrutiny and review and made it expedient to tolerate narrowness of thought. Most exercises tended to demonstrate doctrine rather than to test it. As time went by, the Army grew less patient with Air Force support, even though it showed sympathy towards the plight of a shriveled TAC.

Finally, after the B-36 controversy, TAC convened an air board of review that consisted of top fighter pilot leaders to address the doctrinal and technical problems of tactical aviation. The board came up with substantive recommendations and concerns regarding TAC's bureaucratic impotence, the illusion of flexibility and indivisibility (SAC knew little and cared less about TAC roles), problems of specialization, and concerns over Army desires to build its own tactical air force. In response to the board's recommendations, the CONAC commander, Lt Gen Ennis C. Whitehead, an experienced Pacific bomber commander, stated that CONAC was doing fine by the Army; that joint cooperation was good; that TAC did not need units assigned to it; that emphasis on CAS would hurt air defense; and that "the very best support bomber available is the B-36, the second best one the B-50, and the third best the B-29," all the Air Force's largest bombers.[63]

Efforts to improve tactical capabilities proved too little, too late. The Air Force was flying bigger and faster planes, flying them higher and farther, and using longer runways. Fighter pilots had accepted the preeminence of the bomber pilots' Strategic Air Command as America's first line of defense, and as time went on, those responsible for interdiction and close air support in Tactical Air Command found the Air Force moving further away from its mission. Certainly, small defense budgets and concern over the Soviet Union advanced investment in SAC, but the Air Force appeared more interested in exploiting the national demand for a global strategic striking force than it was in bringing substance to airpower's indivisibility and flexibility. Yet the Air Force was not alone, for despite the National Security Act, each service promoted the strategic outlook that best protected its interests. A nervous General Vandenberg expressed deep concern in May 1950 over the widening "gap between Air Force requirements and capabilities that was nothing short of tragic."[64] In less than a month, the neglected tactical capabilities of the Air Force would begin to cost the lives of many American soldiers.

One month after voicing concern over Air Force capabilities, General Vandenberg confidently claimed airpower could halt the sudden communist invasion of South Korea.[65] Soon the process of public assurances again masked private concerns. Spurred by Army complaints concerning CAS, secret Air Force investigative teams returned from Korea and reported on poor training, doctrine, and equipment.[66] Unpreparedness precipitated improvisation. Jet F-80s yielded to propellered F-51s, which were more accurate, could carry more ordnance, could loiter longer, and could work from more primitive fields. Doctrinal understanding was in short supply (still unpublished formally within the Air Force), as were qualified forward air controllers and communications equipment.[67] Yet, the Air Force theater leaders and staffs (most of them fighter pilots) created a system that worked and did much to preserve the Pusan perimeter and impede enemy offensive capabilities. Unpreparedness and neglect led to a desperate situation; it was a hard and an embarrassing lesson the fighter leaders would not soon forget.

Predictably, the Air Force in Korea performed best in those missions it had emphasized since the previous war—strategic bombing and air superiority. The strategic bombing campaign lasted eight weeks, from 1 August to 27 September 1950, and it destroyed virtually all strategic targets of significance in North Korea.[68] Once China entered the war, B-29s fell as easy prey for the Soviet-made MiG-15 jet fighters. Nevertheless, American jet fighters quickly gained air superiority with the F-86. The ground commanders remained unimpressed with the interdiction campaign though. The campaign was confounded by an enemy whose divisions required only 50 tons of supplies a day and remained resilient by relying on camouflage, a diverse supply network, and the cover of night and inclement weather. Prohibited from striking China, airpower denied the enemy victory but it could not provide the same victory for the allies. The death of Joseph Stalin, unacceptable costs of a successful offensive, exhaustion, threats to destroy irrigation dams, and Eisenhower's threat to use atomic weapons compelled the armistice.[69] With some justification again, the Air Force preferred to believe the threats to destroy irrigation dams and Eisenhower's threat to use atomic weapons made the difference, and once more airpower could claim the starring role.

The long-term implications of the Korean War on Air Force culture were twofold. First, it introduced to combat a new generation of future leaders, the "Korean War generation." These leaders differed from the World War II generals in that they did not experience total war, and 60 percent were first generation jet fighter pilots. They also would achieve higher levels of civilian and professional education and follow broader career paths to dominate top leadership roles from 1978 to 1987. Their formative combat experience occurred in the complexities of limited war, and few felt the passions of the struggle for autonomy. The Korean War and the junior World War II generations would gain the most experience from fighting the limited war in Korea.[70]

Second, the Korean War highlighted a growing split between the bomber and fighter communities. The split began with the founding of the semiautonomous Twentieth Air Force in the Pacific war. The Twentieth Air Force formed the conceptual origins of SAC, a global atomic striking force that reported directly to the JCS and received clear funding priority in the Air Force from 1946 until the mid-1960s. While TAC paid the price for its neglect during the Korean War, SAC continued to receive more funding and preference.

But what really exacerbated relations between the two communities was the difference between each service component's view of the war's meaning. Within the Air Force, the predominantly bomber-oriented senior Air Force leadership's view held that war would not have occurred if SAC had received greater funding; hence, it would have been stronger before the war and thus offered a more credible deterrent. Joint Chiefs of Staff chairman Omar N. Bradley asserted that striking Manchuria would involve us in the "wrong war, at the wrong place, at the wrong time, and with the wrong enemy." Many senior Air Force leaders used this statement to characterize the whole war. Their posture seemed ironic when one realizes how many of them did want to bomb Manchuria.[71] Senior Air Force leaders "chafed under the prospect of political constraints" that reduced the decisiveness of airpower and surrendered initiative to the enemy.[72]

But many in the fighter community had a different perspective. General Weyland, European war veteran, senior fighter cohort, and commander of the Far East Air Forces (FEAF) in the Korean War, wrote in his after-action report that tactical air forces needed more joint training, a better command and control system, and greater preparation for more limited wars in the future. He recommended a TAC coequal with SAC, one that was mobile and well funded.[73] Many in TAC saw the Korean War as a means to establish a need for a greater rapid-response tactical capability.[74]

The Korean War contributed to an increase in defense spending to cope with the cold war, but the allocation of resources was uneven. TAC felt it had proved a need and right for more proportional funding, but to no avail. TAC pointed to *National Security Council* 135/3 of September 1952, which indicated the United States should be ready to fight conventional wars.[75] Nevertheless, SAC would continue to get funding and institutional preference, which served to harden feelings between the Air Force's two combat communities. By 1953 TAC and SAC began to march farther apart institutionally and philosophically.

With few exceptions, the World War II bomber generals, especially the senior generation, had developed an absolutist perspective towards war and airpower.[76] These generals were the natural descendants of the prewar "airpower enthusiasts" (whom several of them knew) and the postwar "romantics" (whom most of them knew or were themselves). Their central tenet held that airpower, specifically strategic bombing, not only could win wars but also could end them. These generals cared not for Carl von Clausewitz, for they believed when politics failed, war began, and "narrow military strategy concerned with complete military victory" reigned supreme.[77] Instead, they clutched to the gospels according to a reborn Douhet and an aerial Alfred T. Mahan. From the former, they embraced the efficacy of a relentless atomic air offensive; from the latter, the economic and strategic framework. Shrinking budgets amidst perceptions of a growing threat nourished interservice radicalism and strategic monism. Absolutism was a natural product of the traditions of their romantic promises (decisiveness), their most destructive and singular means (strategic bombing), and their unconditional ends (total victory). Absolutist views coincided with a strategy of annihilation that could envision only suitable total ends by way of massive means. The perspective was unambiguous, simple, and easy to embrace. If the nation decided to declare war, it should use all means in this punitive crusade, unhampered by political interference, to achieve total military victory quickly. Simply put, air absolutists believed resolute strategic bombing was decisive in and of itself.

The bomber-dominant senior World War II generation, who would occupy top leadership positions in the Air Force through 1965, displayed a remarkable similarity in their career paths. Eighty percent of these bomber pilots fought in the Pacific war. Of those, 75 percent served in the Twentieth Air Force. Isolated on the Pacific Islands and under the able leadership of senior bomber cohort major general LeMay, they developed a strong, disciplined cohesion. Reporting directly to the JCS, they received less political, allied, or interservice interference.[78] Responding with resolution and autonomy, in part to avenge the disaster at Pearl Harbor, the Twentieth Air Force felt its air assault ended the war in the Pacific just as dramatically as it had begun. Highly centralized, undistracted, and relentless strategic airpower managed by airmen had brought about total military victory over the Japanese in spectacular fashion. Their memories were consumed by two total wars fought to exhaustion. Little wonder that they, in large measure, supported their Pacific brother in arms, Douglas MacArthur, both in his belief "that there is no substitute for victory" and in his absolutism. As one noted analyst concluded: "The MacArthur legacy was taken over less by his own service than by . . . the air force."[79] Clearly, they perceived the Korean War as an anomaly. Now, the imminent danger of the gigantic communist threat coupled with the primacy of the strategic nuclear mission, rekindled the absolutist mentality, especially in SAC and amongst most of the senior Air Force leaders.

On the other hand, those pragmatists who existed came chiefly from the fighter community.[80] Pragmatists viewed war and airpower in more ambiguous terms. War contained rivalries, conflicting interests, changing priorities, distractions, and complexities that demanded patience. Airpower was multidimensional and flexible and sometimes demanded improvision. Pragmatists inclined more than absolutists towards the Clausewitzian notion of war as a "political instrument" and respected that politics ultimately governed the conduct of wars. Pragmatists favored relative interests over absolute values, and the air pragmatists were more comfortable with alliances and working with other services. They also preferred the massive application of airpower but accepted the measured use of force in proportion to costs and benefits—that limited aggression could be repelled with limited response. In short, they accepted the political and military realities of war better, especially limited war.

Curiously, two-thirds of the senior fighter cohort and three-quarters of the junior fighter cohort fought in the European theater of World War II.[81] They were accustomed to the difficulties of working intimately with the Army and the other Allies. That the Allied air strategy responded to political redirection on occasion was not surprising to them. These fighters frequently experienced shifts in roles and missions as well as the need for improvisation and flexibility. They fought and deployed with the Army and witnessed victory as a combined effort (as had their southwest Pacific brethren). And their numbers swelled in the new fighter-dominated Korean War generation.

Though they came from common roots and a common war, the two communities which produced the future Air Force leadership did not have a common experience. They bonded together to win a war and to gain service independence, but postindependence absolutism and strategic monism, exacerbated by a tight defense budget, frustrated the subordinated fighter community. After initial difficulties stemming from long neglect, the fighter community perceived that its ultimate contribution to the Korean War justified more attention and funding for the "more plentiful" future. Yet, it took the demands of the Korean War and the compassion of Congress to reestablish TAC as a coequal command in 1951. Nevertheless, 1953 portended the advent of more troubled times for the subordinated TAC. Those senior leaders with more pragmatic views left Washington, and in came Eisenhower's new chiefs of staff, with two Pacific war bomber generals in the Air Force's top two positions—Nathan F. Twining and Thomas D. White.[82]

As events later revealed, under Twining and White, the new chief of staff and vice chief of staff, respectively, SAC continued to overshadow TAC. Yet it was through the insightful work and far-reaching efforts of LeMay, oftentimes called the father of SAC, that SAC became a formidable force. Equally important, these men brought with them their absolutist views. The ascendancy of this trio helped to shape military thinking for years to come.

Notes

1. Tami D. Biddle, "How Much Can an Economy Devote to Defense?", presentation on defense budgets during the Truman and Eisenhower administrations delivered to International Security and Arms Control Program, Yale University, New Haven, Conn., 2 October 1988. On the influence of the Bureau of Budget's effect on Truman, see Mark Perry, *Four Stars: The Inside Story of the Forty-five Year Battle Between the Joint Chiefs of Staff and America's Civilian Leaders* (Boston: Houghton Mifflin, 1989), 21. For the influence of George Kennan's "Long Telegram" on Truman's thinking, see Caroline Ziemke, "In the Shadow of the Giant: USAF Tactical Air Command in the Era of Strategic Bombing, 1945–1955" (PhD diss., Ohio State University, 1989), 21.

2. Herman S. Wolk, *Planning and Organizing the Postwar Air Force, 1943–1947* (Washington, D.C.: Office of Air Force History [OAFH], 1984), 211.

3. *New York Times*, 6 October 1945, 12. Gen Carl A. Spaatz, first chief of staff of the Air Force, "thought that the major lesson of the war was that prolonged ground wars of attrition would now be relegated to the past." See Wolk, 41; Harry R. Borowski, *A Hollow Threat: Strategic Air Power and Containment Before Korea* (Westport, Conn.: Greenwood Press, 1982); and David Alan Rosenberg, "The Origins of Overkill: Nuclear Weapons and American Strategy, 1945-1960," *International Security* 7 (Spring 1983):

3–71. In fact, the public and most officials in the United States did not know there were only a few atomic bombs available in the late 1940s.

4. Bernard Brodie, "The Heritage of Douhet," *Air University Quarterly Review* 6, no. 2 (Summer 1953): 126–27. "If we disregard the over-all vision and consider only specific assertions, it is clear in World War II Douhet was proved wrong on almost every important point he made. . . . But it is also true that he was able to create a framework of strategic thought which is considered by many responsible airmen to fit the atomic age astonishingly well."

5. Wolk, 211.

6. Richard K. Betts, *Soldiers, Statesmen, and Cold War Crises* (Cambridge, Mass.: Harvard University Press, 1977), 127.

7. Philip Selznick, *Leadership in Administration: A Sociological Interpretation* (Evanston, Ill.: Row, Peterson, 1957), 57.

8. John T. Greenwood, "The Emergence of the Postwar Strategic Air Force, 1945–1953," in *Air Power and Warfare: The Proceedings of the 8th Military History Symposium, United States Air Force Academy, 18–20 October 1978,* eds., Alfred F. Hurley and Robert C. Ehrhart (Washington, D.C.: OAFH, 1979), 218–19.

9. Gen Leon Johnson, transcript of oral history interview by Arthur K. Marmor, 14 April 1965, Air Force Historical Research Agency (cited hereinafter as AFHRA), Maxwell AFB, Ala. Senior bomber generation brigadier general Johnson, former chief of the Personnel Services Division, remembered, "We didn't demobilize; we merely fell apart. . . . We lost many records of all the groups and units . . . because there was no one to take care of them. . . . It was not an orderly demobilization at all. It was just a riot, really." Eugene M. Zuckert, an assistant secretary of the Air Force, recalled the period as one of the "saddest," characterized by a "high degree of inexperience in Washington. People serving [from the field] as colonels and brigadier generals . . . who didn't understand Washington, didn't understand what a headquarters was like." See Eugene M. Zuckert, transcript of oral history interview by Dr. George M. Watson, 27 April 1982, 3, AFHRA.

10. Richard H. Kohn and Joseph Harahan, eds., *Air Superiority in World War II and Korea: An Interview with Gen James Ferguson, Gen Robert M. Lee, Gen William Momyer, and Lt Gen Elwood R. Quesada* (Washington, D.C.: OAFH, 1983), 18.

11. Perry McCoy Smith, *The Air Force Plans for Peace, 1943–1945* (Baltimore: Johns Hopkins University Press, 1970), 25. Smith also argues that autonomy was the primary focus for postwar planning in the Air Force (p. 14).

12. Robert Frank Futrell, *Ideas, Concepts, Doctrine: Basic Thinking in the United States Air Force, 1907–1960,* vol. 1 (Maxwell AFB, Ala.: Air University Press, December 1989), 231. In fact, there was cautious optimism by General Kenney and others that "nuclear bombers without fighter escort might be strategically feasible." See Joseph W. Caddell, "Orphan of

Unification: The Development of United States Air Force Tactical Air Power Doctrine, 1945–1950" (PhD diss., Duke University, 1984), 119. Furthermore, no Air Force war plans from 1945 to 1950 addressed a conventional surface campaign.

13. Arthur T. Hadley, *A Report From the Field: The Straw Giant* (New York: Random House, 1986), 77.

14. House Subcommittee on Appropriations, *Military Establishment Appropriations Bill for 1948*, 80th Cong., 1st sess., 1947, 600.

15. Wolk, 39.

16. Vance O. Mitchell, "The First Generation: A Policy History of the Air Force Officer Corps, 1944–1973" (unpublished manuscript, OAFH, May 1991), 723.

17. Smith, 13, 19, 60.

18. Wolk, 41.

19. Mitchell, 736.

20. Wolk, 179–80.

21. Ibid.; and Flora Lewis, "The Education of a Senator," *The Atlantic*, December 1971, 56.

22. Futrell, 228.

23. Ibid.

24. Wolk, 209.

25. Walter Millis ed., *The Forrestal Diaries* (New York: Viking Press, 1951), 463–64.

26. Futrell, 239; Stuart Symington, transcript of oral history interview by Hugh N. Ahmann and Herman S. Wolk, 2 May 1978, 110, AFHRA. Some in the Air Force strongly advocated a preemptive strike. Maj Gen Orvil Anderson, a bomber advocate and commandant of the Air War College, was quoted by the press as advocating a preemptive strike against the Soviet Union in response to the Korean invasion. As a result, an irritated President Truman pressured for Anderson's sudden retirement.

27. Alexander P. de Seversky, "A Lecture on Air Power," *Air University Quarterly Review* 1, no. 2 (Fall 1947): 25–41.

28. Lt Col Joseph L. Dickman, "Douhet and the Future," *Air University Quarterly Review* 2, no. 1 (Summer 1948): 3–15.

29. Lt Col Frank R. Pancake, "The Strategic Striking Force," *Air University Quarterly Review* 2, no. 2 (Fall 1948): 48–56; Lt Col John Healy, "Air Power and Foreign Policy," *Air University Quarterly Review* 2, no. 2 (Fall 1948): 15–26; and Wolk, 120. The provocative nature of some of these statements induced bomber advocate Haywood Hansell to admit later that "proponents of the two ideas soon lost all sense of proportion in the very intensity of their zeal. Airmen tended to advocate strategic bombing to the exclusion of all else; and . . . ground soldiers to view bombardment as simply as more artillery. If the Army belittled airmen claims, it must also be admitted that, at least in some very small measure, we may possibly have overstated our powers and understated our limitations."

30. Walt W. Rostow, *The United States in the World Arena: An Essay in Recent History* (New York: Harper, 1960), 224.

31. Ibid., 223.

32. James Parton, "The Thirty-One Year Gestation of the Independent USAF," *Aerospace Historian* 34, no. 3 (Fall/September 1987): 155.

33. War Department, FM 100-20, *Command and Employment of Air Power* (Washington, D.C.: Government Printing Office, 1943), 2.

34. Parton, 155.

35. Though conceptually and politically vindicated, the Twentieth Air Force was hardly global. See Michael S. Sherry, *The Rise of American Air Power: The Creation of Armageddon* (New Haven, Conn.: Yale University Press, 1987), 185. Sherry notes, "It was global only in the sense of air force ambitions, not in terms of current realities."

36. Ibid., 184.

37. John T. Greenwood, "The Atomic Bomb—Early Air Force Thinking and the Strategic Air Force, August 1945–March 1946," *Aerospace Historian* 34, no. 3 (Fall/September 1987): 165.

38. House Subcommittee, *Military Establishment Appropriations Bill for 1948*, 401–2.

39. Futrell, 242–43. New SAC commander, senior generation bomber General LeMay, in October 1948 recommended that "the fundamental goal of the Air Force should be the creation of a strategic atomic striking force capable of attacking any target in Eurasia from bases in the United States and returning to the points of take-off."

40. Ibid. Two months after LeMay's speech, senior Air Force leaders decided officially that "to launch the atomic offensive must be considered as the primary mission of the Air Force and must be given the greatest consideration and priority."

41. FM 100-20, 9.

42. Small defense budgets no doubt contributed to shortcomings in the ability of the air advocates to achieve their doctrinal promises, but they alone were not necessarily causal. Technological, doctrinal, and organizational obstacles remained significant.

43. Richard H. Kohn and Joseph Harahan, eds., *Strategic Air Warfare: An Interview with Curtis E. LeMay, Leon W. Johnson, David A. Burchinal, and Jack J. Catton* (Washington, D.C.: OAFH, 1988), 93. This account indicates that SAC needed five to six days to go pick up atomic weapons and fly to forward bases before launching atomic air strikes. Also in March 1946 only 27 B-29s were atomic capable. Nine bombs were available in 1946, 13 in 1947, and 50 in 1948. AEC (arms export control) teams could prepare only two bombs each day by mid-1948 (p. 95). Rosenberg, 14.

44. Betts, 117.

45. Robert Perry, "The Interaction of Technology and Doctrine in the USAF," in *Air Power and Warfare: The Proceedings of the 8th Military History Symposium United States Air Force Academy, 18–20 October 1978*, eds. Col Alfred F. Hurley and Maj Robert C. Ehrhart (Washington, D.C.: OAFH,

1979), 390. "It is not a great oversimplification to suggest that the new United States Air Force sensibly concluded—en masse—that new technology, shaped and applied as rapidly as circumstances (most budgetary) would permit, could dominate military capabilities for the foreseeable [sic] future. . . . Evolution of doctrine through the gradual application of revolutionary new technology was preferred."

46. Futrell, 221.

47. Ibid., 275–76. An Air University study found that focus on day-to-day concerns prevented a solid research and development program (p. 277).

48. Caddell, 303. According to Caddell, an unreleased Air Force investigation in 1949 concluded that all postulated Air Force fighters after the F-90 would have poor performance below 20,000 to 25,000 feet. Also, an Air Force board endorsed fast jets as they "doubted that propellered aircraft would survive in the next conflict" (p. 306). The narrow focus on strategic bombing also hampered development of rocket/missile technologies, drones, transport, and fighter-bomber aircraft.

49. Hoyt S. Vandenberg was basically a fighter general from the European theater. Symbolic of his orientation was the reduction in the number of college professors on his consulting list and their replacement by political and press figures. See John L. Frisbee, ed., *Makers of the United States Air Force* (Washington, D.C.: OAFH, 1987), 215.

50. Futrell, 307. In 1951, however, General LeMay cautioned Congress that employing "strategic air power against tactical targets [was] not getting the full use of the weapon."

51. For the best analysis of the B-36 controversy, see Paul Y. Hammond, *Super Carriers and B-36 Bombers: Appropriations, Strategy, and Politics* [Interuniversity Case Program no. 97] (New York: Bobbs-Merrill Company, 1966). For other analyses see Caddell, chap. 4, and Ziemke, 99–106. Privately, the Army told the Air Force it was concerned about TAC's limited ability.

52. Earl H. Tilford Jr., *Setup: What the Air Force Did in Vietnam and Why* (Maxwell AFB, Ala.: Air University Press, 1991), 14.

53. History, Tactical Air Command, 1946, vol. 1, 7. The AAF established TAC in March 1946 to gain the Army chief of staff's (General Eisenhower) favor on its road to independence. TAC suffered from overcommitments without the rank in its leadership and without funding priority to build a credible capability. The TAC commander, General Quesada, remarked that TAC was in "a helluva state."

54. Ziemke, 58.

55. Ibid., 75.

56. Ibid., 68–73. Later, he would admit he felt "personally offended" and "let down" (as did the retired Spaatz), but insisted he wasn't bitter at his beloved Air Force. For Spaatz's reaction, see Caddell, 201.

57. Ziemke, 75.

58. Kohn and Harahan, *Air Superiority*, 64.

59. Dickman, 3–15. Dickman also anticipated conditions where TAC should be given to the Army.

60. Jerome V. Martin, "Reforging the Sword: United States Tactical Air Forces, Air Power Doctrine, and National Security Policy, 1945–1956" (PhD diss., Ohio State University, 1988), 56.

61. Ziemke, 130.

62. Ibid., 80–82. The F-84 was not suitable for low-altitude operations, nor was any jet that was in development at the time.

63. Caddell, 299–300.

64. Futrell, 291.

65. Perry, 25.

66. Caddell, 66–70; Ziemke, 190.

67. On doctrine, see David MacIsaac, "The Evolution of Air Power Since 1945: The American Experience," in *War in the Third Dimension: Essays in Contemporary Air Power*, ed. R. A. Mason (Washington, D.C.: Brassey's Defence Publishers, 1986), 16; and Martin, 337. On forward air controllers, see Ziemke, 148; and on communications equipment, see Caddell, 60, 66.

68. Robert F. Futrell, *The United States Air Force in Korea, 1950–1953* (New York: Duell, Sloan and Pearce, 1961), 157–58. Hydroelectric dams were spared deliberately.

69. Mark Clodfelter, *The Limits of Air Power: The American Bombing of North Vietnam* (New York: Free Press, 1989), 22–24; Edward C. Keefer, "President Dwight D. Eisenhower and the End of the Korean War," *Diplomatic History* 10 (Summer 1986): 280; and Tilford, 19.

70. Author spreadsheet. The senior World War II generation had 18 percent of its generals directly involved in Korea; the junior World War II generation, 29 percent; and in both generations, the majority were fighter pilots (more in demand in this limited war).

71. Senior generation bomber major general Emmet O'Donnell Jr., Far East Air Force bomber commander, stated at the outset of the war: "It was my intention and hope that we would be able to get out there and to cash in on our psychological advantage in having gotten into the theatre and into the war so fast by putting a very severe blow on the North Koreans . . . and then go to work burning five major cities in North Korea into the ground, and to destroy completely every one of about 18 major strategic targets." See Gen Emmet O'Donnell, transcript of oral history interview by Dr. Edgar F. Puryear Jr., 2 December 1967, 28, AFHRA; and Futrell, *United States Air Force in Korea,* 186. O'Donnell later strongly supported MacArthur's desire to bomb Manchuria after Chinese intervention: "I was all for the bombing of Manchuria, and I wanted very badly to do it as soon as we recognized the Chinese forces . . . as bona fide forces. I think we could have gotten in and, for a very small cost in casualties, we could have really hit them hard and perhaps even stopped them." See Futrell, *Ideas*, vol. 1 (p. 298); and Curtis E. LeMay with MacKinlay Kantor, *Mission with LeMay: My Story* (Garden City, N.Y.: Doubleday, 1965), 454. Senior generation bomber lieutenant general LeMay made the following statement: "The B-29s were trained to go

up there to Manchuria and destroy the enemy's potential to wage war. The threat of this impending bombardment would, I am confident, have kept the Communist Chinese from revitalizing and protracting the Korean War." See Carl H. Builder, *The Masks of War: American Military Styles in Strategy and Analysis* (Baltimore: Johns Hopkins University Press, 1989), 71.

72. Martin, 286; M. J. Armitage and R. A. Mason, *Air Power in the Nuclear Age* (Urbana, Ill.: University of Illinois Press, 1983), 44. In 1955 former secretary of the Air Force Thomas K. Finletter stated the following: "The Korean War was a special case, and airpower can learn little from there about its future role in United States foreign policy in the East. . . . Any attempt to build an Air Force from the model of the Korean requirements could be fatal to the United States." See also Futrell, *United States Air Force in Korea*, 644. The official Far East Air Force report claimed Korea was "unlike wars of the past and was not necessarily typical of the future."

73. Ziemke, 177.

74. Martin, 92, 95.

75. Ibid., 97. *National Security Council* 135/3 stated the following: "Although there is continuing danger of general war, the most immediate danger facing the United States is that a progressive and cumulative loss of positions of importance to the United States (either as a result of deterioration within the free nations or of communist cold war actions or a process involving both) could eventually reduce the United States, short of general war to an isolated and critically vulnerable position."

76. I borrow the term *absolutist* from Morris Janowitz, *The Professional Soldier, A Social and Political Portrait* (Glencoe, Ill.: Free Press, 1960), xi. I have modified the definition.

77. Russell Frank Weigley, *The American Way of War: A History of United States Military Strategy and Policy* (New York: Macmillan, 1973), xix. Weigley argues this approach to war was America's dominant strategy from the Civil War through World War II.

78. The Twentieth Air Force was not entirely insular. It did rely on the Navy for supplies and bombed Japanese airfields at the request of the Navy.

79. Betts, 83; Janowitz, 268; and Clodfelter, 25. Emmet O'Donnell Jr., a senior World War II bomber general, stated, "It [American objective in Korea] is contrary to everything that every military commander that I have been associated with or from all of our history. He has never been in a position where he could not win the war he started to win. That is not American. . . . And who did it?—I don't know. I know that General MacArthur's hands were tied, I am sure, not by the Joint Chiefs of Staff, but by the . . . State Department."

80. I also borrow this term *pragmatists* from Janowitz, xi, 270–77, but I have refined the definition. Other related terms come from James M. Gavin, *War and Peace in the Space Age* (New York: Harper, 1958), 250–52. Gavin refers to them as liberals. See also Sam C. Sarkesian, *The Professional Army Officer in a Changing Society* (Chicago: Nelson-Hall Company, 1975), 199.

Sarkesian refers to them as transitionalists. In addition, see George Lowe, *The Age of Deterrence* (Boston: Little and Brown, 1964), 2–4. Lowe calls them traditionalists.

81. Although several generals, including Curtis E. LeMay, Carl A. Spaatz, and Jimmy Doolittle, served in both theaters, the preponderance of European experience within the fighter community of the World War II generations was found to have strongly influenced their future perspectives.

82. Those demonstrating pragmatism and departing Washington, D.C., included Hoyt S. Vandenberg, Lauris Norstad, and Otto P. Weyland. Vandenberg, who had discouraged the bombing of Manchuria, retired. Norstad, though displaying absolutist tendencies as the Twentieth Air Force chief of staff to end the war, returned to more pragmatic views after World War II. Norstad was transferred to Europe and NATO duties. Weyland took command of Pacific Air Command Air Force then Tactical Air Command. All had been associated with fighters in the European theater at one time or another. See Lawrence J. Korb, *The Joint Chiefs of Staff: The First Twenty-five Years* (Bloomington, Ind.: Indiana University Press, 1976), 148. Korb claims Sen. Robert Taft convinced Eisenhower that Vandenberg and the other chiefs were too closely wedded to the Truman administration and limited war, so an entirely new JCS was brought in. Ike claimed the timing was coincidental.

Chapter 3

Curtis E. LeMay and the Rise of the Strategic Air Command (1948–57)

Up until 1945, the theory that airpower, by itself, could be decisive in war remained a theory whose proof was arguable. But with the dropping of the atomic bombs on Japan, few could doubt that airpower, with this kind of bomb, could be a decisive instrument of war, all by itself.

—Military analyst Carl H. Builder
The Masks of War

Flying fighters is fun. Flying bombers is important.

—Attributed to Gen Curtis E. LeMay

From its inception in March of 1946, the Strategic Air Command was a favorite of the Air Force and later of America. It was the country's economical, yet increasingly powerful, first line of defense against the Soviet Union. As the only military force capable of delivering atomic weapons deep into enemy territory, SAC would receive, except during the Korean War, the lion's share of military appropriations for the next 15 years. Under the command of the outspoken Gen George C. Kenney, MacArthur's former air deputy in the Pacific war, the command quickly released a bold statement: "Destruction is just around the corner for any future aggressor against the United States. Quick retaliation will be our answer in the form of an aerial knock-out delivered by the Strategic Air Command."[1]

From birth SAC professed more capability than it actually possessed.[2] Kenney spent much of his time away from the command delivering speeches on airpower and serving as senior US military advisor for air to the new United Nations. In his many absences, Kenney granted broad authority to his deputy, Pacific war veteran Maj Gen Clements McMullen. With the tacit support of Kenney, McMullen purged SAC of nonflying officers and forced the aircrew to absorb those nonflying duties, as well as to cross-train into other crew duties—often before they were adequately trained in their primary duty.

McMullen was determined to implement the mandated force reductions while increasing efficiency, as long as pilots remained in key positions. Characterized as a "stern taskmaster," he once made the following suggestion: "Give them half of what they ask for, work them twice as hard, and they will get twice as much done."[3] SAC's deputy commander absorbed other staff positions and organizations into his headquarters and soon wore down the command and its morale. By the end of 1947 only two of SAC's 11 groups were combat ready.[4] The Air Force chief of staff, Gen Carl A. Spaatz, chided Kenney for this problem, but nonetheless tolerated the situation for 18 months. Finally, at the request of several high-ranking officers, and in the context of the Berlin and Czechoslovakian crises, the new chief of staff, Gen Hoyt S. Vandenberg, sent the highly regarded Charles A. Lindbergh to inspect six SAC bases. Lindbergh spent more than one thousand hours in the air with SAC crews. His September 1948 report cited low standards of professionalism, poor morale, low proficiency, personnel disruptions, and command training policies that "seriously interfered with training in the primary mission of the atomic squadrons."[5] Upon the advice of Lauris Norstad, Vandenberg replaced Kenney the following month with the fast-rising Curtis E. LeMay.[6]

The laconic LeMay was the greatest operational commander in Air Force history. Winston Churchill claimed LeMay was the savior of the Western world.[7] This senior World War II bomber general climbed from major to major general in four years. After the war LeMay became the youngest four-star general in US history since Ulysses S. Grant. But perhaps his greatest contribution was to create from the ashes of postwar demobilization a professional fighting force of unprecedented destructive power, not to mention a strong cultural legacy that persists in the Air Force today.

LeMay's road to fame began before the war when, as a lieutenant, he gained a reputation as the best navigator in the Army Air Corps. He was also one of its top test pilots and often his own mechanic. He was noted for completing tasks to perfection by working harder than anyone else. As war approached, the young LeMay was given a few bombers and raw crews to prepare for combat. He worked 12 hours a day, seven days a week, at a barren old base out west, where he drove aircrews through a grueling flight and ground training schedule and taught them to be mechanics (arrival of his mechanics had been delayed). LeMay led by example and suffered every discomfort with his men. Even at this early age, he believed his harsh methods ultimately would save lives as well as build pride and competence. His bomb group was shipped off to England before LeMay thought it ready and soon found itself in combat.

From England LeMay led the toughest missions, shared his men's danger, and learned not to count on fighter support. He was the top tactician and innovator in the theater. He designed instrument departure procedures, bomber formations, level bombing procedures, lead-crew training programs, and target-study folders that were soon adopted commandwide. He trained and disciplined his unit harder than others did, and it soon demonstrated higher mission success rates and lower attrition. Consequently, at a remarkably early age, LeMay felt the heavy sense of responsibility and witnessed the horrible price in lives lost through inexperience and lack of training. His reputation for toughness grew, accentuated by a permanent facial scowl from Bell's palsy. He didn't mind being called tough: "In this racket," he said, "it's the tough guys who lead the survivors."[8]

LeMay's rapid promotions chased his growing reputation. After LeMay had established the standards for the Eighth Air Force in Europe, General Arnold sent him to fashion the B-29 bomber as a "decisive" weapon against the Japanese. First, LeMay operated out of India and China, where he trained crews to his standards, worked bugs out of the B-29, and continued to innovate by improving weather forecasting and experimenting with incendiaries. Second, Arnold transferred him to the Pacific to direct the B-29 bombings against Japan. Under intense pressure from Arnold to defeat Japan quickly with the B-29, LeMay faced his greatest challenge.

The Twentieth Air Force was LeMay's crowning combat achievement. Working from remote sites was familiar and preferable to the battle-hardened, 38-year-old major general.

On remote Pacific islands, he and his men would be without the social or political distractions of England, for example. Having high priority and reporting directly to the joint chiefs in Washington gave the resolute LeMay the freedom and support he needed to fulfill the promises of strategic airpower. First, he began a rigorous training program to bring aircrews up to his standards. Most particularly, he trained lead crews to fly in adverse weather using radar-aimed deliveries. Second, he centralized maintenance to reduce waste and increase sortie production. Having learned in China that Japanese fighters had difficulty in intercepting the fast, high-flying B-29s, LeMay commanded fighters to escort the bombers at the front of the bomber formation to force Japanese fighters into rear attacks, where the B-29s' speed and guns were most effective.[9] With high-altitude precision daylight bombing largely foiled by bad weather and jet stream winds, LeMay boldly decided to attempt unescorted, low-altitude, incendiary attacks at night—without gunners so more bombs could be loaded. Many thought he was crazy, but his loyal crews flew the risky missions, which set Japan aflame in the spring of 1945. To LeMay and the Twentieth Air Force, the atomic bombs were anticlimactic. As LeMay stood on the USS *Missouri* to witness the Japanese surrender, he gazed proudly upward to see 462 of his "war-winning" B-29s fly overhead.[10]

LeMay, destined to become the most significant of the young senior World War II generation absolutists, was a true believer. He judged that "conventional airpower would have won the war in Europe if we had delayed the invasion until we had built sufficient air power" and that we beat the Germans "by keeping supplies from them."[11] Absolutists also contended that the B-29 won the Pacific war and that airpower was decisive because it directly assaulted the enemy's ability to wage war, which was more important than isolating or attacking his army.[12]

After a brief postwar assignment to the Air Research and Development Command, LeMay was dispatched as commander of United States Air Forces in Europe (USAFE) to handle the trouble that was brewing in Berlin. The Air Force's top operational crisis manager was ill at ease with the political obligations of his job, but he rose to the occasion when the

Berlin blockade began in June 1948.[13] LeMay organized the airlift of supplies to the isolated population in Berlin—a counterbalance to his previous role as destroyer. He also concocted a "pretty good plan" with Army lieutenant general Arthur G. Trudeau to force open the autobahn to Berlin. He recommended that Trudeau's small military force start up the autobahn while LeMay provided air cover, with SAC B-29s poised to destroy Soviet airfields should Trudeau run into trouble. Though the plan was disapproved, LeMay recalled that "had we done that, the fracas would have ended right there. There would have been no opposition."[14] His confidence in strategic airpower was absolute.

When he took command of SAC after the Berlin crisis, LeMay may have reconsidered. He began by visiting headquarters at Andrews AFB near Washington, D.C., and soon discovered there was "not one crew—*not one crew*—in the entire command who could do a professional job. Not one of the outfits was up to strength—neither in airplanes nor in people nor anything else" (emphasis in original).[15] LeMay postponed his remedy to help move SAC headquarters to remote Offutt AFB, Nebraska, a move that was more than symbolic. LeMay had grown accustomed to working in isolated places and cringed at the political and social distractions of the Washington area. The 42-year-old lieutenant general had concluded from his Berlin experience that upon his shoulders would lie the onerous responsibility for the security of the free world. He had built from scratch three flying organizations with a sense of urgency before; now, he must do so on a grander scale and with that same sense of wartime urgency: "We had to be ready to go to war not next week, not tomorrow, but this afternoon, today. . . . We had to operate every day as if we were at war."[16] LeMay desired to build a force "so professional, so strong, so powerful, that we would not have to fight."[17]

But the people in SAC had to be convinced they weren't as good as they thought. So LeMay directed all available SAC units to conduct high-altitude simulated bombing runs over Dayton, Ohio, on short notice. The results were abysmal; not one airplane "finished the mission as briefed," and the average crew missed the assigned target by more than two miles.[18]

With fresh and fond memories of the Twentieth Air Force in the Pacific war, LeMay sought to replicate it on a grander scale at SAC. He replaced virtually all of SAC's command structure and headquarters' staff with his warriors and absolutists from the Twentieth Air Force.[19] LeMay was determined to rebuild SAC in his image—one unit at a time.

LeMay had to get top priority in Air Force funding, research, and personnel. In December 1948, the same month that TAC and ADC were consolidated into CONAC, LeMay convinced senior Air Force leaders that "the fundamental goal of the Air Force should be the creation of a strategic atomic striking force capable of attacking any target in Eurasia from bases in the United States and returning to the points of take-off." It should be able to strike "in one fell swoop telescoping mass and time."[20] With supreme confidence in strategic bombers, especially those equipped with atomic weapons, LeMay and his absolutists began a nine-year journey to build capability to match doctrinal claims for strategic airpower—a theory built on globalism, indivisibility, and decisiveness.

LeMay sought global capability by improving a trusted technology; he pushed for bigger, higher, faster, and longer ranged bombers. B-36s set new distance records, and SAC's air-to-air refueling capability extended the range of SAC's bombers. Meanwhile, LeMay pushed for the development of the speedy jet B-47 and the intercontinental jet B-52 that were expected to be difficult to intercept. By the end of the Korean War, SAC was expanding beyond its 29 US and 10 overseas bases.

LeMay next sought to manage his dispersed global command and to make it responsive. Like the Twentieth Air Force, LeMay's new command would be highly centralized and would report directly to the Joint Chiefs of Staff. His persistence produced a viable command and control center in 1953. By then atomic weapons were more plentiful, and the need for centralized control and coordination of a growing atomic arsenal was becoming paramount. The expanding Soviet nuclear capability, which by the mid-1950s could threaten America proper, required a credible deterrent and war-fighting force from SAC—a challenge which called for even more centralization and instant and reliable communication systems to ensure control over such a destructive force.

The demanding and omnipresent LeMay again created a disciplined command. He continued to select bomber crews for their ordered and deliberate thinking. They always had been screened for reliability and dependability and had grown accustomed to close supervision, routine, and disciplined procedural compliance. LeMay preferred control and centralization, especially when the stakes were high.

LeMay also professed the indivisibility of his bomber fleet. His centrally managed bombers would convey such a destructive capability that they would deter war at any level.[21] Failing deterrence, they could win war at any level through relentless strategic bombing. Furthermore, a force designed to defeat the Soviets, the absolutist leader maintained, would provide a "strategic umbrella" under which limited wars could be controlled.[22]

Besides enhancing control, centralization at the huge headquarters at Offutt AFB also would improve targeting efficiency, streamline the conduct of the strategic air offensive, and facilitate that long-sought decisiveness. Effective targeting relied on accurate intelligence and reconnaissance. LeMay built a fleet of reconnaissance aircraft, and asked his crews to study modified versions of his World War II target folders, which eventually included photographs and radar predictions of targets. SAC headquarters developed an ambitious intelligence program and forged carefully integrated war plans for a simultaneous assault that required strict routing and timing.[23] SAC's "positive control" minimized the possibility of mistakes, as no one moved until told, and every order had to be verified by others; if it varied in prescribed form, it was considered invalid and crews returned to base.[24] To ensure that nothing went wrong, SAC wrote manuals for every job, demanded strict adherence to checklists, and drilled aircrews in a rugged routine of training and alerts that created a body of "perfect specialists" who were consumed with executing their mission flawlessly from their isolated bases.[25] LeMay's lifetime in flying more than 75 different types of aircraft colored his diction, analogies, and perceptions—in this instance his view of teamwork:

> If you removed that plate from the body of SAC, you could look in and
> see people and instruments. They would be as the intricate electronic
> physiology of an airplane today: each functioning, each trained, each
> knowing his special part and job—knowing what he must do in his
> groove and place to keep the body alive, the blood circulating. Every
> man a coupling or a tube; every organization a rampart of transistors,
> battery of condensers. All rubbed up, no corrosion. Alert.[26]

Frequent inspections and competitions kept the command
compliant, busy, and honed. As one senior World War II
bomber general recalled, "It was a twenty-four-hour, seven
day-a-week job, and you didn't look upon it as anything
else."[27]

LeMay's high standards and resolute leadership fashioned
SAC into a disciplined and proud, if regimented, command. As
in World War II, LeMay's men were busy with routine and
perfecting technique, and they had little time or inclination for
innovation. Once again innovation came largely from LeMay
and his experienced lieutenants. Initiatives for centralized
maintenance, codification of measurable results, high-
frequency radios, elite security police, inspector teams,
survival schools, accident investigations, safety programs, and
expanding bomb and reconnaissance competitions generally
came from headquarters.

The peerless LeMay was the absolute ruler of SAC, and he
ruled absolutely. He fired those who could not or would not
meet his standards: "I couldn't afford to differentiate between
the incompetent and the unfortunate," he rationalized.[28] And
he got results. He remarked with typical brevity, "Our job was
to produce. And we produced."[29] LeMay shouldered much of
the formidable responsibility for war planning and strategic
deterrence in a dangerous nuclear age, always trying to build
and maintain a strategic supremacy that could monopolize
initiative, maximize deterrence, and *win*.[30]

LeMay favored the hardworking people of SAC, sometimes
too much.[31] He personally designed barracks and created
hobby and auto-hobby shops, family services centers, and
aero clubs that remain standard features of many bases
today. He did all he could to instill pride and professionalism
in his men and women and reminded them they were the
nation's first line of defense. LeMay thought his officers
assumed more responsibility than their Air Force peers and

deserved rank commensurate with that responsibility. In late 1949 he received authority to grant "spot promotions" to SAC aircrews of his choosing up to a 15 percent limit. This private promotion system was LeMay's alone, and he used it to reward performance of his best crews. As long as the crews continued to perform well, they received the pay and privileges of the advanced rank. In his first year, LeMay promoted 237 first lieutenants to captain. The spot promotion system in SAC would remain as long as LeMay remained in the service, and it peaked in 1959 with more than nine hundred spot promotions.[32] SAC personnel consistently enjoyed higher promotion rates than the other commands through 1965.[33] LeMay fought hard to get the best for his command and his people. He usually did so but not without making a good many enemies along the way.

LeMay's lukewarm support of the Korean War was one notable instance. The absolutist recommended that SAC go north and burn the principal communist cities. When that proposal was rejected, LeMay resisted attempts to use his strategic bombers for interdiction and close air support. The SAC commander believed that massive fire bombing of cities in North Korea and, if necessary, strategic targets in Manchuria would get the war over quickly and would save lives in the long run. When ordered to participate in a limited war, he reluctantly sent Maj Gen Emmett "Rosie" O'Donnell Jr. and two conventional bomber units "low on the totem pole [for atomic conversion]."[34] For LeMay, airpower was misused in the Korean War as "flying artillery." The bomber fleet, he felt, should be preserved for the supreme strategic campaign against the "real" enemy's heartland. Senior Air Force leaders recognized that and continued to give SAC programs priority during the Korean War.[35]

Whereas SAC maintained remarkable institutional stability and growth during the Korean War, TAC was overextended. Manning shortages, diverse missions, and a surge in training requirements strained TAC. The simultaneous buildup in Korea and USAFE drained TAC of its talent and funding.[36] It also had to deal with demands from the Army, manage the airlift mission, and cope with changing technologies. Additionally, TAC helped write and rush conventional doctrine to Korea and atomic doctrine to the North Atlantic Treaty Organization (NATO) as well as organize, train, and equip forces for those two diverse theaters. What resources did not go to Korea seemed bound for NATO and its growing demand for nuclear-capable fighters, despite SAC's opposition.[37] Morale was low and the command overworked. The TAC commander, fighter general Joe Cannon, complained in 1950 to senior Air Force leaders that he could not meet his growing commitments without more funds and personnel. He asked for better allocation, but the new vice chief of staff, senior World War II bomber general Nathan F. Twining, replied that Cannon would have to wait for a review.[38] Cannon would find few allies among the new Air Force leadership.

The "noncontroversial" Twining had been recommended by the ailing but popular Gen Muir S. Fairchild, Vandenberg's vice chief of staff, as his own replacement in 1950. A trusting General Vandenberg concurred, only to find himself suddenly stricken by cancer as he extended into his fifth year as chief of staff. As the Korean War ended, a dying Vandenberg also had to recommend a successor for his job. The first two candidates to come to mind were noted rivals: pragmatist Lauris Norstad, currently commander of USAFE, and absolutist Curtis E. LeMay, then commander of SAC. Vandenberg, increasingly estranged from the outspoken secretary of the Air Force Finletter, realized how critical these men were to their important jobs. He also recognized how diligent Twining had been as his vice chief, and more important, how well Twining got along with Finletter. And so to the surprise of many, Twining succeeded Vandenberg.[39]

Twining had graduated in the middle of his West Point class, five years ahead of Vandenberg. He was consistently described as simple, hard working, well liked, honest, patient, commonsensical, and "an old soldier . . . down-to-earth, sort of old salt-type of fellow."[40] He lacked guile and sophistication and was not perceived as a strategist or an intellect. But he was an experienced combat bomber commander, who succeeded LeMay at the close of the Pacific war and supervised (indirectly) the dropping of the atomic bombs on Japan. Though more seasoned and less boisterous than most romantics, Twining remained an absolutist.[41]

Twining's views on war were typical of those colored by an indelible and formative experience in World War II. Like his associates, the new chief believed in total means to achieve total ends. He recognized victory only in brinksmanship and total war.[42] He believed in America's crusade for "life, liberty, and the freedom of men everywhere" and that the great victory of World War II had been forfeited by failing to take Berlin ourselves and to dictate terms to the Soviets. Subsequently, he thought "this unfortunate program of appeasement set the stage for the eventual loss of China to communist domination and created the circumstances for the Korean War, the French loss of Indochina, and today's untenable situation in Vietnam, Cambodia, and Laos."[43]

Twining's view of airpower in the Korean War also typified absolutist thought. As vice chief of staff, Twining, unlike his boss Vandenberg, endorsed bombing Manchuria: "We felt that [bombing Manchuria] would never bring on a war, and if it did, [the Soviets] couldn't pick a better time to jump the United States. If they wanted to go to war with us, we might have taken them on then much easier than we could any other time."[44] Furthermore, "By September 1950, the United States had actually won the war in Korea, but threw it away precisely in the manner in which this nation threw away the political victories which were possible after our military success in World War II." To Twining, it led to "an inglorious stalemate; 'limited war' became a fad and a convenient excuse for deferring hard decisions and sweeping fundamental principles [maximum means for decisive ends] under the rug."[45] Twining's strongest belief sought to maintain military supremacy and a resolve sufficient to "win" and dictate the peace. Like other Air Force absolutists, he claimed superior strategic airpower would guarantee "ultimate military victory."[46]

To retain Vandenberg's political skill on Capitol Hill and to complement Twining's extensive operational experience, Thomas D. White was selected as vice chief of staff. At age 18 White was the youngest person ever to graduate from West Point. His early career was spent in attaché life: China, the Soviet Union, Italy, Greece, Panama, and Argentina; and he was fluent in six languages. Colleagues described him as intellectual, aloof, polished, patient, articulate, well read, humane, gracious, imaginative, and of the highest integrity. Longtime Air Force associate and former secretary of the Air Force Eugene M. Zuckert recalled that White "was a sharp contrast to the usual World War II Air Force general. He was a deep and thoughtful individual. He impressed me more than any officer I had ever met. When he got that [first] job [legislative liaison to Congress], it became obvious that this man was a man of superior qualifications in an area where the Air Force was very, very poor."[47] White built a tremendous reputation in Washington for his role in legislative liaison during the B-36 hearings. He also briefly had commanded a bomber unit in the Pacific war—which ingratiated him to the Pacific absolutists. White's intellect and political acumen greatly assisted Twining.[48]

White's boss was a welcome addition to the JCS formed by the early Eisenhower administration.[49] Mindful of the influence that his threats to use atomic weapons in Korea had on the Korean armistice and cognizant of public fatigue with that war, Ike decided to use atomic weaponry as an economical way to build a defense policy that would not weaken the US economy. He believed that economic vitality and diplomatic alliances backed up by a credible military strength—"security with solvency"—provided the best formula for containment. This New Look relied on bolstering an atomic striking force (SAC) that would have enough strength to deter war at any level. Drafted by the JCS in August 1953, the JCS war plans gave top priority to strategic airpower and secondary priority to air defense. Two months later National Security Memorandum (NSM)162/2 stated, "Air power and nuclear weapons should provide the nation's primary means of defense—plans should be developed to use nuclear weapons whenever *desirable* militarily" (emphasis added).[50] From this military belief leaders thought they would have the nuclear option across a wide range of possible military conflicts with relatively few political restraints.[51] The perceived decisive effects of Hiroshima and atomic intimidation in Korea would remain closer to the minds of the dominant military absolutists than to American civilians.

The new national security policy strongly favored the young Air Force; it would receive on average 46 percent of the defense budget from 1952 to 1960.[52] It pleased no one more so than the dominant bomber generals, who, under their new chief, General Twining, now filled 71 percent of the Air Force's rated positions (positions occupied by aviators) above the rank of major general.[53]

The vastly changed political situation in the post-World War II era had thrust the United States into a leadership role against the perceived menace of communism. With a series of crises culminating in the Korean War, ill will between the two superpowers, each equipped with growing numbers of nuclear weapons, made warfare too important to be left to generals. The dangers of high-stakes nuclear warfare, coupled with new communication technologies, necessitated and enabled an increase in civilian control of the military. One noted sociologist made the following observation:

> Interpenetration of the civil and military sectors has deeply modified the insularity of the military profession. The new skill requirements, the growing importance of academic rather than strictly military education, modifications of the military rank hierarchy mirroring changes in civilian society, and a diversification of military careers are all elements in this process. One can speak of these developments in their entirety as a "civilianization" of the military; yet the militarization of society proves an equally apt image, describing dependence of the military on the total national resources as a base of mobilization.[54]

The fusion of military and foreign policy in the cold war era bewildered Air Force absolutists. Although the Eisenhower administration asked the JCS to consider "a wide range of domestic and international economic and political factors" in their advice during this complex era, Air Force senior leaders generally refused and provided strictly professional military advice that protected Air Force interests.[55] As a result, many argue the JCS generally lost relative influence over foreign policy and budgetary matters.[56] After rendering military advice, the JCS awaited National Security Council policy and interpreted it within service doctrine if possible to further service interests. Additionally, the services were unable to keep expanding foreign policy commitments in line with military capabilities to support those commitments. The State

Department's desire to function in a world of ambiguity, and often bluff, maximized leverage and diplomatic freedom of maneuver. The military, on the other hand, sought firm policy and priorities as a foundation to structure forces and generate achievable strategies. The polarity between these diverse imperatives was inevitable; for the State Department to "articulate priorities of national interest is to create political liabilities, since they could embarrass allies, antagonize neutrals, and even assist opponents in their political propaganda."[57] The frustration of increasing requirements with limited military budgets encouraged the military to search for ways to guard against a growing threat with fewer weapons. Extensive reliance on nuclear weapons was a natural offspring.

In 1953 the Air Force's first published doctrinal manual reflected absolutist beliefs that accommodated the new president's defense policy. The manual argued that attacking a nation's "heartland . . . can effectively reduce its will to fight," and furthermore "no nation can long survive unlimited exploitation by enemy air forces utilizing weapons of mass destruction."[58] The doctrine manual would change little over the next decade.

Favorable technological, economical, and political factors boosted the nation's youngest military service and its absolutist doctrine into budgetary and doctrinal preeminence during the Eisenhower years. However, the Air Force leadership was ill equipped to influence the direction of national security policy. Dominant Air Force leaders generally were young operational commanders from World War II and were growing up with their young service. They were mostly bomber pilots who remained primarily interested in building the chief military arm of the emerging national security state. They prided themselves in "doing" versus "thinking" and tended to define the latter only in terms of their absolutist beliefs and in the interest of service well-being. Few had extensive professional schooling, and their operational and traditional focus encouraged more extensive incursions by educated civilians in the formulation of defense policy.

Early Air Force personnel policy illuminates senior and junior World War II generational experience and concerns during the post-World War II period. The explosive growth of officers in World War II left little age difference between those who would lead and those who would follow for the next 20 years. The Air Force always had treasured its youth as well as its inclination to be "forward looking." General Arnold "felt that anybody past about 45, if not earlier, never had an original idea."[59]

The immediate postwar Air Force faced an enormous problem concerning promotions in its drastically reduced officer corps. Gen Laurence Kuter, charged to address the problem, recalled that the Air Force had a World War II "hump" of officers that included "hundreds of young generals" who were blocking promotions of "second generation talent" who, in turn, were leaving the Air Force early. As a result, the Officer Personnel Act of 1947 included legislation that ended the strict seniority system and replaced it with an "up or out" promotion-by-selection system. Kuter's policy "forced early retirement in accordance with the earliest provisions of the Personnel Law."[60] Additionally, to spread rank distribution within the hump, beginning in 1948 the Air Force received permission to use "spot promotions," which advanced many officers to a temporary rank far in advance of normal progression.[61]

The major problem resided in the flying community. Flying officers had enjoyed a 70 to 30 percent numerical advantage over those who didn't fly in the early Air Force. After having demobilized from a V-J day population of 413,890 aircrew members to a mere 24,079 by June 1947, the shrinking rated force soon was unable to meet the demands of SAC, NATO, and the Korean War effort. Thousands of reservists had to be called up, and a rejuvenated aviation cadet program produced more than 20,000 pilots during this period to meet demands.[62] The legacy of this disruption after the Korean War produced a larger "hump" of young officers (especially pilots), who, after service in World War II and recall for the Korean War, were too old or committed to return again to civilian life. By the end of 1954, 50 percent of the officers in the Air Force had been commissioned within four years of each other.[63] Again, the air arm utilized "one shot promotions" to trim the rank structure of the hump. In 1954 Congress passed the

Officer Grade Limitation Act (OGLA), which placed numerical ceilings on each grade (rank) for each of the services, exacerbating the Air Force's problem. That same year the Air Force "hump study" admitted that while the hump had "previously been a wave that carried many into positions of responsibility, it was [now] becoming a dam that would cripple the career plans of many."[64] The hump of primarily World War II officers, if not reduced by 1,700 officers each year, would number a staggering 54,000 officers nearing retirement eligibility (20 years in service) in the mid-1960s—with insufficient positions to accommodate their rank.

In deference to the loyalty and cohesion developed during World War II, senior Air Force leaders were reluctant to lay off fellow combat veterans; instead, they received annual waivers to the OGLA and tried their best to keep their peers employed at least through 20 years of service. Warily, in 1956 Secretary of the Air Force Donald A. Quarles convened a panel to examine officer quality. Compelled by the panel's adverse findings, Air Force Chief of Staff Twining ordered an aggressive campaign to raise standards. Improvements were slow but sure in coming; yet, force reductions mandated by the Eisenhower administration in 1957 "provided a quick and easy alternative to the quality control mechanisms just put in place."[65] The effect of protecting the predominantly pilot hump of World War II veterans was to populate the Air Force with pilots who grew up with their Air Force, occupied flying and absorbed nonflying jobs, and to a certain extent, blocked the promotion of subsequent generations—at least until the World War II generation retired. It also reflected paternalism and a broad dissemination of World War II combat experience throughout an Air Force that was aging by the early 1960s.[66]

The infusion of tens of thousands of aviation cadets during World War II also lowered average officer education levels to the lowest by far of all services.[67] Despite the extensive combat experience of Air Force officers in the postwar period, the officer ranks still needed an academic education to comprehend the "lessons" of the war, to keep pace with rapid advances in science and technology, and explore better alternative strategies for the security of both the United States and its interests. The *Air Force Times* recognized education as the veteran's best protection against manpower cuts after World War II.[68] The young service established the Air Force Institute of Technology (AFIT) in 1946 and pushed an aggressive Reserve Officer Training Corps (ROTC) program on college campuses. But the Korean War disrupted the stable establishment of education programs. The Air Force hoped to get most of its pilots from the ROTC program but found that college graduates preferred low-risk, nonflying jobs, a four-year-draft deferment, and the opportunity to serve as an officer in a reserve unit.[69] In 1953 officer education levels had risen only to 43.6 percent college graduates, termed "far too low" by Secretary of the Air Force Harold E. Talbott.[70]

The Air Force of the 1950s continued to value experience over education, action over contemplation. As Roger Hilsman, a highly decorated West Point graduate and subsequent civilian academic, observed in 1953:

> There are, of course, intelligent generals, highly intelligent ones; but intelligence is not the same as intellectuality. . . . Military men are not thinkers. Intellectuality is not a highly prized trait because, in training a modern armed force, and in battle, decisiveness and interpersonal and executive skill are more essential.[71]

Traditional skills of action-oriented generalship and leadership dominated the senior World War II generation. If education held any value, it was a technical education for this service. But even in this effort, the Air Force fell short of its desired levels.

Professional military schooling could compensate somewhat for a lack of civilian education in matters of strategy, doctrine, and policy. Partially for this reason, the Army Air Forces created in 1946 an air university to match the Army and Navy War Colleges. In the charter for the new school, General Fairchild, the new commander of Air University, established that "the Air University will seek most earnestly to develop in students the power to solve problems by well ordered, resourceful and original thought, rather than merely to train them in information and the routine performance of techniques."[72] The founders established three schools: Air Tactical School (ATS) for junior officers, Air Command and Staff School (ACSS) for midlevel officers, and Air War College (AWC) for senior officers.

Early evaluations of this Air Force foray into officer education brought mixed reactions. An outside board, chaired by consultant Dr. Jacob S. Orleans, evaluated ACSS in 1949 and found officers were evaluated on the extent of information they could consume, versus their ability to reason, interpret, or reach sound and justifiable decisions.[73] The 1949 Board of Visitors (BOV) for Air University agreed and found the schools lacking explicit mission statements, functional curricula, and faculty skilled in stimulating new ideas, doctrine, technological vision, and good staff work.[74] The following year the Fairchild Board verified the desperate need to raise the educational level of Air Force officers and recommended that 100 percent of all officers attend ATS, 60 percent ACSS, and 25 percent AWC.[75]

These recommendations, however, ran up against the Korean War. As with other institutional programs, professional schooling within the Air Force gave way to the demands of military emergency. During the Korean War, the Air Force shortened year-long courses to five and one-half months, sent much of the faculty to the field, and, at the direction of General Twining, crammed information into the abbreviated school year.[76] After the Korean War, the chronic problems of a faculty limited in number and quality remained as the Air Force preferred to draft officers to populate the rapidly increasing number of wings. SAC was particularly reluctant to send people to school, and Air University facilities could not accommodate the "hump" anyway.[77] Try as it might, Air University did not receive the support needed from senior Air Force leaders to educate officers to a level where they could better understand and influence policy and chart new courses.

In sum, the disruptions of World War II and the struggle for service independence, precipitous postwar demobilization, remobilization for the Korean War, and rapid growth to meet the challenges of the cold war dominated the attention of the young institution and kept its officers busy—often too busy to attend civilian or professional military educational programs of substance. Figure 1 offers a comparison of the civilian and professional education of fighter and bomber generals of the senior and junior World War II generations. The figure reveals that fighter pilots were generally made more available for professional military and graduate schooling than bomber pilots in both generations.[78] It also shows how World War II and the Korean War interrupted professional military education, especially senior service school, for the senior generation and intermediate service school for the junior generation.

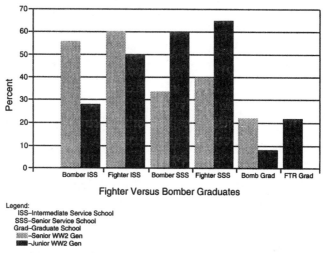

Fighter Versus Bomber Graduates

Legend:
ISS—Intermediate Service School
SSS—Senior Service School
Grad—Graduate School
▨—Senior WW2 Gen
■—Junior WW2 Gen

Figure 1. Advanced Schooling of Air Force Four-Star Generals (World War II Generation)

Ever reliant on the competence of its combat experience and unshakable doctrine, the World War II generation hump and its leaders grew up with the young service largely preoccupied, comfortable, and qualified primarily in operational matters. In the complexity of the new era, defense policy formulation fell to civilians by right and by default.[79] The resultant policy of "massive retaliation" in the post-Korean era was a welcome luxury for the Air Force and its absolutist generals. It mirrored their doctrine of total victory in total war. Absolutist bomber general Twining, Air Force chief of staff from 1953 to 1957 and chairman of the JCS from 1957 to 1960, believed the policy of massive retaliation was "one of the greatest things we ever did."[80] Under massive retaliation the Air Force flourished, SAC expanded rapidly, and the dominant absolutists pushed for more destructive capability to insure military victory over the communists by way of overwhelming airpower.[81]

Yet, excessive reliance on massive retaliation failed to deter limited war. Ho Chi Minh's communist Vietminh had surrounded the French forces at Dien Bien Phu in northern Vietnam in the spring of 1954, and France called on the United States for help. General LeMay quickly drew up plans and desired to "up the ante" with his superior SAC. General Twining favored a onetime atomic strike with three small atomic weapons: "You could take all day to drop a bomb, make sure you put it in the right place . . . and clean those Commies out of there and the band could play the 'Marseillaise,' and the French could come marching out . . . in great shape."[82] However, pragmatic general Earle E. Partridge, commander of FEAF and a fighter general with extensive experience in the European theater of World War II as well as the Korean War, had a different view. As the theater commander, he recognized that "this is basically a civil war, with pacification and unification (as opposed to destruction) being the prime objective. Air operations, without the required political and psychological programs, can be regarded only as destructive."[83] This difference of opinion among generals reflected the philosophical difference growing within the Air Force between many in the strategic and tactical communities.

The fall of North Vietnam to the communists fewer than six months after the Dulles massive retaliation speech stimulated a flurry of analyses that questioned the deterrent credibility of the new policy of massive retaliation.[84] Army chief of staff Matthew B. Ridgway claimed in 1954 that we had designed our military strategy and foreign policy to fit the weapon rather than the reverse. He argued that massive retaliation may trap us into using atomic weapons, if for no other reason than to demonstrate we weren't bluffing. Consequently, he concluded, the Soviets would attempt to fight at a level below nuclear war.[85] But most of the pressure came from the rising community of civilian defense intellectuals from RAND and other interested circles.[86] The Eisenhower administration also showed a concern regarding *limited war*, a term that entered the lexicon in 1954. In 1955 the Basic National Security Policy acknowledged the possibility that the United States might have to choose between massive nuclear destruction and yielding to local aggression, unless the country developed a limited war capability. Budget-minded Eisenhower, bolstered by air absolutist claims, hoped forces for general war (nuclear conflict with the Soviet Union) could operate effectively in limited wars also to, as stated in NSM 422/2, "punish swiftly and severely any local aggression in a manner and on a scale best calculated to avoid the hostilities broadening into total nuclear war."[87] Nevertheless, the possibilities and practicalities of limited war seriously interested only the other services and Tactical Air Command.

TAC's fight for survival in the SAC-dominated Air Force during the Eisenhower years centered around pragmatist fighter general O. P. Weyland.[88] His Nineteenth Tactical Air Command had supported Gen George S. Patton Jr.'s dash across France in World War II and earned accolades for Weyland from Patton as "the best damn general in the Air Corps." Weyland later commanded the FEAF during the Korean War, and his reconstruction of the Japanese air defense forces led to his fame as "the father of the new Japanese Air Force." His breadth of operational experience was matched by extensive professional military schooling, which included stints as assistant commandant of the Army's Command and General Staff School and as deputy commander of the National War College. Opie knew "ground forces forward and backwards" and recalled his greatest frustration during the Korean War was that "few other commanders were educated in other services."[89]

Weyland's goal as TAC commander was to "hold together and improve a small, but very, very proficient tactical air force structure" and remain "obnoxious enough" to secure organizational, doctrinal, and technological improvements.[90] But, in the shadow of SAC and massive retaliation, Weyland, like Cannon, his predecessor, spent much of his time simply trying to preserve his force and mission. To fight for missions that supported the Army or conventional war ran counter to Air Force and national defense policy (massive retaliation). In an era when budget limitations hampered US attempts to contend with a growing target list, the military clutched its growing atomic arsenal. Like everyone else, TAC was forced to split up in its own way and did so by the end of 1954.[91] The tactical air forces (TAF) proffered that the "decisive" use of tactical nuclear weapons in Europe, for example, might halt a Soviet onslaught while providing an option short of a global conflagration for which SAC forces were trained.[92] Nevertheless, TAC still risked absorption by SAC unless it found a mission outside the scope of SAC and atomic warfare.

During the French crisis in Indochina, General Weyland suggested at a commander's conference that TAC organize and maintain a highly mobile tactical air force that could meet contingencies anywhere in the world.[93] While Twining and White accepted the idea in principle, they could not spare manpower for a new organization, especially when they needed every flyer to man the growing numbers of atomic capable wings.[94] Aided by a convincing and widely distributed Air War College paper which asserted that "the so called 'New Look' at national security policy quietly died as a viable blueprint for defense with the fall of Dien Bien Phu," Weyland and the TAC advocates argued what many defense intellectuals were stating—that coming nuclear parity would neutralize the utility of general war with the Soviet Union and permit, indeed encourage, "brushfire" or limited wars.[95] After a year of briefing various audiences on the concept of a rapidly responding global tactical strike force capable of coping with any military situation at any level, Weyland secured approval for his Composite Air Strike Force (CASF), but only as a planning headquarters.[96] One month earlier senior Air Force leaders had seriously considered dispensing with conventional ordnance and training. However, Weyland and tactical commanders rebuked their consideration, alleged that eliminating conventional capability was a political decision, and warned that exclusive reliance on nuclear weapons was fraught with "myriads of political, psychological, and other implications." Furthermore, they contended, the Air Force needed to be "psychologically prepared" for limited wars and retain a variety of munitions.[97] At the same time, the Air Staff professed the indivisibility of airpower and asserted that SAC could do the TAC mission. Weyland responded that SAC was ill equipped and ill trained to handle limited war because of the heavy demands of a potential general war; TAC, on the other hand, was more flexible.[98]

TAC fought for survival and modest funding under the covetous eyes of the insatiable SAC and its growing list of newly discovered strategic targets—a list that expanded with Soviet military growth and was accentuated by improving US reconnaissance capability to find targets.[99] To contribute to the nuclear destruction of Soviet targets was TAC's most marketable option in support of the national defense policy and the absolutist doctrine of the Air Force.[100] For TAC to obtain the favor of the bomber-dominant senior Air Force leadership, the "life insurance policy" had to address the three pillars of Air Force doctrine.[101]

Though the CASF emanated from Weyland's Nineteenth Air Force, it struggled to build a ready force without any assigned aircraft. The CASF promised globalism through air refueling and improved mobility and communications systems. It sought decisiveness through nuclear weapons. But, like SAC, it was unable to address fully the tenet of indivisibility because the national focus on strategic targeting overshadowed other missions. Additionally, training to deliver tactical nuclear weapons was complex, leaving little time and money for much else, even within TAC. This focus on the numerous requirements of nuclear drill diluted training and thought on the versatility of airpower across the spectrum of war. Consequently, this focus caused other Air Force roles and missions to suffer and made it difficult to support TAC's CASF when it did not have a visible enemy as SAC did.[102] Nevertheless, under accusations of harboring a "battleship mentality" and following Weyland's campaign for CASF, the broadminded Vice Chief of Staff White acknowledged the role of TAF in rhetoric typical of the time. On 7 May 1955 he stated,

> Our tactical air forces, with enormous firepower, global mobility, operational invulnerability and versatility, have become a deterrent to aggression and a decisive force in war. As such, our Tactical Air Command assumes a place alongside our Strategic Air Command as a potent force for peace.[103]

But the CASF remained an underfunded and poorly supported concept for some time.

To the predominantly bomber senior Air Force leadership, limited war and the CASF were necessary adjuncts that demonstrated the institution's concern for "covering all bases." The Air Force saw its primary task in its more exclusive and far more important realm—strategic deterrence. Many absolutists felt limited war was a distraction. As Chief of Staff Twining summarized, "The United States has always done what was necessary to totally win. . . . There is no such thing as limited war. Merely discussing limited war inspires the enemy."[104]

As the preeminent Air Force expanded to 137 wings in the mid-1950s, SAC bombers continued to receive top priority. In 1955 SAC received its first B-52 intercontinental bombers and was directed to give highest priority to the development of intercontinental ballistic missiles (ICBM). In the summer of that year, Air Force attachés attending an air show at Tushino airport near Moscow witnessed a distressing number of Soviet jet Bison bombers fly by in an air parade. (The Soviets duped the attachés by circling the bombers to overfly the viewing area again and again.) The outcome stimulated a drastic revision of the projected Soviet bomber force size. The revised estimates predicted that the long-range Soviet bomber force would double that of SAC by 1959.[105]

The perceived "bomber gap," in part, prompted the Congressional Air Power Hearings of 1956. Air Force intelligence attempted to prove the existence of the gap when other intelligence agencies could not substantiate Air Force assessments. Faced with uncertainties, organizational interests guided choice among competing interpretations of evidence. According to John Huizinga, director of the Central Intelligence Agency's Board of National Estimates, "The Air Force was judged the least competent of the services, and it was very hard to deal with Air Force assertions. You had to prove a negative, a hopeless position to be in."[106]

At the congressional hearings, General LeMay warned against the dangers implicit in the bomber gap and reminded congressional leaders and the public that manned strategic bombers were still the weapon of choice: "We believe that in the future the situation will remain the same as it has in the past, and that is a bomber force well-equipped, determined, well-trained, will penetrate any defense system that can be devised." Over the objections of Secretary of Defense Charles Wilson and in spite of Eisenhower's responsive supplemental funding, Congress granted a bonus of $928.5 million to the strategic forces.[107] The inadvertent consequence to the Soviets of their deception at Tushino was to enlarge SAC.

These years comprised the heyday of SAC. The aggressive LeMay was building, modernizing, and expanding the most destructive military force in history. SAC fed on perceptions of a growing Soviet threat. As improved intelligence and reconnaissance uncovered more targets in the Soviet Union, SAC and the Air Force convinced the US government of the need for more bombs and delivery systems.

LeMay held tremendous power and influence. As a commander, he was operationally responsible only to the JCS and the president. But LeMay held substantial clout even over the JCS and the Air Staff because he determined operational limits and strategy.[108] His first war plan in 1949 attempted to use 133 bombers on 70 cities at one time, an enduring absolutist strategy to use overwhelming force in one assault to end war quickly and decisively. As the proliferation of bombers and nuclear weapons (begun with increased defense spending during and after the Korean War and the availability of small H-bombs) exceeded the growing target list, the atomic strength of the United States enabled LeMay by 1960 to turn to the use of a "counterforce" strategy, versus reliance on a weapons-limited "city-busting" campaign.[109] The Air Force felt more comfortable with counterforce, in part, because it more closely reflected the Air Force's doctrinal roots of precision bombing against military-industrial targets and much of its World War II experience. More importantly, the demands of counterforce exceeded in numbers, accuracy, and range the Navy's new submarine-launched ballistic missile (SLBM).[110] In any case, counterforce demanded more weapons (to hit more targets accurately) for a larger Air Force.

Blocking the route to military expansion stood President Dwight D. Eisenhower. In 1955 he had warned the Air Force against overemphasizing the numbers of aircraft and units while neglecting maintenance and spare parts, base improvements, and training of personnel. Claiming the Air

Force had more than enough money, the president slowed the growth of Air Force wings as early as 1955.[111] He also directed the Air Force to pursue ICBM development that same year. Eisenhower subsequently offered reassurances against the existence of a bomber gap. The new U-2 spy plane and other classified sources had provided the president with evidence of low Soviet jet bomber production. Despite repeated efforts, Ike could not contain Air Force growth entirely. The Democratic Congress and an influential press favored Air Force growth. By 1957 Air Force manpower nearly equaled that of the Army, and Air Force assets exceeded those of the 55 largest US civilian corporations combined.[112]

The year 1957 proved significant for the Air Force. General Twining became chairman of the Joint Chiefs of Staff, General White became Air Force chief of staff, General LeMay became the Air Force vice chief of staff, and Gen Thomas S. Power became the new commander of the Strategic Air Command. Furthermore, in October the Soviets launched sputnik, the world's first man-made satellite which instigated not only a space race but a public debate over a "missile gap."

As vice chief of staff, the articulate White developed a nuclear strategic expertise "that overwhelmed others," at least in the military.[113] A former aide remembered "his grasp of overall strategy and his ability to sort of look out beyond today's world and see what might be important in the future is what really set him apart."[114] Though White was a former bomber commander in the Pacific war and ardently supported a deterrent SAC, his background and perspective were broader than those of most absolutists. He saw the need to push technologies and expand the Air Force's vision. In a 1956 speech to the Air War College, he noted stagnation in Air Force thought:

> We see too few examples of really creative, logical, far-sighted thinking in the Air Force these days. It seems to me that our people are merely trying to find new ways of saying the same old things about air power without considering whether they need changing to meet new situations and without considering the need for new approaches to new problems.[115]

White's expansive background, Capitol Hill experience, and progressive views served the Air Force well, but he lacked the operational credibility of a Twining. It was partly for this reason that he brought LeMay to Washington as his vice chief of staff. White respected LeMay's record in SAC, desired to give LeMay's force of character a broader arena, and felt LeMay would be "the greatest complement to me. . . . His experience, background, and probably his personality were quite different than mine. I knew it might be tough, but if it worked, it would be terrific for the Air Force."[116] It worked, somewhat. While White concerned himself most with JCS and political issues, he allowed LeMay considerable leeway to run the Air Force. The contrasting personalities produced disagreements, but in the end LeMay remained loyal to his chief.[117]

LeMay's greatest problem as vice chief was that he unconsciously "paid inordinate attention to SAC after he left it."[118] Shortly after becoming the vice chief, LeMay presented a speech to the major commanders that claimed the United States "could no longer afford the luxury of devoting a substantial portion of our Air Force effort to support ground forces."[119] LeMay believed so strongly in the strategic air role that he continued to permit spot promotions in SAC and to foster disproportionate research and development funding for SAC.[120] In the late 1950s Secretary Zuckert remembered how White had expressed concern over the brigadier generals' promotion list, which had a disproportionate number of SAC names on it. Zuckert and White returned the list to LeMay and the Air Staff for more equitable distribution.[121] TAC commanders also had difficulty in getting support for their programs and people under LeMay.[122] When the Air Force faced budget cuts in 1957, LeMay advocated the absorption of TAC into a SAC-dominated "air offensive command."[123]

If LeMay were biased slightly, the person who replaced him at SAC was obsessed with the absolute dominance of the Strategic Air Command. LeMay left his successor a thriving command that had expanded from 837 to 2,711 aircraft and from 21 stateside bases to 38, with an additional 30 bases overseas. "Tough Tommy" Power, in the words of LeMay himself, was "a mean son-of-a-bitch."[124] LeMay selected Power, the only senior World War II-generation general who had neither a civilian nor a military education beyond high school, as his vice commander at SAC "because he could get things done."[125] One retired four-star general claimed, "LeMay was a pussycat compared to Power."[126] Another noted that Power was "hard and cruel" and loved to "perform in front of an audience" and "ridicule briefers."[127] Power had been LeMay's strong man at SAC from 1949 to 1954, after which he had commanded Air Research and Development Command (ARDC). Power had personally led the first incendiary attack on Tokyo in March 1945 and orbited the area to assess the conflagration. General Power was the ultimate absolutist. In his apocalyptic book, *Design for Survival*, Power claims that "it was strategic bombing more than any other factor that ultimately forced the unconditional surrender of Germany and Japan. . . . We could have won Korea with nukes overnight. . . . We should have intervened in Hungary when we had strategic superiority."[128] He further asserts that the first principle of war was to "maintain a credible capability to achieve a military victory under any set of conditions and circumstances" and that deterrence could be achieved only through "superior military strength."[129] Power was a parochial, hard-driving autocrat at SAC. He presided over significant growth in SAC, including the incorporation of intercontinental ballistic missiles.

The ICBM became a widespread national concern only in response to the shock of the Soviet launching of the sputnik missile into space in October 1957. The Air Force absolutists slowly supported ICBM development. The US ICBM program began on paper in 1951 with the Atlas, which was in developmental testing by 1955. In reaction to the new Soviet H-bomb and new technical breakthroughs, Eisenhower directed that the ICBM receive the highest national priority in 1955. In November 1955 Headquarters Air Force directed ARDC and SAC to get ready to develop and employ ICBMs. After considerable interservice controversy, Secretary of Defense Louis A. Johnson assigned the ICBM program officially to the Air Force in 1956. In August 1956 the ARDC commander, bomber general Power, warned of a "somewhat distorted and exaggerated picture" of missile capabilities and potential which "cannot cope with contingencies."[130] Additionally, Power did not push Air Force research in solid-fuel technologies until threatened by the success of the Navy's solid-fuel Polaris program.[131] Finally, at the September 1957 conference, Chief of Staff White, concerned about the successes of Polaris and his generals' "lukewarm" attitude towards ICBMs, scolded his subordinates for allowing their dedication to aircraft to turn into a "battleship attitude." He noted that "all truths change with time" and, that furthermore, the missile was "here to stay."[132] Despite White's enthusiasm for missiles, LeMay and Power worried that these unproven weapons would draw funds from bombers. LeMay briefed the Gaither Committee in September 1957 that he doubted Soviet missiles posed a threat to the United States or that they would be significant in his military lifetime.[133] Power testified before Congress in December (after sputnik) that emphasis on missiles was "maybe a little bit strong."[134] Despite White's efforts to influence his generals, only strong public and congressional reaction to the "shocking" Soviet capability demonstrated by the launching of sputnik sparked interest in ICBMs within the senior leadership of the Air Force.

The impact on Air Force strategic doctrine was twofold. Foremost, the Air Force did not want to slow the growth of its treasured and mighty bomber force. SAC responded to allegations of a new vulnerability to Soviet ICBMs by dispersing those bombers to numerous satellite bases leased to SAC, placing one-third of its forces on alert, and beginning construction on a network of radars, known as the ballistic missile early warning system (BMEWS). Next, fears of a missile gap could be countered by an ambitious Air Force ICBM program. As in the now-defunct "bomber gap," the new missile gap looked wider to the Air Force than to other intelligence agencies. When U-2 evidence, human intelligence, and eventually satellite photos could not substantiate the existence of a missile gap, the Air Force, which claimed "every flyspeck on film was a missile," responded that the Soviets were hiding and camouflaging their missiles.[135] And, as in the illusory bomber gap, public and congressional furor compelled an increase in funding, this time a 52 percent increase in the ICBM budget, as well as a presidential move in 1959 to grant ICBMs top priority again.[136]

Despite civilian interest in ICBM, the bomber generals preferred the proven past over the uncertain future. LeMay continued to list long-range missiles last on his military priorities.[137] Missiles would, he argued, gain "satisfactory state of reliability" only after "long and bitter experience in the field," a reaffirmation of the senior World War II generation's emphasis on experience.[138] Pacific war absolutist and bomber general Clarence S. Irvine ridiculed the deterrent effect of a submerged missile: "I don't know how to show your teeth with a missile."[139] Even White relented in 1959, voicing his concern over "a great downgrading of our manned bomber force" in favor of "romantic and exotic" missiles that he was "not prepared to stake the existence of the nation on."[140] To the absolutists, manned bombers had brought victory in World War II; now, they could fly higher, faster, and farther to deliver a destructive power that far exceeded any in history. A carefully orchestrated, simultaneous assault by SAC's nuclear bombers would be unstoppable and decisive. After witnessing the favorable results of war games amidst the imposing growth of SAC, Eisenhower complained that bomber advocates wanted "to kill every Russian three times."[141]

Though a few missile advocates did exist within the institution, the Air Force began to see the need for ICBMs primarily in reaction to external factors. First, a Soviet surface-to-air missile (SAM) shot down a high-flying American U-2 spy plane over the Soviet Union in 1960—a capability that bode ill for SAC's bombers. Second, a more resolute Eisenhower again demanded that ICBMs become top priority, in August 1959. Third, the Navy was quickly developing a submarine-launched ballistic missile which would challenge SAC's monopoly on strategic deterrence. After less-than-enthusiastic support within the Air Force for Atlas and Titan missiles, by 1960 (when SLBM-capable Navy Polaris submarines became a reality) the JCS requested 1,600 new Minuteman ICBMs. SAC now wanted 10,000.[142]

The Air Force's expanding arsenal fostered advocacy for a counterforce strategy, which would aim overwhelming numbers of nuclear weapons at military targets with great precision, in hopes of preempting damage from follow-on enemy strikes. The advocates also hoped that focusing solely on military targets might induce the Soviets to restrict their targeting of US cities. But absolutist general Power and SAC opposed counterforce in 1960 on grounds that anything less than an ability to destroy enemy society completely would weaken deterrence. Power testified that SAC was small and needed more modernization to maintain its essential overwhelming strength. Furthermore, Power still preferred reliance on the strategic bomber: "We never put anything to work in SAC unless it has proven that it can do a man's job, can carry the load."[143]

Sputnik's major casualty in the Air Force was TAC and the tactical air forces.[144] While TAC had received research and development funds sufficient to develop 23 different fighter aircraft types from the end of World War II to 1954, it would receive only one new production series aircraft from 1955 to 1964.[145] SAC had complete dominance in the selection of new technologies, and usually the best TAC could do was to accept SAC rejects.[146] In 1957 Eisenhower's restrictions in defense spending cost the Air Force 10 tactical fighter wings.[147] From 41 wings in 1957, TAC would shrink to 23 wings by 1960. In the interim, Weyland's Composite Air Strike Force had responded to crises in Lebanon and Taiwan in 1958. Though marginally trained and ill equipped for conventional war, the deployed tactical striking force did serve its political purpose; fortunately, it did so without extensive combat. TAC officers felt they had proven the legitimacy of the CASF; SAC claimed its mobilization and alert capability limited the crises.[148] TAC was still spread thin with multiple missions: airlift, support of the Army, air escort for SAC, air defense augmentation, retardation (tactical nuclear weapons), the CASF, and requirements to train and man the tactical air forces. By 1959 General Weyland claimed his TAC no longer could support its missions to augment Air Defense Command and escort SAC.[149] At his retirement that year, he further warned "that the Pentagon's preoccupation with strategic bombing and long-range missiles may soon leave us unprepared to fight a limited war."[150] TAC was trapped by its own commitment to nuclear warfare. After sputnik, enemy targets expanded greatly. Now, with fewer forces, the tactical air forces were even more committed to an exclusively nuclear role.

The Air Force's final response to sputnik was to assess its educational programs. Sputnik spawned numerous study groups that found disturbing weaknesses in the Air Force's educational system. By 1954 the Soviets were producing 50,000 engineers each year; the United States only 20,000.[151] Studies revealed Air Force personnel with the highest skills were the least likely to stay in the service. The Rawlings Board of 1956 noted that the Air University professional schools "produced few truly educated officers," and the schools were too small to accommodate the "hump" of aging World War II veterans.[152] In 1957 SAC and TAC had approximately 31 percent of its officers with bachelor's degrees and 1.5 percent with master's degrees.[153] A 1957 study noted that the Air War College emphasized strategic air operations with no formal discussion of the American political system or of arms control and observed the school "lacked critical analysis."[154] Yet, sputnik alerted the Air Force, as well as the country, to its educational shortcomings and contributed to the tremendous expansion of education in the 1960s. Still, it would affect mostly future generations; the Air Force had to ride with experience in the interim.

While the lack of education surely could narrow Air Force capabilities, the defining phenomenon of the institution's first two decades of existence was the ascendancy of SAC within the Air Force. SAC received clear budgetary, procurement, doctrinal, and personnel preference. Figures 2, 3, and 4 indicate the extent of SAC's domination in funding, numbers of aircraft, and personnel, respectively, during this period. Figure 5 shows a comparison in the growth in the number of wings in SAC and TAC.

More wings for SAC meant additional air divisions, which meant more positions for command and general officer assignments. The forced dispersal of bomber units in response to the Soviet ICBM threat positioned this phenomenon to SAC's advantage. Force structure growth in response to the guiding national security policy of massive retaliation created more bomber pilots in the treasured "operational" leadership positions. From this population, the future ruling elites would be selected. Appendix A samples the backgrounds of the Air

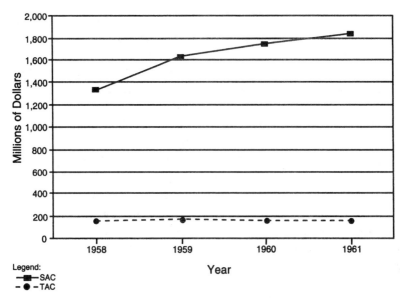

Source: Headquarters USAF, *U.S. Air Force Statistical Digest, FY 1958–1961.*

Figure 2. Strategic Air Command versus Tactical Air Command Operational Costs (1958–61)

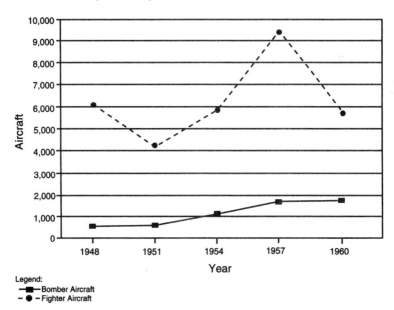

Source: Headquarters USAF, *U.S. Air Force Statistical Digest, FY 1948–1960.*

Figure 3. Bomber versus Fighter Aircraft Inventory (1948–60)

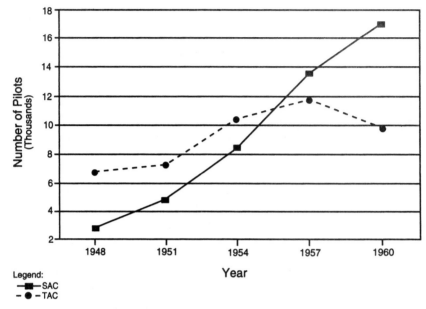

Source: Headquarters USAF, *U.S. Air Force Statistical Digest, FY 1948–1960.*

Figure 4. Number and Distribution of Pilots (1948–60)

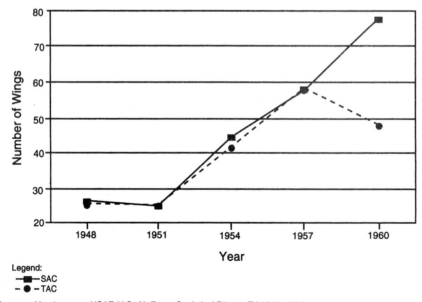

Source: Headquarters USAF *U.S. Air Force Statistical Digest, FY 1948–1960.*

Figure 5. Number and Distribution of Air Force Wings (1948–60)

Force's senior leaders in 1960.[155] Bomber domination appears evident, and it would increase in the next few years.

The apex of bomber domination within the Air Force came with the selection of LeMay as Air Force chief of staff in 1961. New secretary of defense Robert S. McNamara purportedly asked White to stay on, but the physically ailing White declined.[156] The logical successors were LeMay and Norstad. Lauris Norstad claimed he preferred to continue as Supreme Headquarters Allied Powers Europe (SHAPE) commander at NATO.[157] That situation left the well-known LeMay, who had built the great Strategic Air Command and had spent the last four years "running the Air Force" and learning to operate in Washington, as the only other alternative.

Among LeMay's first actions as chief was to promote his people into key leadership positions.[158] Within three months LeMay had replaced the last of the fighter generals in senior positions at USAFE and TAC. By 1 October 1961 all major operational commanders, and the vast majority of the Air Staff leadership, had become ardent bomber generals—most of them SAC absolutists. SAC's methods became Air Force methods.[159]

Observed noted military sociologist Morris Janowitz, "In the military, as in any organization, the 'big issues' are personified by outstanding men and the factions that develop around them. Within the elite nucleus the hypothesis is also relevant that an officer's perspectives are influenced by his personal alliances and contacts."[160] Unknowingly, the Air Force fulfilled the Janowitz hypothesis while the print was still wet.

Notes

1. Robert Frank Futrell, *Ideas, Concepts, Doctrine: Basic Thinking in the United States Air Force, 1907–1960*, vol. 1 (Maxwell AFB, Ala.: Air University Press, December 1989), 216.

2. Harry R. Borowski, *A Hollow Threat: Strategic Air Power and Containment Before Korea* (Westport, Conn.: Greenwood Press, 1982). Borowski offers a good discussion of the early problems in SAC.

3. Ibid., 57–74; Vance O. Mitchell, "The First Generation: A Policy History of the Air Force Officer Corps, 1944–1973" (unpublished manuscript, Office of Air Force History [OAFH], May 1991), 127; Thomas M. Coffey, *Iron Eagle: The Turbulent Life of General Curtis LeMay* (New York: Crown Publishers, 1986), 274; and Richard H. Kohn and Joseph Harahan,

eds., *Strategic Air Warfare: An Interview with Curtis E. LeMay, Leon W. Johnson, David A. Burchinal, and Jack J. Catton* (Washington, D.C.: OAFH, 1988), 75.

4. Mitchell, 129.

5. Ibid., 131–33; and Kohn and Harahan, 77.

6. Borowski, 149; Gen John McConnell, transcript of oral history interview by Dr. Edgar F. Puryear Jr., 1975, Air Force Historical Research Agency (cited hereafter as AFHRA), Maxwell AFB, Ala., 25; and Gen Frank F. Everest, transcript of oral history interview by Dr. Edgar F. Puryear Jr., 16 July 1979, AFHRA, 11.

7. Lawrence J. Korb, *The Joint Chiefs of Staff: The First Twenty-five Years* (Bloomington, Ind.: Indiana University Press, 1976), 76.

8. Coffey, 59.

9. Curtis E. LeMay and Bill Yenne, *Superfortress: The Story of the B-29 and American Air Power* (New York: McGraw-Hill, 1988), 140.

10. Ibid., 1; and Curtis E. LeMay with MacKinlay Kantor, *Mission with LeMay: My Story* (Garden City, N.Y.: Doubleday, 1965), 390.

11. LeMay and Yenne, 2–3; and Gen Curtis E. LeMay, transcript of oral history interview by the OAFH, January 1965, 2–3, AFHRA.

12. LeMay and Yenne, 2–3.

13. Coffey, 266–69; and LeMay with Kantor, 401.

14. Gen Curtis E. LeMay, transcript of oral history interview by John T. Bohn, 9 March 1971, 14, AFHRA.

15. Edward G. Longacre, *Strategic Air Command: The Formative Years (1944–1949)* (Offutt AFB, Nebr.: Office of the Historian, 1990), 23; and LeMay with Kantor, 430.

16. LeMay, interview by Bohn, 29.

17. Kohn and Harahan, 84.

18. Longacre, 24; and LeMay with Kantor, 433.

19. They included cold, hard Thomas S. "Tommy" Power,* vice commander; Augie Kissner, chief of staff; J. B. Montgomery, deputy chief of staff for Operations; Walter C. "Cam" Sweeney,* deputy chief of staff for Plans; Jack J. Catton,* chief of Requirements; Al Kalberger, public affairs; William "Bill" Irvine, 509th commander; Emmet "Rosie" O'Donnell,* Fifteenth Air Force commander; Roger Ramey,* Eighth Air Force commander; William H. "Butch" Blanchard,* Eighth Air Force director of operations; Jack D. Ryan,* 509th commander. (The asterisk indicates future four-star general World War II generation bomber pilots.) See also Coffey, 277.

20. Futrell, 243; David MacIsaac, "The Air Force and Strategic Thought, 1945–1951," *International Security Studies Program Working Paper Number 8* (21 June 1979): 37–38; and David Alan Rosenberg, "The Origins of Overkill: Nuclear Weapons and American Strategy, 1945–1960," *International Security* 7 (Spring 1983): 13–15, 48.

21. Futrell, 450–51.

22. History, Tactical Air Command, July–December 1958, 59; and Air Force Manual (AFM) 1-2, *United States Air Force Basic Doctrine* (1959), 4, as cited in Mark Clodfelter, *The Limits of Air Power: The American Bombing of North Vietnam* (New York: Free Press, 1989), 30–31.

23. Rosenberg, 13–15.

24. David A. Anderton, *Strategic Air Command: Two-Thirds of the Triad* (New York: Charles Scribner's Sons, 1976), 16. On SAC's control of war plans, see Kohn and Harahan, eds., 90; and Rosenberg, 14–15.

25. LeMay, interview by Bohn, 30; LeMay with Kantor, 439, 441. LeMay recounted: "*Everyone needed training.* You train enough, and you can be practically unconscious, but your reflexes will pull you through."

26. LeMay with Kantor, 496.

27. Kohn and Harahan, 97; and Morris Janowitz, *The Professional Soldier: A Social and Political Portrait* (Glencoe, Ill.: Free Press, 1960), 30. Janowitz notes the development of technological routines in SAC consumed their attention.

28. Kohn and Harahan, 98.

29. LeMay with Kantor, 482.

30. Kohn and Harahan, 90; and Rosenberg, 8–15, 37, 44. Rosenberg has an interesting analysis of SAC's responsibility for operational planning, as well as its semiautonomous status and remarkable power during the 1950s.

31. Coffey, 379–82. Coffey cites instances where LeMay protected his people simply because they were "his people."

32. Mitchell, 181, 281. LeMay, interview by Bohn, 40. Many spot promotions went to reward "lead" crews and reservists who had difficulty competing. See also Charles K. Hopkins, *The Development of Strategic Air Command: 1946–1981 (40th Anniversary)* (Offutt AFB, Nebr.: Office of SAC History, 1986), 27.

33. Ludrew B. Grappe, Ray W. Alvord, and James V. Poland, *Air Force Officer Performance Evaluation: Rating Trends and Relationships from 1954 through 1965* (Lackland AFB, Tex.: Personnel Research Laboratory, October 1967), 22–25. SAC is not specifically identified as command "A," but its identity rather obvious from close examination of related data.

34. LeMay with Kantor, 458; Kohn and Harahan, 87. LeMay's opposition to using strategic bombers in interdiction roles contradicted the doctrinal tenet of indivisibility.

35. LeMay with Kantor, 459–64; and Kohn and Harahan, 88–89.

36. Caroline Ziemke, "In the Shadow of the Giant: USAF Tactical 9Air Command in the Era of Strategic Bombing, 1945–1955" (PhD diss., Ohio State University, 1989), 255. TAC spent 4 percent of its budget in that period on personnel relocation alone. History, Tactical Air Command, January–June 1954, vol. 1, "Personnel Instability and Unit Manning in TAC, 1953–1954." This report states that the average duty assignment for officers in TAC during this period lasted seven months. TAC trained its personnel and usually sent them overseas.

37. Curtis E. LeMay, transcript of oral history interview by John T. Bohn, 9 March 1971; 43, AFHRA. LeMay opposed the bids of TAC and USAFE for a "retardation mission," which proposed the use of tactical nuclear weapons to disrupt the Soviet air defenses and the onslaught of Western Europe. LeMay didn't like the incursion of others into his plans and felt there would be duplication of effort when SAC itself didn't have enough weapons—despite TAC's assertion that it would enhance SAC survivability. See Jerome V. Martin, "Reforging the Sword: United States Tactical Air Forces, Air Power Doctrine, and National Security Policy, 1945–1956" (PhD diss., Ohio State University, 1988), 221; Ziemke, 236; and Samuel Huntington, *The Common Defense: Strategic Programs in National Politics* (New York: Columbia University Press, 1961), 307. SAC also opposed Air Force programs Project Lincoln (1951) on air defense and Project Vista (1952) on tactical nuclear weapons. See William R. Gray, "The Case for Combining SAC and TAC" (Maxwell AFB, Ala.: Air University, March 1957), 22.

38. Martin, 207; LeMay, 214, 377; and Ziemke, 194. Twining later told Joe Cannon to absorb cuts in the aftermath of Korea. See Ziemke, 196, 236–38. Opposed by SAC, TAC pushed for an atomic role when atomic weapons became plentiful. Futrell, 310–11. Cannon responded with resentment: "A tactical fighter-bomber unit capable of delivering atomic weapons promises to be one of the most devastating striking forces that will be available to the military establishment. I personally consider it extremely important to have the strategic air forces tend to their own knitting, keep their minds on their own jobs and not be diverted from their primary mission" [insularity and rivalry were building both ways]. See Ziemke, 215. Secretary of the Air Force Finletter and senior Air Force leaders were concerned that too much money for TAC in NATO might mean the Air Force would lose control over the direction of its growth.

39. Gen Lauris Norstad, transcript of oral history interview by Dr. Edgar F. Puryear Jr., 22 August 1977, 15–17, AFHRA; Gen Frank F. Everest, transcript of oral history interview by Dr. Edgar F. Puryear Jr., 16 July 1979, 5, 131, AFHRA. See Herman S. Wolk, *Planning and Organizing the Postwar Air Force, 1943–1947* (Washington, D.C.: Office of Air Force History [OAFH], 1984), 175; and Futrell, 279, on Norstad's political skills and pragmatic beliefs.

40. Edgar F. Puryear Jr., *Stars in Flight: A Study in Air Force Character and Leadership* (San Rafael, Calif.: Presidio Press, 1981), 206.

41. Martin, 112. In response to *National Security Council 68*, Twining had written to the Air Staff: "Air power is deterrence *par excellence.* Naval power and ground power are not. . . . I can conceive of air power of such dominating quality that it could win a war by itself, or less than this could be the power which could dominate a country and force its yielding to one's will."

42. Nathan F. Twining, *Neither Liberty nor Safety: A Hard Look at U.S. Military Policy and Strategy* (New York: Holt, Rinehart and Winston, 1966),

3. Twining began this book with "World War II carried the United States to a pinnacle of self confidence and world respect . . . and things have generally gone downhill since."

43. Ibid., 7–8.

44. Mark Clodfelter, *The Limits of Air Power: The American Bombing of North Vietnam* (New York: Free Press, 1989), 20.

45. Twining, 53; and Puryear, 260–61. Twining also defends the absolutist statements of Orvil Anderson that led to Anderson's "early retirement" by the Truman administration.

46. Martin, 116.

47. Eugene M. Zuckert, transcript of oral history interview by George M. Watson, December 1986, 79–80, AFHRA; Eugene M. Zuckert, interview by Dr. Edgar F. Puryear Jr., 28 September 1977, 20, AFHRA.

48. Puryear, 160.

49. C. Wright Mills, *The Power Elite* (New York: Oxford University Press, 1956), 188. Mills notes that new JCS members had held major commands in the Pacific.

50. Ziemke, 243.

51. Richard K. Betts, *Soldiers, Statesmen, and Cold War Crises* (Cambridge, Mass.: Harvard University Press, 1977), 106; Robert F. Futrell, "The Influence of the Air Power Concept on Air Force Planning, 1945–1962," in *Military Planning in the Twentieth Century: Proceedings of the Eleventh Military History Symposium USAF Academy, 1984* (Washington, D.C.: OAFH, 1986), 264.

52. Lawrence J. Korb, *The Joint Chiefs of Staff: The First Twenty-five Years* (Bloomington, Ind.: Indiana University Press, 1976), 109.

53. Data from "USAF Leaders Through the Years," *Air Force Magazine*, May 1989, 56–57; Jacob Neufeld, *Organizational Charts, Headquarters USAF, 1947–Present: AFP 210-5* (Washington, D.C.: OAFH, May 1989); and Air Force biographies. See also Gen O. P. Weyland, oral history interview by Arthur Marmor, 1971, AFHRA. Weyland was a senior World War II European-experienced fighter general who would command TAC from 1954 to 1959. He commented on Air Force senior leadership in 1953: "We had 'very little' tactical experience, and the people in the tactical business were outnumbered and outvoted."

54. Kurt Lang, "Technology and Career Management in the Military Establishment," in Morris Janowitz, ed., *The New Military: Changing Patterns of Organization* (New York: Russell Sage Foundation, 1964), 77.

55. Korb, 107; and Maxwell D. Taylor, *The Uncertain Trumpet* (New York: Harper and Brothers, 1959), 110. Taylor, an Army general, alleges that Twining, as chairman of the JCS, voted with the Air Force on all split decisions.

56. Korb, 107.

57. Janowitz, xvii.

58. Air Force Manual (AFM) 1-2, *United States Air Force Basic Doctrine* (Washington, D.C.: Government Printing Office, 1953), 12–13. See also

Andrew D. Dembosky, "Meeting the Enduring Challenge: United States Air Force Basic Doctrine Through 1992" (master's thesis, North Carolina State University, 1993), 16–19.

59. Lt Gen Fred M. Dean, transcript of oral history interview by Maj Richard H. Emmons, 25 February 1975, 52, AFHRA.

60. Gen Laurence S. Kuter, transcript of oral history interview by Thomas A. Sturm and Hugh N. Ahmann, 1–3 October 1974, 509–10, AFHRA. The law prescribed that lieutenant colonels must retire after 28 years of service; colonels and brigadier generals, 30 years; and major generals and above, 35 years. Officers twice passed over for promotion had to leave the service. The act also limited permanent grades (ranks) by percentages, which prescribed a "pyramid" rank structure (fewer officers as rank increased).

61. Ibid., 84–87. By 1949 nearly 40 percent of Air Force officers served in a temporary rank higher than their permanent rank. Janowitz, 72–73. Janowitz claims 49 percent of Air Force generals in 1950 made general before 21 years of service (Army 6.6 percent and Navy 1.5 percent).

62. Alfred Goldberg, ed., *A History of the United States Air Force, 1907–1957* (Princeton, N.J.: D. Van Nostrand, 1957), 105; and Vance Mitchell, "The First Generation: A Policy History of the Air Force Officer Corps, 1944–1973" (unpublished manuscript, OAFH, May 1991), 57. The massive influx of aviation cadets served to lower the average age of Air Force officers to 29. Over 80 percent of the hump was composed of reservists. See also Wolk, 74.

63. Mitchell, 282.

64. Ibid., 283, 250. By 1955 the average temporary colonel reached that rank a full decade before being eligible for it in permanent rank; high rank was a result of the demands of World War II, populating a new service, and early promotions to reduce the hump of World War II peer groups. Thirty-eight percent of the Air Force colonels in 1956 held that rank in World War II. The Regular Officer Augmentation Act of 1956 also authorized the secretary of the Air Force to grant regular officers two extra years of seniority to mitigate the effect of the hump.

65. Ibid., 268–70.

66. Janowitz, 63. The average age of an Air Force general officer in 1945 was 46.9 years. By 1951 it stood at 51.2 and was increasing.

67. Mitchell, 100. Fewer than 2 percent of the aviation cadets held college degrees. See also Richard L. Davis and Frank P. Donnini, *Professional Military Education for Air Force Officers: Comments and Criticisms* (Maxwell AFB, Ala.: Air University Press, 1991), 3. The average educational level of an Army Air Forces officer at the end of World War II was one year of college. See also Henry Willis Easterling Jr., "Nonmilitary Education in the United States Air Force, 1945–1979" (PhD diss., Indiana University, 1980), 54. By 1948 the Air Force had from 35 to 40 percent college graduates, by far the lowest of the services (Army and Navy had approximately 70 percent each). See also Arthur T. Hadley, *A Report From*

the Field: The Straw Giant (New York: Random House, 1986), 82. Hadley claims that the statistics in 1947 were 50 percent college graduates in the USAF, 77 percent in the Army, and 85 percent in the Navy.

68. "Education Level Must be Higher, Air Force Warns Again," *Air Force Times* 10, no. 18 (8 October 1949); and Goldberg, 121.

69. Mitchell, 104.

70. Harold E. Talbott, "Statement of Policy, Information, and Education of the Armed Forces," *Air Force Letter 34-23* (Washington, D.C.: Department of the Air Force, 24 September 1953). Talbott cited poor prisoner of war performance by Air Force members as reflective of its poor educational levels.

71. Roger Hilsman, "Research in Military Affairs," *World Politics*, no. 7 (1954): 502.

72. Davis and Donnini, 29.

73. Jacob S. Orleans, *A Report to the Commanding General, Air University, of an Educational Survey of the Air Command and Staff School, Headquarters Air University (Orleans Report)*, September 1949, Air University Library, Maxwell AFB, Ala.

74. Davis and Donnini, 18, 54, 56.

75. Muir S. Fairchild, *Report of the USAF Military Education Board on the Professional Education System For USAF Officers (Fairchild Board)*, 24–25 January 1950, Air University Library, Maxwell AFB, Ala., 20; and Janowitz, 141. Twenty-two percent had attended AWC by 1950 (70.7 percent Army, 33.3 percent Navy war colleges). See also Davis and Donnini, 3. The 1950 Board of Visitors observed there was still little time for reflective thinking in the schools.

76. Mitchell, 167. The tendency to "cram information" acknowledges the lack of breadth and professional literacy in a body of preoccupied specialists.

77. Davis and Donnini, 52; Gen Horace M. Wade, transcript of oral history interview by Hugh N. Ahmann, 1–12 October 1978, 215, AFHRA; and Robert Frank Futrell, *Ideas, Concepts, Doctrine: Basic Thinking in the United States Air Force, 1961–1984*, vol. 2 (Maxwell AFB, Ala.: Air University Press, 1989), 161.

78. Author spreadsheet: sample size small for senior generation fighter generals (only four), none of whom went to graduate school.

79. Betts, 84. Betts observes that the military evaluated tactical capabilities better than it did basic policy and strategy.

80. Twining, 32, 36. In 1966 Twining commented, "I still don't think it's quite out of date. Now they talk about flexible response and control—which to me is a bunch of junk . . . [massive retaliation] worked and now we're nice. . . . We must go into wars to win victory."

81. Betts, 116. "The fundamental principles that guided Air Force advice in Cold War decisions on use of force were that strategic bombing can cripple an enemy in its homeland, aerial interdiction of supply lines can cripple an enemy at the front, and either form of bombing is an effective

coercive tool independent of other military operations. These made Air Force attitudes the most consistently radical of those of all the services in the Cold War." See also Russell Frank Weigley, *The American Way of War: A History of United States Military Strategy and Policy* (New York: Macmillan, 1973), 396; and John Prados, *The Soviet Estimate: U.S. Intelligence Analysis and Soviet Strategic Forces* (Princeton, N.J.: Princeton University Press, 1982), 21. The Air Force expanded urgently to meet the "year of expected vulnerability" in 1954, when it was expected the Soviets could launch an atomic strike on the United States.

82. Betts, 21, 106. When LeMay was asked what would happen to the French, he responded, "Well, I guess they'd have gotten it too." See David Alan Rosenberg, "The Origins of Overkill: Nuclear Weapons and American Strategy, 1945–1960," *International Security* 7 (Spring 1983): 18. LeMay was confident SAC could deliver a "Sunday punch" of 600 to 750 atomic bombs on the USSR within two hours, incurring negligible losses to SAC—this assumption was verified by the JCS study the following year. See John Prados, *The Sky Would Fall: Operation Vulture* (New York: Dial Press, 1983), 92, 154.

83. Martin, 270; and Weyland. Weyland and other pragmatists also counseled against involvement, saying that American involvement simply would replace the French with Americans as the object of hatred within Indochina.

84. Objections to the concept of massive retaliation began as early as July 1950 when Eugene Rabinowitz responded *to National Security Council 162–2.* See also Eugene Rabinowitz, "Atomic Weapons and the Korean War," *Bulletin of Atomic Scientists* 6, 194. "If we have nothing but atomic bombs with which to strike back, we will obviously be forced to use these weapons—even if the enemy does not do so first, and even if our leaders have grave doubts about the political wisdom and moral justifications of their use."

85. Ziemke, 248–49; and Mark Perry, *Four Stars: The Inside Story of the Forty-five Year Battle Between the Joints Chiefs of Staff and America's Civilian Leaders* (Boston: Houghton Mifflin, 1989), 62.

86. Weigley, chap. 17; Fred M. Kaplan, *The Wizards of Armageddon* (New York: Simon and Schuster, 1983); Lawrence Freedman, *The Evolution of Nuclear Strategy* (London: Macmillan Press, 1981); Gerard H. Clarfield and William M. Wiecek, *Nuclear America: Military and Civilian Nuclear Power in the United States, 1940–1980* (New York: Harper & Row, 1984); and Bernard Brodie, *Strategy in the Missile Age* (Princeton, N.J.: Princeton University Press, 1959). All discuss in detail the role of the defense strategist in the nuclear age.

87. Martin, 268–70.

88. Janowitz, 316–17; and Betts, 106. Each author notes that Weyland was the latest in the pragmatic heritage of European-experienced fighter generals: Elwood Quesada, Hoyt Vandenberg, and Lauris Norstad.

89. Weyland.

CURTIS E. LeMAY AND THE RISE OF SAC

90. Ibid.

91. Ziemke, 267; and Martin, 180. By the end of 1954, TAC units were qualified to deliver nuclear weapons.

92. TAF consisted of USAF theater commands that generally employed fighters: TAC, United States Air Forces in Europe (USAFE), Alaskan Command (ALASCOM), and Pacific Air Forces (PACAF)—formerly Far East Air Forces (FEAF).

93. Futrell, *Ideas*, vol. 2, 449.

94. Ibid., 450.

95. Richard P. Klocko, "Air Power in Limited Military Actions," graduate study group thesis number 7 (Maxwell AFB, Ala.: Air University, 1954); Ziemke, 273; and Futrell, *Ideas*, vol. 2, 225–26.

96. History, Tactical Air Command, January–June 1955, 6; and Martin, 275. Weyland had briefed the concept to the Air Staff, a meeting of Air Force four-stars, the Air Force Association, industrialists, the press, Congress, and the Air War College before he gained final approval in June 1955.

97. See Martin, 281, 294–95; and Futrell, *Ideas*, vol. 2, 461–62, for the debate regarding conventional munitions between the two communities.

98. Martin, 279; Ziemke, 268; United States Congress, House Committee on Un-American Activities, *Soviet Total War: Historic Mission of Violence and Deceit*, 85th Cong., 2d sess., 380, 389, 391; History, Tactical Air Command, July–December, 1958, 36; and Futrell, *Ideas*, vol. 1, 442, 450.

99. Wade, 248. Wade, a junior World War II generation bomber general, admitted that only "dyed in the wool" TAC (fighter) types kept the command alive during the fifties. See Rosenberg, 22–23.

100. Each military service and branch searched for a role in general war: The Navy sought a nuclear strike role and the Army focused on missile air defense; Air Defense Command concentrated on intercepting Soviet bombers; and TAC's forte centered around offensive air support in theater warfare.

101. Futrell, *Ideas*, vol. 2, 452. Futrell discusses the difficulty TAC had in meeting globalism and decisiveness. See also Leverett G. Richards, *TAC: The Story of Tactical Air Command* (New York: John Day Company, 1961), 29–30, 241–43.

102. History, Tactical Air Command, January–June, 1959; Levi R. Chase, "A Global Mission for TAC" (thesis, Maxwell AFB, Ala.: Air University, April 1956), 25. Chase documents the dominance of SAC, problems of TAC, and the parcelling out of tactical resources to various regions and missions.

103. Thomas D. White, *Army, Navy, Air Force Journal*, 7 May 1955, 1063. For "battleship mentality," see Martin, 273.

104. Twining, 104, 106.

105. Thomas A. Keaney, *Strategic Bombers and Conventional Weapons: Airpower Options* (Fort Lesley J. McNair, Washington, D.C.: National

Defense University Press, 1984), National Security Affairs Monograph Series, no. 84-84, 15.

106. John Newhouse, *War and Peace in the Nuclear Age* (New York: Knopf, 1989), 110.

107. US Congress, *Study of Airpower*, 145, 171, 218, 1481, 1504; For more on the bomber gap, see Prados, *Soviet Estimate*, 43–45; George Reed, "U.S. Defense Policy, U.S. Air Force Doctrine and Strategic Nuclear Weapon Systems, 1958–1964: The Case of the Minuteman ICBM" (PhD diss., Duke University, 1986), 20; Thomas M. Coffey, *Iron Eagle: The Turbulent Life of General Curtis LeMay* (New York: Crown Publishers, 1986), 338; and Newhouse, 110–11.

108. Rosenberg, 8–10. SAC's planning resources and computers exceeded any in the Pentagon.

109. In the early 1950s the United States developed cheaper, smaller, and more powerful "nuclear" weapons called hydrogen bombs (H-bombs), which could be delivered by smaller aircraft like fighters.

110. Reed, 17, 19, 27–28; Fred M. Kaplan, *The Wizards of Armageddon* (New York: Simon and Schuster, 1983), 42. SLBMs did not have the range nor accuracy nor numbers to play a role in this more ambitious strategy. For an excellent analysis of LeMay's power and SAC's semiautonomy during the Truman and Eisenhower years, see Rosenberg. For SLBMs see Donald A. MacKenzie, *Inventing Accuracy: A Historical Sociology of Nuclear Missile Guidance* (Cambridge, Mass.: Massachusetts Institute of Technology Press, 1990).

111. Martin, 205. Buying aircraft and adding new organizations first help to make subsequent appropriations to supply easier and help to maintain what has been procured.

112. Mitchell, 231.

113. Mark Perry, *Four Stars: The Inside Story of the Forty-five Year Battle Between the Joints Chief of Staff and America's Civilian Leaders* (Boston: Houghton Mifflin, 1989), 74.

114. Lt Gen Royal B. Allison, transcript of oral history interview by Dr. Edgar F. Puryear, 6 July 1977, AFHRA, Maxwell AFB, Ala., 4–5.

115. Robert C. Richardson III, "In the Looking Glass," *Air University Quarterly Review* 9, no. 4 (Winter 1957–1958): 46–47.

116. Coffey, 345; Allison; and Gen Jacob E. Smart, transcript of oral history interview by Dr. Edgar F. Puryear Jr., 17 July 1979, AFHRA, 17.

117. Allison. Allison adds: "There were times that I think General White really wondered if he had made a wise move in bringing General LeMay in." See Coffey. LeMay and White were not friends; LeMay considered White too compromising: "Tommy wouldn't get in the mud and fight."

118. Smart, 2.

119. Futrell, *Ideas*, vol. 1, 398.

120. Ibid.; and Eugene M. Zuckert, history interview by Dr. Edgar F. Puryear Jr., 28 September 1979.

121. Zuckert, interviewed by Puryear, 23, 30; Eugene M. Zuckert, transcript of oral history interview by Dr. George M. Watson, 27 April 1982, AFHRA, 26; and Zuckert, interviewed by Watson, 9 December 1986, 3–5, 79–80.

122. Everest, 6, 50. Everest, as commander of USAFE and then TAC, noted how White remained accessible and sympathetic. On the other hand, LeMay was not and often denied requests.

123. Futrell, "The Influence of the Air Power Concept on Air Force Planning, 1945–1962," 266.

124. Coffey, 49.

125. Ibid., 51.

126. Gen Theodore R. Milton, transcript of oral history interview by Dr. Edgar F. Puryear Jr., 28 June 1979, AFHRA, 15.

127. Gen Horace M. Wade, transcript of oral history interview by Hugh N. Ahmann, 10–12 October 1978, AFHRA, 306–10.

128. Thomas S. Power, *Design for Survival* (New York: Coward-McCann, 1965), 31, 50, 106.

129. Ibid., 39, 126.

130. Thomas S. Power, "How Much Can Missiles Really Do?" *Air Force*, September 1956, 105–6.

131. Reed, 54–63.

132. Ibid., 48–49, 64. In June 1957 White asked a board of senior officers chaired by Lt Gen Donald Putt to review ICBM development. They cited lack of Air Force interest and understanding by most top-level officers. They also noted lack of Air Force vision and support of education. For the best analysis of the social and cultural dynamics that led to conservatism in accepting the ICBM, see MacKenzie.

133. The Gaither Committee, chaired by longtime RAND trustee and adviser H. Rowan Gaither, was originally chartered by the National Security Council in the spring of 1957 to analyze US civil defense needs but later received permission to expand the scope of the study to include the entire question of national defense in the ballistic missile era.

134. Kaplan, 132; and Herbert F. York, *Race to Oblivion* (New York: Simon and Schuster, 1979), 52–53.

135. Kaplan, 159, 167; David Wise and Thomas B. Ross, *The Invisible Government* (New York: Vintage Books, 1964), 212–13; and Prados, *The Soviet Estimate*, 117–19.

136. Reed, 75; Prados, *The Sky Would Fall*, 80–81. The Air Force admitted the disappearance of the bomber gap because of new Soviet emphasis on missiles.

137. York, 30; cited in Morton H. Halperin, *Bureaucratic Politics and Foreign Policy* (Washington, D.C.: Brookings Institute, 1974), 30. After sputnik LeMay's prioritized list of weapons systems included (1) B-52, (2) B-70, (3) the nuclear aircraft, and (4) ICBMs at the bottom.

138. Coffey, 335; see also Curtis E. LeMay, "Future of Manned Bombers," *Ordnance* (September–October 1958), 202–5.

139. "Missiles Have No Discretion, Reliability Still Low, AFA Told, 'Need Man in Airplane,'" *Army, Navy, Air Force Journal*, 1 March 1958, 3.

140. Edgar F. Puryear Jr., *Stars in Flight: A Study in Air Force Character and Leadership* (San Rafael, Calif.: Presidio Press, 1981), 199.

141. Reed, 73.

142. Prados, 114.

143. Kaplan, 237–46; Rosenberg, 59–60; and *Department of Defense Appropriations for 1960*, pt. 1, 390, 855; pt. 2, 384–85.

144. The TAF consists of the Air Force's worldwide fighter assets. They are assigned to TAC, USAFE, Pacific Air Forces (PACAF), and Alaskan Air Command (ALASCOM). TAF forces, during much of this time, included much of the airlift forces.

145. Martin, 374; and Marcelle Size Knaack, *Encyclopedia of US Air Force Aircraft and Missile Systems*, vol. 1, *Post-World War II Fighters, 1945–1973* (Washington, D.C.: OAFH, 1978).

146. Ziemke, 229.

147. History, Tactical Air Command, July–December 1958, 36. The Air Force considered eliminating the Nineteenth Air Force (CASF) in 1957. Gen T. R. Milton, interviewed by author, June 1991. Milton recalled a conversation between Twining and LeMay in 1957. LeMay wanted 19 wings of B-52s. Twining refused the proposal, saying it would emaciate TAC's budget. LeMay responded, "Well, what is TAC's mission?" Twining is said to have responded, "Hell, I don't know, but the Air Force has to have fighters."

148. David A. Anderton, *Strategic Air Command: Two-Thirds of the Triad* (New York: Charles Scribner's Sons, 1976), 55–56. Also see Martin, 381–82.

149. Martin, 376.

150. Huntington, 406.

151. Goldberg, 158; and Mitchell, 336. The Air Force had a difficult time retaining pilots, ROTC graduates, scientists, and engineers.

152. Gen E. W. Rawlings, USAF, chairman, *Report of the USAF Educational Conference of 18–19 October 1956* (Maxwell AFB, Ala.: 8 November 1956), 65–70.

153. Headquarters USAF, *USAF Statistical Digest* (Washington, D.C.: Directorate of Data Systems and Statistics, Comptroller of the Air Force, Headquarters USAF, May 1957).

154. John W. Masland and Laurence I. Radway, *Soldiers and Scholars: Military Education and National Policy* (Princeton, N.J.: Princeton University Press, 1957), 374, 380, 417.

155. The author wishes to thank Maj Mike Flood, a student at the School of Advanced Aerospace Studies, Maxwell AFB, Ala., for assistance in the construction of the appendices.

156. Gen George S. Brown, transcript of oral history interview by Dr. Edgar F. Puryear Jr., 14 September 1977, AFHRA, 11.

157. Ibid.; and Norstad, 19.

158. LeMay kept close control of persons promoted to general officer. Lt Gen Robert Kelley, interviewed by author, July 1993.

159. Coffey, 340. As his vice chief, Gen Fred Smith, recounted, "I think Curt, as the years went by . . . became more and more dictatorial and more and more insistent on SAC being it. Anything else was purely secondary."

160. Morris Janowitz, *The Professional Soldier: A Social and Political Portrait* (Glencoe, Ill.: Free Press, 1960), 293.

Chapter 4

The Apogee of Strategic Air Command and the Missile Challenge (1961–62)

I think we have been consistent in our concepts since the formation of the GHQ Air Force in 1935. Our basic doctrine has remained generally unchanged since that time.

—Gen Curtis E. LeMay

The senior World War II generation reached the apex of power in the early 1960s. As shown by figure 6, these bomber generals, led by Curtis LeMay, rose to four-star rank faster than most of their peers.

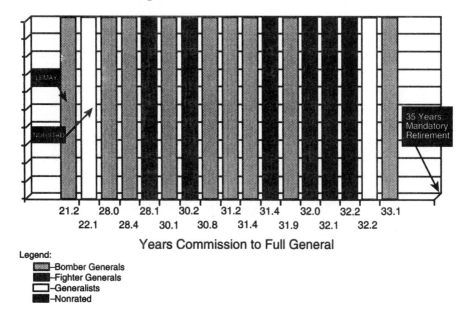

Legend:
- ▨ –Bomber Generals
- ▦ –Fighter Generals
- ☐ –Generalists
- ■ –Nonrated

Figure 6. Rapidity to Full General: Senior World War II Generation

In the early 1960s, bomber generals held more than one-half of the four-star positions (fig. 7).

The generalists, those not insulated within fighter or bomber tracks, were hard pressed to make full general at all.

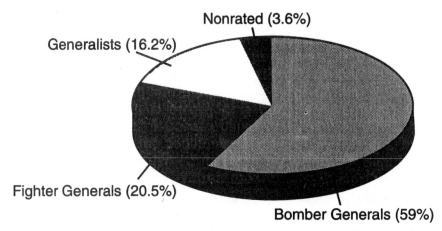

Figure 7. Time as Full General: Senior World War II Generation

In 1961 Secretary Zuckert concurred with the dominant bomber generals that LeMay, the last of the "World War II superstars," was most deserving of the top uniformed position in the Air Force.[1] The new Kennedy administration respected LeMay's popularity within the Air Force and felt LeMay "had the toughness . . . the country needed most in the wake of the Bay of Pigs."[2]

Within the Air Force LeMay's popularity was conditional, his toughness unconditional. LeMay's removal of nonbomber generals from key positions exacerbated the already bad relations between the bomber and fighter communities. One general recalled, "In the early sixties SAC and TAC were like two rattlesnakes. They would hardly talk to one another."[3] A case in point focused on LeMay's dismissal of fighter general Frank F. Everest as commander of TAC. When LeMay personally notified Everest of his involuntary "retirement" for medical reasons—Everest had a recent history of heart problems—the incensed Everest responded, "You are far from a politician. You are the bluntest bastard I have ever talked to in my life, and you are highly opinioned and not inclined to adjust yourself to the political atmosphere that any Chief of Staff, all Chiefs of Staff, must operate in. You don't have that sort of a faculty."[4] Unmoved, LeMay appointed SAC bomber general Walter C. "Cam" Sweeney Jr. as the new commander of TAC because TAC was "behind the times."[5]

The unwelcome Sweeney brought in bomber major general Walter E. Arnold as his chief of staff and began to "do for TAC what LeMay did for SAC."[6] Sweeney began to "professionalize" TAC with the "high standards" and programs of SAC. He implemented SAC's centralized management control system which quantified, measured, and evaluated virtually every element of TAC's supply, maintenance, and operational system.[7] Resisted at TAC, Sweeney set up a liaison office with SAC, centralized TAC maintenance organizations, reorganized TAC's numbered air forces from a functional to a geographic orientation, and built command posts in each wing. Additionally, he implemented new standardization, evaluation, and safety programs. Sweeney based most of his changes on the SAC model.[8]

While some changes were warranted, the speed and manner in which Sweeney implemented them caused much resentment. Influential fighter major general Momyer was removed as TAC's deputy chief of staff for plans upon Sweeney's arrival, and that position remained vacant for months. Everest's recently appointed vice commander of TAC, fighter lieutenant general Gabriel P. Disosway, "didn't see eye to eye on anything" with his new commander and was replaced by bomber lieutenant general Charles B. Westover the following year.[9]

As TAC felt the incursions of the SAC community, so did the other commands that housed mostly fighter units. USAFE received a bomber general, Truman H. Landon, as its commander the same day LeMay became chief of staff. LeMay asked the former USAFE commander, fighter general Frederic H. Smith Jr., to become his vice chief—the only fighter general on LeMay's Air Staff. Smith was reluctant to work for LeMay and sought counsel from Gen Lauris Norstad, the Supreme Allied Commander Europe (SACEUR). Norstad advised Smith to accept the job, as the Air Force needed Smith as a "mellowing influence."[10] Smith accepted the job as vice chief of staff and soon disagreed with LeMay on whether to reduce the number of SAC personnel. LeMay replaced Smith with a Zuckert nominee, nonflyer general William F. "Bozo" McKee, a year later.[11] LeMay had no regrets: "I was satisfied; I didn't think I had [Smith's] complete loyalty. We disagreed. Once I made a decision, I expected whole-hearted cooperation. He was happy to leave."[12]

Until Disosway was removed from TAC and transferred to the Air Staff, that organization was thoroughly dominated by SAC's bomber generals, with the exception of the nonrated General McKee. Director of Military Personnel, fighter brigadier general Albert P. Clarke, recalled,

> SAC was bleeding us white. [General Thomas] Power was CINCSAC [Commander-in-Chief Strategic Air Command] and didn't have any patience for anything else in the Air Force. He was absolutely single-minded on SAC, and ruthless in that regard. Whenever I tried to get any policy implemented that in any way infringed on what Tommy Power thought was right for SAC, he would just call up General LeMay and say, "Get Clark[e] off my back," which usually happened. So it was a pretty tough time to try to protect any equity in personnel programs. We had an elite air force within an air force. It was an unhealthy situation. People in SAC were frozen. They were trying to get every good man in the Air Force and nobody ever came out of SAC. So everybody else was second-class citizens. It was a difficult time for anybody to run a personnel program.[13]

When Disosway arrived as the lone fighter lieutenant general on the Air Staff in 1962, he remembered being "smothered" by SAC generals who soon got accustomed to his usual dissenting vote.[14]

The bomber monopoly on the key leadership positions in the Air Force not only alienated non-SAC elements, it also led to more dogmatic doctrine. The Air Staff never was more populated with absolutists zealously in pursuit of technology to vindicate a timeless faith in the efficacy of strategic bombing. In 1959 senior staff evaluation officers at Air University concluded,

> Our studies on new weapon systems foreseen during the next 15 years have concluded that the present strategy of deterrence will continue essentially unchanged and so will the basic tasks of our military forces. . . . The key to changes in future strategy will rest with scientific development; for the nation which can gain a clear ascendancy over all the rest in adequate numbers of more highly effective weapons, whether offensive or defensive, will be in a position to dominate other nations in all forms of military conflict.[15]

Shortly thereafter, General White expressed the same zeal for technology: "We in the Air Force . . . always want to see technology move faster because we realize that it is from the area of new developments that our lifeblood stems."[16] In 1961 two Air Force analysts added: "Technology wins wars. . . . Technology paces strategy and determines its nature. Strategy can place demands on technology in order to meet momentary requirements. But over the long haul, changes in strategy come primarily from technology."[17] Technological zeal continued as the primary means of refining the three tenets of airpower theory: *globalism, indivisibility,* and *decisiveness.*[18]

The air advocates improved global access with higher, faster, longer range "aerospace" vehicles, preferably manned and coupled with improved communication systems. The KC-135 jet tanker was developed to extend the range of the intercontinental B-52 jet bomber as well as the faster B-47 and B-58 jet bombers. The high-flying U-2 strategic reconnaissance aircraft was followed by the high-flying, high-speed SR-71. Ground and airborne command posts, early warning radars, high frequency radios, computerized systems, and soon communications and reconnaissance satellites also pushed the Air Force closer to true global access and responsiveness through the centralized control preferred by SAC.

Indivisibility, however, remained largely an illusion. SAC and TAC never were farther apart than under the leadership of the bomber generals. The Air Force was distancing itself doctrinally from the battlefield. In a major speech in September 1961, LeMay defined the problem of service unity, with a slight strategic bias, to unify his Air Force.

> Our problem then, as I see it, as we reach *higher* and *farther,* is that we must maintain our unity of mission and unity as an organization. . . . To be a credible deterrent, aerospace power must consist of flexible and diversified forces that have a war-waging and war-winning capability. . . . We need to restate firmly that the United States Air Force is an entity. Its elements all contribute to the aerospace power that is vital for our defense.[19]

Indivisibility was difficult when the training and technical demands, as well as philosophies, of nuclear and limited war were so disparate. But might equaled right. The SAC-dominated Air Force consumed itself so much with its chief challenges—the growing nuclear target list, the missile threat, alerts, and dispersals—that it had little time for conventional or nonstrategic considerations.

Driven by the same imperatives, the tactical air forces continued to struggle for a piece of the nuclear mission, if only for fiscal and doctrinal survival.[20] Its planes, however, did not have the range to reach strategic targets in the Soviet Union, and SAC had no inclination to share its mission with another branch. In the meantime, the conventional capabilities of TAF atrophied, as did its budget. The Air Staff planned to cut TAC's budget even further in fiscal year 1964.[21] Munitions stocks fell too low to support training in conventional war, and the TAF remained divided geographically (three separate commands) and functionally with airlift, fighter, reconnaissance, and tanker elements.[22] Ironically, the monolithic mind-set of bomber generals divided the Air Force into SAC and all others, undermining the indivisibility of airpower that LeMay had called for.

Finally, the proliferation of atomic weaponry, delivered primarily by way of strategic bombers, some fighter-bombers, and now ICBMs, gave the air advocates, they believed, the arsenal of decisiveness. The Single Integrated Operation Plan (SIOP), first developed by the SAC-dominated Joint Strategic Targeting Planning Staff in August 1960, would deliver LeMay's (now Power's) all-out offensive, "the Sunday punch," which could demolish the Soviet Union.[23]

By the early 1960s, the senior World War II generation's Air Force continued to prefer methods of the proven past over the uncertain future. In its view manned bombers remained preferable to ICBMs, so bombers remained at the top of the Air Force's procurement list.[24] The Air Force sponsored a weapons-rich counterforce strategy, in part, to justify national procurement of bombers and ICBMs versus the Navy's relatively inaccurate Polaris missiles. The air arm had returned to the traditional strategy of precision attacks against military targets. This return offered a feasible option because of plentiful, accurate weapons of differing yields and methods of delivery. Absolutist generals insisted upon clear military superiority so instrumental in the victory of World War II.

Conveniently preeminent in the national strategy of massive retaliation and under the guise of bomber and missile gaps, the Air Force was building and maintaining LeMay's goals of "overwhelming strength so powerful that nobody would dare attack us" and an ability "always to be able to prevail at the highest level of intensity so that any kind of an escalation would be to the disadvantage of the enemy."[25] The Air Force showed a determination to build the military superiority necessary to "prevail" in a nuclear war.[26] The confidence of the absolutists grew with the size and lethality of their forces. In June 1961 an Air University Research Studies Institute study boasted, "There would be no necessity for expensive 'balanced forces' and 'combined operations' if the proven irrefutable fact that aerospace power is the dominant and decisive force were accepted."[27] This attitude fueled the arms race, hindered the development of conventional war capabilities within the Air Force, and furthered conservatism.

The comfort of doctrinal preeminence during the 1950s and other systemic ailments yielded conservatism and dogmatism by the early 1960s. Oron P. South, a civilian historian and member of the Research Studies Institute, had argued in 1958 that the process of doctrinal revision involved such lengthy coordination between staff and operational agencies that it inevitably resulted in a justification of present forces and ideas. South added that the process "discourages any change more radical than minor updating of paragraphs."[28] Coordinating two- or three-page doctrinal or plans papers took an average of 10 months.[29] At the same time fighter colonel Robert C. Richardson III, an Air Staff planner, complained of "the curse of bigness," which promoted a "status quo attitude" and a "growing tendency to hold what we have rather than risk untested organizational and doctrinal changes."[30] One observer of the period noted that World War II had the effect of reducing visionary energy, accompanied by a "shift from forecast to review" and preferring lessons to formalize rather than theories to test.[31] The Air Force was having difficulty coping with change and was developing a reactive rather than proactive posture by the late 1950s.

Alarmed, Curtis E. LeMay, then vice chief of staff, had called for an internal study on the Air Force's alleged conservatism in late 1959. The study bluntly concluded that "today there is little evidence of any substantive conceptual change nor is the Air Staff now organized so as to best generate and process proposals for change." Air Force planning, the report continued, "has been largely limited to considering the impact of adding forecast weapon systems to projections of current concepts," and the current structure was not capable of giving advice on new strategy and concepts "not influenced by Air Force interests or past Air Force positions and policies." The report claimed the Air Force had "defensive, status quo, reactionary positions on most issues" and found it hard to "list any policy or strategic goals . . . that the Air Force is publicly fighting for, other than 'more of the same.'"[32]

The study warned that Air Force doctrine was losing touch with military realities by attempting to fight the next world war with the weapons, strategies, and tactics of World War II. It concluded that Air Force visionaries were increasingly nearsighted, while farsighted civilian strategists were beginning to fill the void. No one acted upon the study's recommendations, but responsibility for the development of doctrine was moved from the "ivory tower" of Air University in distant Maxwell AFB, Alabama, to the Pentagon, where, despite the study's warnings, doctrine and concepts were subordinated to short-term requirements of current policy battles.[33]

As the bomber-dominated Air Force became increasingly dogmatic, the new John F. Kennedy administration championed change and favored a choice other than holocaust or humiliation.[34] Kennedy's new national defense policy of Flexible Response challenged the Department of Defense (DOD) to bolster conventional and counterinsurgency capabilities to master the full spectrum of warfare. Kennedy wanted more options to achieve political objectives. He desired survivable, flexible, and cost-effective forces and weapons whose judicious use could send effective political signals, preserve maximum political options, and retain initiative at all levels of warfare. He desired a close, cooperative relationship between the State and Defense Departments to achieve a more coherent policy.

After the Bay of Pigs, Kennedy issued National Security Action Memorandum 55, which instructed the military chiefs to become active in the policy-making process by providing "their best judgment on economic, political, and psychological matters as well as strictly military matters."[35] With a few exceptions, LeMay felt most comfortable with providing strictly professional military advice. Consequently, the new administration soon considered him "a political actor without a political conscience"—much to the detriment of his influence.[36] To make things more difficult for the chiefs, Kennedy abandoned Eisenhower's formal National Security Council Planning Board, the process of deducing specific policies from consistent general goals, as well as the process of disseminating National Security Council memoranda for guidance. Kennedy preferred ad hoc consultation and task forces to handle crises. Military participation decreased and political scrutiny of military plans and options increased.[37]

Kennedy's agent of change within the DOD was the resolute taskmaster and new secretary of defense, Robert S. McNamara, who caught the Air Force off guard as much as the new policy did. Secretary McNamara drove from the head of Ford Motor Company into the Pentagon determined to adjudicate interservice rivalries and impose competitive decision making according to the rational principles of sound management and budgetary restraint. The resultant efficiency, in his mind, would be essential for the country to afford the forces and weapons befitting the new policy of Flexible Response. McNamara demanded subordination of service interests to national goals, of military judgment to quantitative analysis, and of military chiefs and service secretaries to the department secretary and his deputies. He relied on systems analysis to explore trade-offs between costs and capability. Within the span of a few years, he elevated and expanded the Office of the Secretary of Defense (OSD) from 500 civilians to more than 2,500.[38] Accompanied by a growing host of "whiz kids," he introduced managerial innovations and a hectic pace of change that left the services dumbfounded. Few expected the new defense secretary to wield the full authority of the Defense Reorganization Act of 1958 so quickly and so thoroughly.[39]

111

The Air Force's honeymoon with the new administration proved short-lived. Kennedy was dismayed equally by LeMay's failure to incorporate economic considerations into his military advice and by the cumbersome bureaucratic processes of the Air Force. Deputy Secretary of Defense Roswell L. Gilpatric recalled that the president was "not one for men in uniform with pointers reading aloud sentences off flip charts he could read much faster himself." In the spring of 1961 an Air Force general presented "The Net Evaluation," an annual doomsday briefing, Gilpatric continued, "as though it were for a kindergarten class. . . . Kennedy got up and walked right out in the middle of it, and that was the end of it. And we never had another one."[40] A frustrated McNamara occasionally left Air Force briefings early too and often remarked to Secretary Zuckert on the Air Force's "lousy papers" that didn't "support your position."[41]

By and large, the new administration was not impressed with Air Force policies, either. McNamara recalled the Air Force of the early sixties as extremely parochial, "so parochial that they were acting contrary to their own interest and the interests of the nation."[42] Zuckert, long associated with the Air Force, reflected in 1965: "It took some time for our old attitudes and outlooks to change. . . . New hardware was welcomed with more enthusiasm than were new ideas in the realms of strategy, concepts, and doctrine." He noted especially in 1961 that some senior Air Force leaders

> were still approaching top-level problems of national security in terms of the concepts, doctrine, and study methods of the early 1950s. There were too many who took a parochial view of the big problems of planning, programming, and budgeting; who refused to believe that national policy and strategy were what the Administration said they were—not what an element of the armed forces thought they ought to be. I suppose this was a hangover from the ten or more years when we had been the principal guarantor of Free World security and in many ways the favored service.[43]

Kennedy's people found the Air Force striving stolidly for strategic nuclear supremacy with a doctrine generally suited only to unleash it, should deterrence fail. Kennedy wanted options.

McNamara was determined to give the president a flexible military instrument, regardless of the methods or opinions of the venerable World War II generals. His move to strengthen the defense secretariat downgraded the service secretaries and created a buffer of civilians between the service chiefs and the secretary of defense. Consequently, more civilians had to say yes before an Air Force initiative could be approved. Soon OSD officials bypassed service secretaries and chiefs and worked directly with action officers.[44] At the same time, McNamara directed 93 studies, 75 of which recommended curtailment of some authority in the services, a move fellow civilian Zuckert found "troublesome."[45]

Then the defense secretary flooded the services with projects, demands for statistics, and position papers—most of them with short deadlines. Consensus, particularly in the JCS or on controversial matters, took time. Short deadlines encouraged split decisions, which, according to one Air Force colonel, gave McNamara the leverage to play services against each other while he determined policy himself.[46] Additionally, the multitude of individual projects with different deadlines made it difficult for the services and the JCS to relate the projects to each other and to overall strategic problems. When different organizations were assigned the same problem, varying solutions again gave McNamara the option of choosing for himself. The net effect was to keep the military bewildered and reactive. As one senior World War II general remembered, "We spent most of our time in the Air Force trying to cope with McNamara and little towards enhancing airpower."[47]

Noting the institutional crisis his Air Force faced and appalled by the dogged resistance of many of his "older officers who . . . did not really see why it was necessary to buttress our positions," Secretary Zuckert called for a conference at Homestead AFB, Florida, in December 1961 to "try to find out what was wrong with the way the Air Force was doing business vis-à-vis McNamara and the Office of the Secretary of Defense. I wanted to find out just what the hell we could do."[48] As a representative of the secretary of defense, Zuckert was finding that the Air Staff was too doctrinaire, relied on "military judgment" versus facts and figures, was generally poor with statistics, and was not articulate or persuasive. The Air Force needed more intellectual planners, more and better research and development people, and "good staff officers that are better in a litigative atmosphere."[49] As an official responsible for addressing the concerns of the Air Force, Zuckert was having a difficult time convincing his impatient boss that the Air Force was adequately responsive.

Out of the conference at Homestead grew Project Alamein, a confidential study under Maj Gen Glen W. Martin. It sought primarily to determine how the Air Force could maintain control of its destiny, particularly through sound long-range planning. The study noted how the concepts of the other services prevailed over Air Force concepts. It recommended that the Air Force combat the perception that it was single-minded and suggested it must adopt the methods of others, including a broader perspective with increased "weight given to political, economic, and psychological considerations, [and] encourage thought and writing on air issues, and make the results available to the people in OSD and the JCS."[50] Zuckert added a call for more postgraduate education to prepare "military statesmen."[51] Furthermore, the Air Force secretary brought to the conference Dr. Edward Learned of the Harvard Business School, whom McNamara held in high esteem. Zuckert commissioned Learned the following year to help the Air Force develop better management practices and write better position papers.[52]

An example of Air Force attempts to adapt to OSD's new methods was to increase enrollment in intensive, multiweek advanced management programs, most notably the Harvard Advanced Management Program. In a survey of all 1,156 line Air Force generals serving between 1953 and 1972, one researcher found operator and staff generals were least likely to attend the highly recommended program (fig. 8). Apparently, operational experience still counted for more than education.

The bomber-dominant Air Force leadership resisted McNamara's new policy. Apparently vindicated by the *United States Strategic Bombing Survey*, the Air Force self-image and definition of purpose seemed directly challenged by the new OSD. The senior World War II generation had deep emotional roots in this doctrine, and the perceived revolutionary change

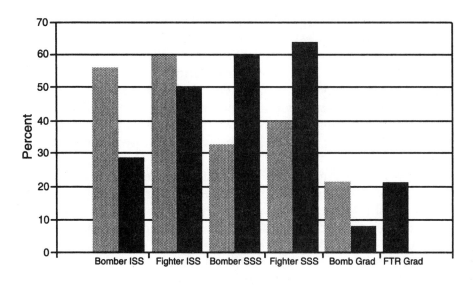

Legend:
ISS–Intermediate Service School
SSS–Senior Service School
Grad–Graduate School
▨–Senior WW2 Gen
■–Junior WW2 Gen

Figure 8. Fighter versus Bomber Generals: Advanced Schooling

facing them threatened who they were and what they had stood for. When McNamara and his whiz kids questioned their credibility as military experts with a flurry of statistics and scientific analyses, the senior cohort responded belligerently. They perceived the threat of doctrinal change as sacrificing a method they had proven with great investment, all for something unproven and championed by young civilians. The senior cohort generally held a suspicious attitude towards civilian defense analysts and intellectuals as well as OSD civilians.

Shortly after his retirement, General White reflected that he did not believe "a lot of these often over-confident, sometimes arrogant young professors, mathematicians and other theorists have sufficient worldliness or motivation to stand up to the kind of enemy we face."[53] LeMay added that defense intellectuals were "'experts' in a field where they had no experience, they proposed strategies based upon hopes and fears rather than upon facts and seasoned judgments."[54] Bomber general Howell M. Estes Jr. was more blunt in assessing McNamara's staff as "a whole bunch of fuzz-cheeked Ph.D.s that didn't know the first damn thing in the world about the military."[55] When McNamara's people obtained classified threat and intelligence information to make their own judgments and when McNamara began to censor the Air Force in late 1961, the Air Force leadership grew increasingly irritated.[56]

LeMay and many of his generation preferred evolutionary change; those concepts and forces his experienced generation had built should be preserved while the young administration matured or passed through office. As leverage against the administration, LeMay and the Air Force cultivated a good relationship with Congress and the public.

Zuckert noticed the foot-dragging. He recalled that the Air Force didn't listen to McNamara for the first 18 months: "I came here to fly generals who were frustrated after World War II. . . . We took too long to realize that national policy had changed and if we wanted to participate in furthering the national policy, we had to change." Zuckert proceeded to say that he visited Nellis AFB, Nevada, in the early 1960s and found that training still emphasized nuclear deliveries, long after "we all knew we should have been going to conventional."[57]

But there was some creative thought going on in the Air Force as the new administration settled in. Pragmatist brigadier general Noel F. Parrish, the assistant for coordination to the Air Force deputy chief of staff, Plans and Programs, was working with William W. Kauffmann of RAND on a renewed RAND "no cities" proposal for strategic targeting.[58] The traditional absolutist strategy was an all-out Sunday punch, appropriate for the national security policy of massive retaliation. The absolutist strategy also proposed limited means since the Air Force had neither satisfactory intelligence, sufficient weapons, and means of delivery nor sufficient command, control, and communication systems. Having made significant progress in each of those areas in pursuit of the tenets of airpower theory, the absolutists in the early 1960s began to consider a new "war-winning" strategy to counter the Navy's Polaris SLBM system and its countervalue (cities only) strategy. They also promised procurement of more Air Force weapons systems. Kauffmann and Parrish proposed a counterforce strategy to aim nuclear weapons exclusively at military targets as opposed to urban-industrial complexes. The United States would use its nuclear forces to reduce damage to its own cities by attacking enemy strategic offensive systems and by providing an incentive to the Soviets to stop targeting US cities. American hardened and dispersed nuclear weapons were poised to retaliate under any circumstance with sufficient might to destroy enemy residual military capability. In fact, some suggested it finally might be possible to make controlled responses to limit the war. This strategy offered an alternative to such a cities-only spasmodic response as that envisioned by the massive retaliation and countervalue strategies.

After the strategy was tested in computer simulations, General White, and then General LeMay, began to support it. However, absolutist general Power opposed anything short of total destruction of Soviet society. In fact, Power argued a no-cities strategy might provoke a Soviet surprise attack.[59] Despite internal disagreements, General White introduced the new strategy to Congress in 1960.

> It is not a "first strike" concept—it is a concept for the development of a capability to prevail under any conditions of attack. This concept has, as its central theme, the application of superior offensive and defensive military force against enemy strengths that directly threaten the continued freedom and security of the United States and her allies [who] must be superior to . . . our enemies in decisive military power.[60]

The absolutists shifted their targeting from cities to military resources while retaining their traditional insistence on "superior decisive military power" and on the ability to "prevail under any circumstances." If the strategy demanded a growth in Air Force warheads and systems and undermined the strategic importance of the Navy's inaccurate, "city busting" Polaris and its "finite deterrence (cities only) strategy," the absolutists would not object.[61] To Air Force absolutists, these advantages occluded any real belief that the war would remain limited. Like the American air campaigns in World War II, the nuclear campaign likely would escalate to destroy cities. The Air Force still would hold unquestionable strategic superiority and hence would retain the strategic initiative, which was the ultimate deterrent.

While the Air Force liked the prospects of counterforce for procurement and continuing doctrinal dominance, the new administration accepted it for a different reason. McNamara visited SAC in February 1961 for a SIOP briefing and was dismayed (like Eisenhower before him) by SIOP's inflexibility and reliance on overwhelming retaliation, a vestige of LeMay's 12-year-old Sunday punch. Before leaving, he received a briefing on the counterforce by Kauffmann and Parrish. Impressed by the contrast between the strategy and SIOP at SAC headquarters, McNamara saw an attraction in the rational control of nuclear operations against strictly military targets. To him this attraction might provide inducements for negotiations and limiting conflagration where previously no option existed.[62]

By early 1962 the new SIOP possessed greater flexibility, and McNamara began to endorse counterforce as America's second-strike alternative to countervalue city bombing. But Air Force satisfaction suffered at the hands of the new *United States Basic National Security Policy* document, which called for qualitative changes without large increases in numbers of weapons. The document also warned that if Soviet nuclear capabilities were improved, the United States might lose its clear strategic superiority. The Air Force responded with a study in 1962 that objected to the idea of strategic parity, because it eliminated the possibility of victory and could damage the traditional US resolve to "win."[63] The absolutists had drawn the line.

The new counterforce doctrine required a restructuring of forces. Central to this process was the challenge posed by ICBMs to the turf of strategic bombers. The Air Force and the Defense Department would quarrel long and hard over this issue.

As the air absolutists sought bigger, higher, faster, and longer range aircraft, the replacement for the B-52 emerged as a hot topic.[64] The Air Force proposed the Mach 3 B-70 high-altitude strategic bomber. The speed and range of the

Valkerie would make it virtually impossible to intercept—except by a missile.[65] Vulnerability to missiles posed part of the problem. The B-70 reflected the inertia of the absolutist's technological zeal to fly higher and faster and farther with a global and responsive capability and relative immunity from fighters. Memories of World War II were not so distant.[66] Additionally, the single-mission focus of the absolutists was not conducive to building flexible technologies. The Air Force continued to push the B-70, which did not carry missiles and could fly only at high altitudes, after Soviet SAMs had demonstrated effectiveness against that capability. In fact, the Air Force had begun modifying B-52s and training crews in low-altitude penetration tactics in 1958. Eisenhower's secretary of defense, Thomas S. Gates, had reduced the B-70 program in 1960 because of suspected vulnerabilities to SAMs as well as concerns over delivery accuracies at such high speeds. Nevertheless, the Air Force thought it might convince the new administration in spite of the other part of the problem—the alleged cost of $1.5 billion for three experimental aircraft.

But the Air Force was understandably concerned about placing too much faith in the "unproven" capabilities of the bomber's rival—the ICBM. In early 1961 Chief of Staff White admitted to Congress that "to say that there is not a deeply ingrained prejudice in favor of aircraft among flyers would be a stupid statement for me to make." But, White insisted, "I do not feel that I am fighting for the life of manned aircraft. I am sure its need is so obvious."[67] He argued that manned bombers offered visible signs of deterrence, and they could be launched and recalled, and they could find difficult targets after the first strike. Furthermore, he voiced concern that an all-missile force would lead to a "Maginot line" mentality; he worried that missile crews waiting in a silo would develop a "static, nondynamic frame of mind."[68] Ultimately, White recommended that the bomber should be pursued, at least until ICBMs were proven reliable.

Despite White's pleas, the new administration stated a different position to Congress in early 1961:

> In reevaluating our general [nuclear] war position, our major concern was to reduce our dependence on deterrent forces which are

[currently] highly vulnerable to ballistic missile attack or which rely for their survival on a hair-trigger response to the first indications of such an attack. Consequently, we sought to place greater emphasis on the second approach—the kind of forces which would ride out a massive nuclear attack and which could be applied with deliberation and always under control of the constituted authority.[69]

By May 1961 McNamara said the Air Force had enough bombers to last until 1967. He gave at least three reasons: They were vulnerable on the ground and in the air; they had to be launched immediately and a recall was problematic; and their long flight time reduced their usefulness for striking time-sensitive targets (counterforce targets). The defense secretary suspected that up to 75 percent would be shot down in a nuclear war against the Soviet Union—if they got airborne. ICBMs, he reasoned, were faster, less vulnerable, easier to maintain and keep on alert, unstoppable, and—most important—cheaper. McNamara concluded ICBMs provided a stronger deterrent to the Soviet Union. OSD's systems analysts calculated the cost of a wing of B-52s and supporting tankers operating for five years could fund more than 250 Minuteman ICBMs or six Polaris submarines.[70] Besides, ICBMs could be operationally ready far quicker than a new bomber.

When LeMay took over as chief of staff in the summer of 1961, his top procurement priority remained the B-70, with ICBMs well down the list. McNamara's list focused on quite the opposite. LeMay's superior operational credibility over his predecessor did little to sway the administration. Frustrated by OSD incursions into military affairs and the impasse with McNamara, LeMay tried an end run to Congress. He secured legislative action to overturn President Kennedy's decision to cancel the B-70 as an operational weapons system. Col David C. Jones, the B-70 briefing officer, felt LeMay's maneuver "left a great deal of ill will in its aftermath and set back attempts by the Air Force to move on to a new bomber program."[71] McNamara felt betrayed and refused to spend the extra moneys.

Next the Air Force attempted to push procurement of the B-70 as an RS-70, a "reconnaissance/strike aircraft." LeMay continued to press: "I want the RS-70 very badly. . . . When something faster comes along I want it."[72] The aircraft was scheduled to fly after the first strike to assess damage and hit undestroyed targets—a unique capability no missile could match. But the argument flew in the face of previous research. In 1959 the JCS's Weapon System Evaluation Group found it doubtful that mobile targets could be located and attacked. The same year, General White told Congress "we feel that the atomic phase of the next war will be a matter of hours, and that reconnaissance will not do us very much good after the war starts."[73] OSD scientists argued that high speed and high altitude would make it difficult for the aircraft to locate and assess targets accurately. Furthermore, technical problems with its radar, communication systems, and missile systems were significant. Despite another tug-of-war with a Congress that backed the Air Force, McNamara stated in 1963 to Congress that "the RS-70, by carrying air-to-surface missiles, would provide only a very small increase in overall effectiveness. In my judgment this increase is not worth the large additional outlay of funds estimated at more that [sic] $10 billion above the $1.35 billion already approved."[74]

Having decided that the secretary of defense was immovable on the B-70 and RS-70, Colonel Jones and Col Russell E. Dougherty approached LeMay and recommended the Air Force pursue a bomber with high speed and low-altitude capability, similar in concept to the tactical fighter (TFX) that former TAC commander General Everest had advocated. LeMay listened and sent the two colonels to brief General Power at SAC on the idea. Power was extremely hostile to any substitute for the B-70. He admonished the colonels and kicked them off the base.[75]

LeMay then directed his staff in 1963 to study various proposals for a follow-on to the B-52. He did not like the OSD position that the Air Force would not need a follow-on until the early to mid-1970s. Nor did he share the belief that the TFX could be accepted as a SAC bomber. By 1964 LeMay lamented that "the B-52 is going to fall apart on us before we can get a replacement for it. There is serious danger that this may happen to us."[76]

The senior bomber cohort in the Air Force influenced Congress on the need to keep a manned strategic bomber in the force. Bombers were proven, visible, and manned; and they had added flexibility. They could be put on alert as a visible political signal. The general's principal argument, though, was the old chestnut of experience. LeMay pointed out the importance of experience and military expertise over systems analysis to Congress: "My generation received its education in combat and learned from actual experience. . . . We have fought a strategic war."[77] The SAC commander, General Power, emphasized experience, too: "I have been in the bombing business since the spring of '29 and yet every other expert in the bombers said we would be shot down. The British said we could not do daylight bombing. Everyone predicted utter failure for the bombing mission. And yet an American bombing mission has never been turned back from its target."[78] Power also insisted "there is absolutely no question about our ability to destroy any target on that target list today." Congress concurred that bombers should remain an essential part of strategic deterrence because it respected military experience and felt strategic bombers added flexibility and insurance should missiles fail catastrophically. A mixed force would be best, at least until missiles could be more fully tested.

To the senior World War II generation bomber generals, strategic bombers provided the preferred weapon system, with ICBMs as an insurance policy. McNamara accepted just the opposite as true. Primarily because of the prohibitive costs of procuring a fleet of complex B-70s, Congress ultimately funded McNamara's ICBMs and did not insist upon an immediate replacement for the B-52. A mixed force is essentially what everyone really wanted; nonetheless, McNamara got the balance he preferred.

Air Force hostility to missiles was not as categorical as many historians have concluded, and it was not based solely on the aversion of pilots to pilotless vehicles.[79] Robert Perry has pointed out that the Air Force leaders believed the testimony of scientist Vannevar Bush. Appearing before Congress in 1945, he argued that an ICBM would be far off and would be plagued by inaccuracies and high cost. Instead of high risk with the radical ICBM, the Air Force initially pursued an evolutionary compromise: air-launched missiles.[80]

The early Navajo, Snark, and Hound Dog missiles gave way to the Skybolt, an air-launched nuclear missile with a range of eight hundred nautical miles. It was scheduled for employment primarily for defense suppression by the B-52s, since the B-70 was not equipped to carry Skybolts. The early 1960s found costs for the Skybolt escalating rapidly while its accuracy remained suspect. The vulnerability of its carrier also posed a concern. Both the US Air Force and the British wanted the missile, but McNamara began to entertain serious doubts about its cost-effectiveness. After cutting the B-70 in early 1962, the OSD preserved the Skybolt program temporarily to avert being, as the director of defense research and engineering, Dr. Herbert F. York, recalled, "picketed by men in light blue suits."[81] In December 1962 the defense secretary canceled the Skybolt and offered to request an additional one hundred Minuteman ICBMs to fill the defense suppression tasks. The Air Force leadership had lost another procurement battle.

McNamara's faith in ICBMs did not come without reservations. He saw the Air Force's new Minuteman ICBM as inflexible, just as he had found the SIOP and the B-70. It too was constructed for an all-out Sunday punch. As with Atlas and Titan, the Air Force had designed Minuteman for launch in one salvo. It had no capability to be retargeted on short notice. All 50 missiles in one squadron had to be launched, or no missiles could be launched from that squadron.[82] In accordance with the new national security policy of Flexible Response and the emerging counterforce strategy, the system needed more flexibility. The Air Force began to look into necessary modifications in 1960. In the spring of 1961, the new OSD requested information on those modifications; the Air Force replied that it could not provide a controlled response to an attack. Unsatisfied, OSD responded by freezing money for Minuteman and withholding approval of the newest developmental version. In June Secretary McNamara directed Secretary of the Air Force Zuckert to organize a group to study Minuteman modifications. The resultant Fletcher committee recommended modifications, many of which eventually manifested themselves in the Minuteman II. Air Force resistance stemmed in part from concern that modifications would incur delays to deployment schedules and would raise costs inordinately.[83]

The defense secretary's interest in Minuteman invigorated the program in 1961 and shifted emphasis from bombers and liquid-fueled ICBMs (Atlas and Titan) to the more cost-effective (especially in terms of maintenance) solid-fueled Minuteman. OSD interest helped improve operational flexibility, accuracy, and penetrability.[84] Although figure 9 shows that serious investment in ICBM procurement began after sputnik, it never exceeded money spent on aircraft.

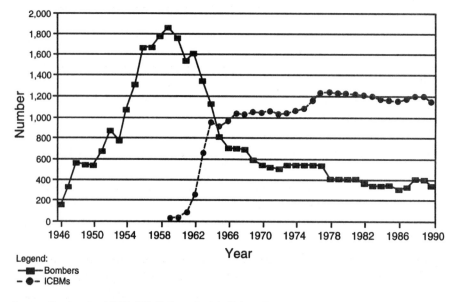

Legend:
- ■ Bombers
- ● ICBMs

Source: Headquarters USAF, *U.S. Air Force Statistical Digest FY 1948–1964.*

Figure 9. Strategic Bombers versus Intercontinental Ballistic Missiles (1946–90)

But money spent on ICBMs fielded many weapons systems quickly, with high alert rates at relatively low cost. The result, as indicated in figure 10, was a shift in emphasis from bombers to ICBMs as the major element of strategic deterrence.

By the end of 1962 the administration had canceled the B-70 and the Skybolt. That same year the last B-52 and B-58

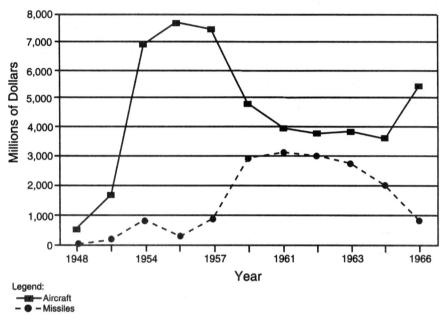

Source: Henry M. Narducci, historian, SAC Office of History, Offutt AFB, Nebr., 6 December 1991, data provided to author.

Figure 10. Total Aircraft versus Missile Procurement (1948–66)

strategic bombers had been delivered to the Air Force, with no follow-on bomber in sight. In October the first Minuteman ICBM site became operational. The apex of SAC and bomber influence within the Air Force coincided with signals of a dimmer future. October also was the month the nation teetered on the edge of nuclear holocaust.

Notes

1. Eugene M. Zuckert, transcript of oral history interview by Dr. George M. Watson, 3, 4, and 5, 9 December 1986, Air Force Historical Research Agency (cited hereafter as AFHRA), Maxwell AFB, Ala., 82–83; Gen George S. Brown, transcript of oral history interview by Dr. Edgar F. Puryear Jr., 14 September 1977, AFHRA, 12; and Stuart Symington, transcript of oral history interview by Herman S. Wolk, 2 May 1978, AFHRA, 60. Former secretary of the Air Force and then senator, Stuart Symington, when asked, nominated Gen Bernard A. Schriever of ICBM fame, "but the big bomber boys didn't want him. Again we get back to tradition as against modernity."

2. The Bay of Pigs debacle, the foiled invasion of Cuba sponsored by the Kennedy administration, proceeded without professional military advice from the JCS. Kennedy was anxious to rebuild his credibility and to mend civil-military relations in the wake of this setback. See Earl H. Tilford Jr., *Setup: What the Air Force Did in Vietnam and Why* (Maxwell AFB, Ala.: Air University Press, 1991), 48; Richard K. Betts, *Soldiers, Statesmen, and Cold War Crises* (Cambridge, Mass.: Harvard University Press, 1977), 70–71; Arthur M. Schlesinger Jr., *A Thousand Days: John F. Kennedy in the White House* (Boston: Houghton Mifflin, 1965), 450; and Thomas M. Coffey, *Iron Eagle: The Turbulent Life of General Curtis LeMay* (New York: Crown Publishers, 1986), 357. Deputy Secretary of Defense Roswell Gilpatric recalled, "We would have had a major revolt on our hands if we hadn't promoted LeMay."

3. Lt Gen Alvan C. Gillem II, transcript of oral history interview by Arthur W. McCants Jr. and Scottie S. Thompson, 13–15 February 1979, AFHRA, 134.

4. Gen Frank F. Everest, transcript of oral history interview by John N. Dick Jr., 23–25 August 1977, AFHRA, 272–74; and History, Tactical Air Command, 1 January–30 June 1961, supporting documents. In his speech to senior Air Force commanders in February 1960, entitled "The Role of Tactical Air Forces in the 'Missile Age,'" General Everest contradicted what the dominant absolutists were saying. He asserted that limited wars could not be fought as a "by product of general war." The senior generation fighter general also advocated advancement of cruise missiles and tactical ballistic missiles to complement ICBMs.

5. Gen Curtis E. LeMay, transcript of oral history interview by Dr. Edgar F. Puryear Jr., 17 November 1976, AFHRA, 47.

6. *U.S. News & World Report*, 27 November 1961.

7. Gen Bryce Poe, USAF, Retired, interviewed by author, 7 April 1992; Gen John Shaud, USAF, Retired, interviewed by author, 6 April 1992; Gen W. L. Creech, USAF, Retired, interviewed by author, 31 May 1992; and Lt Gen Albert Clarke, USAF, Retired, interviewed by author, 16 June 1992. Critics of the management control system noted it became all encompassing and all important to the point of promoting excessive competition between squadrons, wings, and numbered air forces, often to the point of breaching integrity and honesty in reporting to higher headquarters. Unit and leadership success depended to a large degree on how the unit appeared on paper under the management control system.

8. History, Tactical Air Command, 1961–1962, vol. 1, 25, 32, 185; Frederick C. Blesse, *Check Six: A Fighter Pilot Looks Back* (Mesa, Ariz.: Champlin Fighter Museum Press, 1987), 116. Blesse noted that the imposition of SAC's centralized maintenance procedures was "disastrous" for fighter wings and caused sortie rates to plummet. Blesse claims he complained and was told to keep opinions to himself. See Gen David C. Jones, interviewed by author, 22 June 1992. General Jones judged the

condition of TAC in 1964 as very "neglected and abhorrent" and said Sweeney brought much improvement.

9. Gen David C. Jones, transcript of oral history interview by Dr. Edgar F. Puryear Jr., 2 October 1980, AFHRA, 3.

10. Coffey, 360.

11. Ibid., 385; Gen Frederic H. Smith Jr., transcript of oral history interview by J. Ferguson, 19 June 1968, AFHRA, 130. Smith claims he was fired by Secretary of Defense McNamara over Smith's retention of a "stupid major general" in Air Force Logistics Command that McNamara wanted him to fire.

12. Coffey, 386.

13. Lt Gen Albert Clarke, transcript of oral history interview by Scottie S. Thompson, June 1979, AFHRA, 207; Gen Truman H. Landon, transcript of oral history interview by Hugh N. Ahmann, 31 May and 3 June 1977, AFHRA, 452. Landon agrees with Clarke.

14. Gen Gabriel Disosway, transcript of oral history interview by Dr. Edgar F. Puryear Jr., 17 January 1979, AFHRA, 15.

15. Robert Frank Futrell, *Ideas, Concepts, Doctrine: Basic Thinking in the United States Air Force, 1961–1984*, vol. 2 (Maxwell AFB, Ala.: Air University Press, 1989), 162. The Air Force continued to confuse technological achievement with operational success.

16. Ibid., 193.

17. Ibid.

18. Michael S. Sherry, *The Rise of American Air Power: The Creation of Armageddon* (New Haven, Conn.: Yale University Press, 1987), passim. Sherry used *technological fanaticism* to describe the Air Force's chief imperative—one often viewed as both a means and an end. I prefer to use the more cautious term *zealousness*.

19. Ibid., 56.

20. The tactical air forces consist of those units in TAC, United States Air Forces in Europe (USAFE), Alaskan Command (ALASCOM), and Pacific Air Forces (PACAF).

21. History, Tactical Air Command, July–December 1959, 11–13, 26. In February 1958 the Air Force informed subordinate commands that the development of nonnuclear weapons was to be terminated; however, TAC was to monitor the Navy's "energetic conventional weapons development program."

22. History, Tactical Air Command, January–June 1959, vol. 1, chap. 1; and History, Tactical Air Command, July–December 1959, 11–13.

23. The SIOP was a carefully scripted nuclear assault on the Soviet Union. It lent itself to maximize destruction within the Soviet Union for many reasons. Early on, as SAC raced to field adequate weapons to deal with the growing target list, LeMay sought to maximize destruction through his limited means. As the US strategic arsenal grew to excess means, the tendency to deliver a Sunday punch remained. Absolutists perceived rational control of nuclear war as increasing vulnerability and risking

defeat. Besides, in a nuclear war, it would be difficult to communicate a recall or to assess damage in a timely manner. To respond in a measured fashion when warning times were often less than 15 minutes would be equally difficult.

24. Gen Bernard A. Shriever, transcript of oral history interview by Dr. Edgar F. Puryear Jr., AFHRA, 5. Shriever recalls that General Spaatz gave him hell at a cocktail party for "those God–––– missiles that had no pilots on board."

25. Richard H. Kohn and Joseph Harahan, eds., *Strategic Air Warfare: An Interview with Generals Curtis E. LeMay, Leon W. Johnson, David A. Burchinal, and Jack J. Catton* (Washington, D.C.: OAFH, 1988), 108.

26. Futrell, 31, 48, 50; and Thomas S. Power, *Design for Survival* (New York: Coward-McCann, 1965), 39, 49, 84, 126. *Prevail* was a new term, more accommodating than *win* in nuclear parlance.

27. "The Relationship Between Past and Present Strategic and Tactical Concepts," AU/RSI Study, June 1961, AFHRA.

28. Oron P. South, "The Door to the Future," *Air University Quarterly Review* 9, no. 4 (Winter 1957–1958): 117–25.

29. Col R. C. Richardson III, "The Development and Dissemination of Long-Range USAF Plans, Concepts and Policies and Associated Organizational Changes," AFXPD-LR staff study, 23 October 1959, 17–18, AFHRA.

30. Robert C. Richardson III, "In the Looking Glass," *Air University Quarterly Review* 9, no. 4 (Winter 1957–1958): 46–47.

31. Dennis W. Stiles, "Air Power: A New Look From an Old Rooftop," *Air University Review* 27, no. 1 (November–December 1975): 52–54; George A. Reed, "U.S. Defense Policy, U.S. Air Force Doctrine and Strategic Nuclear Weapon Systems, 1958–1964: The Case of the Minuteman ICBM" (PhD diss., Duke University, 1986), 39.

32. Richardson, AFXPD-LR staff study, 1–6, 16, 27, 36; and Reed, 114–17.

33. Reed, 117–18; See also Andrew D. Dembosky, "Meeting the Enduring Challenge: United States Air Force Basic Doctrine Through 1992" (master's thesis, North Carolina State University, 1993), 19–20.

34. Robert F. Futrell, "The Influence of the Air Power Concept on Air Force Planning, 1945–1962," in *Military Planning in the Twentieth Century: Proceedings of the Eleventh Military History Symposium, USAF Academy, 1984* (Washington, D.C.: Government Printing Office (GPO), 267–68.

35. Betts, 35; Jerome Slater, "Apolitical Warrior or Soldier-Statesman: The Military and the Foreign Policy Process in the Post Vietnam Era," *Armed Forces and Society* 4 (Fall 1977): 104; and Futrell, *Ideas*, vol. 2, 86.

36. Betts, 157.

37. Ibid.

38. Lt Gen Richard M. Montgomery, oral history interview, K239.0512-1526, by Capt Mark C. Cleary, 28–30 June 1983, 213.

39. Russell Frank Weigley, *The American Way of War: A History of United States Military Strategy and Policy* (New York: Macmillan, 1973), 449. The Defense Reorganization Act of 1958, in part, attempted to empower the secretary of defense vis-à-vis the service chiefs.

40. Coffey, 391.

41. Zuckert, 13–15.

42. Edgar F. Puryear Jr., *George S. Brown, General, USAF: Destined for Stars* (Novato, Calif.: Presidio Press, 1983), 118.

43. Futrell, *Ideas,* vol. 2, 231; and Eugene M. Zuckert, transcript of oral history interview by Lawrence E. McQuade, 2 May 1964, AFHRA, 10, 11, 15, 18. Zuckert also observed that "there was too much [parochial] thinking along service lines" at the time.

44. Zuckert, interviewed by Watson, 22.

45. Eugene M. Zuckert, transcript of oral history interview by Col John L. Frisbee, 1 September 1965, AFHRA, 11.

46. Col Robert N. Ginsburgh, *U.S. Military Strategy in the Sixties* (New York: Norton, 1965), 35; and Lawrence J. Korb, *The Joint Chiefs of Staff: The First 25 Years* (Bloomington, Ind.: Indiana University Press, 1976), 115–18.

47. Gen Jacob E. Smart, transcript of oral history interview by Dr. Edgar F. Puryear Jr., 17 July 1979, AFHRA, 20.

48. Zuckert, interviewed by Watson, 10–11.

49. Ibid., 13; and USAF interview with Eugene M. Zuckert, 257.

50. Reed, 230.

51. Ibid.

52. George M. Watson Jr., "Man in the Middle: Eugene Zuckert as Secretary of the Air Force," *Air Power History* 36, no. 2 (Summer 1989): 25.

53. Schlesinger, 319.

54. Alfred F. Hurley and Robert C. Ehrhart, eds., "The Perceptions of Three Makers of Air Power History," *Air Power and Warfare: Proceedings of the 8th Military History Symposium, United States Air Force Academy* (Washington, D.C.: OAFH, 1979), 188 (with comment by LeMay during discussion session); and Curtis E. LeMay, *America Is in Danger* (New York: Funk & Wagnalls, 1968), x.

55. Gen Howell M. Estes Jr., transcript of oral history interview by Lt Col Lyn R. Officer and Lt Col Robert G. Zimmerman, 27–30 August 1973, AFHRA, 220.

56. On intelligence access, see Betts, 60. Reed points out that four of the 30 Eisenhower administration-approved articles in the Winter-Spring 1960–1961 issue of the *Air University Quarterly Review,* the dialectical and professional journal of the Air Force, had been removed by the Kennedy administration. He also cites an introductory comment by Air Force general William G. McKee to the audience at the annual Air Force Association Convention in September 1961 regarding his formal presentation: "After the redline action was finished, I don't have a hell of a lot to say." See Reed, 181.

57. Zuckert, interviewed by Watson, 41–42.

58. Brig Gen Noel F. Parrish, transcript of oral history interview by Dr. James C. Hasdorff, 10–14 June 1974, AFHRA, 280. Fighter brigadier general Robert C. Richardson III joined the team soon after.

59. Ibid., 321–22; David Alan Rosenberg, "The Origins of Overkill," *International Security* (Spring 1983), 59–60; and Fred Kaplan, *The Wizards of Armageddon* (New York: Simon and Schuster, 1983), 242–46.

60. Futrell, *Ideas*, vol. 2, 32.

61. The Navy-sponsored "finite deterrence" would limit the bulk of the US nuclear force to "invulnerable" submarines, whose missiles were shorter in range and less accurate than ICBMs, but could hold Soviet cities hostage (a "sufficient deterrent") at less cost overall.

62. Kaplan, 260; and Reed, 176.

63. Reed, 210.

64. Futrell, *Ideas*, vol. 2, 389. Junior World War II generation fighter general James Ferguson, then Air Force director of operational requirements, recalled the B-70 series of aircraft as "a follow-on to the philosophy that we followed for many, many years. For many years we wanted to go higher and faster whenever we could, and as fast and as high as the state of the art would permit." See House, 86th Cong., 2d sess., Appropriations Committee, Department of Defense Appropriations Subcommittee Hearings: *Department of Defense Appropriations for Fiscal Year 1961* (Washington, D.C.: GPO, 1960), pt. 2, 256–67. General White testified "higher and faster is always desirable in the air game."

65. The Soviets had demonstrated their ability to shoot down high-flying US aircraft in 1960 when they downed a U-2 spy plane piloted by Francis Gary Powers.

66. Zuckert, interviewed by McQuade, 114; and Tilford, 50. Zuckert remembered, "LeMay thought of the B-70 as going over enemy lines and dropping bombs as he had dropped them on Germany and Japan."

67. House, *DOD Appropriations FY 1961*, pt. 2, 257.

68. Ibid., 319–20; Futrell, *Ideas*, vol. 2, 33–34.

69. Futrell, *Ideas*, vol. 2, 29.

70. Reed, 184–85; Futrell, *Ideas*, vol. 2, 35.

71. Futrell, *Ideas*, vol. 2, 390–91.

72. Ibid., 96.

73. Rosenberg, 66–67; and House, *Department of Defense Appropriations for 1960*, 86th Cong., 1st sess., pt. 1, 1959, 886–87. The citation predated "counterforce" and graduated response.

74. Futrell, *Ideas*, vol. 2, 56; and Reed, 220.

75. Gen Russell E. Dougherty interviewed by author, 23 June 1992. My account is an understatement.

76. Futrell, *Ideas*, vol. 2, 390.

77. House, *Department of Defense Appropriations for 1964*, 88th Cong., 1st sess., 1963, pt.1, 523; and House, *Department of Defense Appropriations for 1965*, 89th Cong., 1st sess., 1964, pt. 4, 516–18. LeMay added the

following year: "As far as I know, Secretary Zuckert and Secretary McNamara have not ridden on a bomber raid as a lot of us in the Air Force have. I have sat through the last 35 years and listened to stories on the ability to penetrate. The last 35 years, every manned system with a bomber was going to be shot down. . . . My experience tells me that the people who now say that manned systems cannot penetrate are using the wrong substance" (p. 2).

78. Thomas S. Power, "Manned Aircraft Requirement in the 1970s," *Air Force*, November 1963, 96; and Thomas S. Power, "A Sure Way to Prevent Nuclear War," *U.S. News & World Report*, 25 January 1965, 72–76.

79. Jacob Neufeld, *The Development of Ballistic Missiles in the United States Air Force, 1945–1960* (Washington, D.C: OAFH, 1990); and Edmund Beard, *Developing the ICBM: A Study in Bureaucratic Politics* (New York: Columbia University Press, 1976).

80. Robert L. Perry, *The Interaction of Technology and Doctrine in the United States Air Force* (Santa Monica, Calif.: RAND publication no. 197908-18, 1979).

81. Zuckert, interviewed by Watson.

82. Rosenberg.

83. Reed, 196–201.

84. Ibid.

Chapter 5

Flexible Response and the Ossification
of the Senior Absolutists (1963–65)

*I think one of the tragedies of the Air Force was that some
people in it, especially in the 1950s and 1960s . . . became
so wedded to their own thinking that if anybody disagreed,
they were hurt. You had former generals around who could
remember little but the activities of Eighth Air Force in
England, and Fifteenth Air Force in Italy, etc. As a result,
tactical air, troop support, air cargo, etc., were not
adequately represented.*

—Stuart Symington
Secretary of the Air Force (1947–50)

The Air Force role in the Cuban missile crisis was
predictable. Confident that a missile gap existed, but in the
favor of the United States, Gen Curtis E. LeMay and the Joint
Chiefs of Staff advocated resolute and immediate military
action. The Strategic Air Command was at its peak. Bombers
were put on increased alert, many of them placed on airborne
alert. Reconnaissance planes gathered incriminating photos of
Soviet missile sites under construction and continued to map
and monitor ocean traffic near Cuba and activity in Cuba.

The Air Force chief of staff advised that surgical strikes on
missiles alone were not sufficient.[1] He believed only massive
air strikes accompanied by an invasion would remove the
missiles before someone launched them.[2] LeMay believed in
US strategic superiority and assured President John F.
Kennedy that the Russians wouldn't respond to military
action. In fact, LeMay's intelligence held that Russia was not
showing signs of alert or mobilization.[3] But the president
responded that the Soviets couldn't "afford to do nothing" after
what they had been saying.[4] After Kennedy decided to use the
blockade in Cuba, he called Gen Walter C. Sweeney Jr. at TAC
to ascertain how much damage a surprise air strike could
achieve. Sweeney replied that they could not be certain of
destroying all the missiles. Kennedy's brother Robert stated

that Sweeney's judgment removed any lingering doubts in the president's mind.[5] The president settled for a negotiated agreement; he agreed to remove intermediate range ballistic missiles (IRBM) from Turkey after the Soviet Union removed its missiles from Cuba.

LeMay's absolutist behavior in the Cuban missile crisis reflected the prevailing ethos in the Air Force. The absolutists believed SAC's strategic superiority had deterred the enemy at Taiwan and Lebanon in 1958 and in Berlin in 1961. They also believed a fully alerted and imposing SAC had deterred the Soviets in the cold war's greatest crisis. LeMay testified,

> I am convinced that superior US strategic power, coupled with the obvious will and ability to apply this power, was the major factor that forced the Soviets to back down. Under the shelter of strategic power, which the Soviets did not dare challenge, the other elements of military power were free to exercise their full potential.[6]

Other absolutists lauded the decisive contribution of strategic airpower in the crisis. Bomber general David A. Burchinal added, "We could have written our own book at that time, but our politicians did not understand what happens when you have such a degree of superiority as we had, or they simply didn't know how to use it. They were fully engaged in saving face for the Soviets and making concessions, giving up the IRBMs, the Thors, and Jupiters deployed overseas—when all we had to do was write our own ticket." Senior cohort bomber general Leon Johnson agreed.[7] General Power, commander of SAC, felt his command had deterred the Soviets and given Kennedy his confidence. "US forces," said Power, were "ready to invade Cuba and crush the USSR if necessary."[8]

The Cuban missile crisis bolstered absolutist faith in the deterrence of strategic airpower. It was only a small but significant step for them to claim that strategic superiority deters not only general war but limited war, too. As LeMay repeatedly would claim, "If you have the power to stop a big war, certainly the same power ought to be capable of stopping a small war."[9]

On the other hand, McNamara and others believed that the newly added conventional capabilities were the key element in the crisis. The defense secretary opined, "Perhaps most significantly, the forces that were the cutting edge of the action were the nonnuclear ones. Nuclear force was not irrelevant but it was in the background. Nonnuclear forces were our sword, our nuclear forces were our shield."[10] Army generals, of course, agreed. Gen Maxwell D. Taylor and others believed the Cuban missile crisis signaled a strategic stalemate which allowed American conventional superiority in the Caribbean to decide the issue. Limited war was possible, not in spite of nuclear weapons but because of them.[11]

Approximately six months after the crisis, LeMay was considered for reappointment as chief of staff. By 1963 SAC's forces were stronger than ever; its advocates never were more numerous at top levels in the Air Force. But, already some indications gave the appearance that its future might not be so bright. The B-70 and the Skybolt had been canceled with a successor to the B-52 remaining questionable. The growing Soviet threat had compelled an increased alert posture as well as the dispersal of SAC assets. Talk abounded of arms limitations, nuclear parity, and a growing interest in a conventional war in Southeast Asia. These talks challenged long-held Air Force absolutist beliefs.

Within the JCS, LeMay and chief of naval operations Adm George W. Anderson Jr. had given McNamara the most difficulty. The administration decided not to renew Anderson's appointment, and renewed LeMay for only one year of a normal two-year cycle. Vice Chief William McKee suggested LeMay survived because he had much clout with Congress. In any case, most observers agreed the loss of two chiefs at once would draw undue political attention.[12]

In the early1960s significant change occurred for the senior World War II generation. First of all, the Cuban missile crisis heightened the determination of the administration to secure some arms limitations to arrest the spiraling and dangerous arms race. In his inaugural address in January 1961, the president had pledged "to make arms control a central goal of our national policy under my direction."[13] Subsequent Basic National Security Policy (BNSP) documents in 1961 continued to mention bringing an "end to the arms race."[14] In the wake of the frightening Cuban missile crisis in October 1962,

Kennedy accelerated measures. Secretary of State Dean Rusk expressed a new urgency in late 1962:

> Cuba has provided a dramatic example of the deadly dangers of a spiraling arms race. It is not easy to see how far-reaching disarmament can occur. . . . Nevertheless, it is also obvious, as we have seen in recent weeks, that modern weapons systems are themselves a source of high tension and that we must take an urgent and earnest effort to bring the arms race under control and to try to turn it downward if we possibly can.[15]

In June 1963 Kennedy welcomed Soviet acceptance of his proposal for a direct telecommunications link between Moscow and Washington. By then he also had secured agreement with the USSR and Great Britain to renew negotiations for a nuclear test-ban treaty. In July a draft was agreed to, and the president signed it in August. The limited test-ban treaty prohibited tests in the atmosphere, underwater, or in outer space, but it did not prohibit tests underground as long as fallout remained within national boundaries.

The JCS initially opposed the test ban unless it (1) incorporated a detection, identification, and inspection system to detect treaty violations; (2) did not prohibit undetectable testing; and (3) simplified withdrawal procedures. Kennedy met with the chiefs and again privately with LeMay in July and asked that they consider all factors (including political and economic) before providing advice. LeMay wanted to acquire a 100-megaton bomb, to conduct a nuclear air defense detonation, and to detonate one of his missile silos before signing the treaty. The Atomic Energy Commission convinced LeMay they could produce a 50-megaton bomb without testing. LeMay ultimately believed the treaty contained military disadvantages, but he accepted it on the first month of his renewed term because, "I think it might be to our political disadvantage if we did not ratify it."[16]

The members of LeMay's cohort weren't quite as compromising. Power claimed "the surest way to cause a war, nuclear war or any war, is to disarm."[17] More to the point, Power wanted to test his ICBMs and their silos with live weapons to see if they would function in combat conditions.[18] White and Twining also opposed. Twining commented,

"Artificial ceilings on man's acquisition of knowledge are unnatural. The uncertainty of not knowing whether or not one is behind or losing superiority could create great international instability."[19]

Nevertheless, the Limited Nuclear Test Ban Treaty was proclaimed in effect on 10 October 1963. The following week the United Nations General Assembly adopted a resolution by acclamation that welcomed the desire of the United States and the Soviet Union not to station nuclear or mass-destruction weapons in outer space. One month later Kennedy was assassinated.

The fall of 1963 was bewildering to senior absolutists striving to maintain strategic superiority. Such superiority required pushing technologies and procuring weapons to stay ahead of the Soviets. They had been doing this for the past 15 years. As Power stated, "Our security demands that we stay in that [arms] race," and "the name of the game is to stay ahead."[20] But in the aftermath of the Nuclear Test Ban Treaty, McNamara stated,

> The Soviet Union's acceptance of the US proposal for a three-environment test ban offers some evidence . . . that its leadership has at last grasped an essential fact—that the sheer multiplication of a nation's destructive nuclear capability does not necessarily produce a net increase in its security.[21]

Many absolutists had not grasped this fact. As Power remarked, "While I believe in the preservation of military superiority . . . I submit that we can no more arm and disarm at the same time than one can dress and undress at the same time."[22] The dilemma of increasing US military security while decreasing tensions and the level of armaments confronted members of the senior cohort. Disarmament conjured up the 1920s and 1930s to the senior World War II generation. Burdened with the heavy responsibility of national security in the dangerous nuclear era and committed to strategic superiority and "prevailing," many of the senior Air Force leaders grew increasingly frustrated.

An evolution in counterforce during the fall compounded their frustration. After the Cuban crisis the Soviets desired to increase their strategic leverage. Concern about US counterforce first-strike capability, a growing Sino-Soviet split, and a new US conventional buildup contributed to Soviet determination to expand its military capabilities. The defense secretary was not willing to participate further in an expensive, accelerating arms race to keep the counterforce strategy of superiority viable. Other vital economic needs became quite large. Besides, many NATO leaders did not like counterforce, as they felt this "no cities" strategy might lead to a US hesitancy to risk New York for Paris.

In 1963 McNamara drifted slowly to the high ground of compromise between the expensive and rational counterforce strategy and the Navy's cheaper finite deterrence. He put forth two ideas: damage limitation and assured destruction. The counterforce strategy would focus on damage limitation by preempting follow-on Soviet launches; the countervalue strategy would ensure the destruction of Soviet cities after the United States had absorbed a nuclear assault.[23] The secretary of defense thus relinquished support for the absolutists' long-held tenet of maintaining strategic supremacy sufficient to prevail in war, an action LeMay forecast would "inevitably lead to defeat."[24]

Kennedy's New Emphasis

The next difficulty for Air Force absolutists loomed in Kennedy's new emphasis on conventional and limited war. In early 1961 some in the Air Force conceded to the new administration that the Air Force was unprepared for limited war with conventional weapons.[25] Secretary McNamara quickly elevated fighter and airlift procurement on his Air Force priority list behind only ICBM. In late July TAC commander Gen Frank F. Everest, in one of his last official actions, suggested, along with his army counterpart Gen Herbert B. Powell, the immediate establishment of a unified tactical command with a joint headquarters as a highly mobile ready force for deployment to crises worldwide. McNamara concurred, and Strike Command (STRICOM) was established in September with primary responsibility for the Middle East and Africa and secondary responsibility to augment other unified commanders in need.[26]

TAC was looking for opportunities. Its weakened condition showed in the mobilizations for the Berlin crisis of 1961 and the Cuban crisis of 1962. After Berlin, McNamara received approval to expand TAC from 16 to 21, and later to 25, fighter wings. He helped change TAC's dismal prospects.

Chief of Staff LeMay was concerned. In viewing the FY 1963 budget, he complained about the conventional trend:

> I think that your strategic forces should come first. . . . I worry about the trend as established by this year's budget. . . . I do not think you can maintain superiority in this field with that sort of a program. . . . I point out that you cannot fight a limited war except under the umbrella of strategic superiority.[27]

At the same time the Air Force came out with its concept on limited war, which reminded readers that limited war was not a "separate entity from general war," nor should the strategies and force structures be differentiated. "Success in limited war is contingent upon maintaining a superior general war capability," it stated, and "expenditures for forces capable of fighting less than general war must not infringe on the maintenance of a superior general war capability."[28]

Two events in 1962 helped to modify the chief's opinion. First occurred the release of the Howze Board report in August. The Army designated the board to investigate the potential of Army aviation. It recommended the expansion of Army aviation assets to improve its organic firepower and mobility. LeMay judged the board had recommended, in essence, the creation of a second tactical air force. Expansion was unnecessary, LeMay asserted, in that the Air Force could provide the same services.[29] Faced with this doctrinal challenge from the Army, LeMay needed to bolster his fighter and airlift capabilities. Second, Air Force pilots busied themselves training indigenous pilots in South Vietnam under combat conditions, and involvement in war in neighboring Laos loomed as a real possibility. LeMay would have to rebuild TAC if the Air Force wished to become effective in further involvement.

Still, LeMay's focus remained strategic and absolute. As the United States stepped closer to overt involvement in Vietnam, the new president, Lyndon B. Johnson, solicited advice from the JCS early in 1964. LeMay detested the wavering and indecision he noted in the new Johnson administration. If the United States were to get involved, it should "stop swatting flies and go for the manure pile." LeMay went on to say there should be no "going to war kinda" just like "you can't get a little bit pregnant . . . once you get into this you are into it."[30] The veteran of strategic bombing campaigns advocated a massive aerial assault against 94 targets in North Vietnam. LeMay later argued that assault would have ended the war "real quick" (in 10 days). Twentieth Air Force veterans of the Pacific war, bomber generals Burchinal and Jack J. Catton, agreed.[31] Graduated response, LeMay later reflected, "violates the principles of war, and over the centuries we have found that it doesn't work. But we couldn't convince anybody in the Pentagon at the time."[32] The absolutist dogma of using massive and relentless strategic bombing to achieve decisive ends, right or wrong, was passing out of fashion in an era of limited war.

The breeding ground of most Air Force absolutists and of the vast majority of Air Force senior leaders was faring little better. Those principles that had created SAC's greatness were now bringing about its ossification.

SAC's mission was so important that it required the utmost centralization and control. Handling nuclear weapons worldwide required close supervision and strict procedural adherence to maximize control and minimize risk. It fostered a closely supervised, regimented, and regulated daily routine of constant drilling, repetition, and "positive control" (a "don't-go-unless-told" philosophy). A 74-hour-work week of disciplined behavior became the norm. This environment tended to stifle innovation, risk taking, and creativity. The cumulative psychological effect on aircrews was a curious mixture of stress and boredom.

To keep morale up at the mostly isolated SAC bases, the aggressive and strong-willed commanders, most of them veterans of the bloody war of attrition in the skies of World War II, fostered competitions and inspections that permeated every element of the command. The management control system of close quantification, measurement, and evaluation was everywhere, as were intense competitions to build proficiency, pride, and activity. But SAC did not welcome second-place trophies. Though SAC embraced extremely high standards, some of them bordered on the unrealistic. There was ample incentive to "fudge" in competitions and to misrepresent reports to meet standards that everyone else was "meeting."[33]

The cold war kept the pressure on SAC. The threat of Soviet ICBMs after 1957 induced SAC to disperse its bombers and eventually put one-third of them on 15-minute alert. However, CINCSAC would not allow his personnel to be transferred to the theater commands along the periphery of the Soviet Union, where many of his dispersed and isolated bombers sat on alert. He demanded absolute command and control. The consequence was that his deployed units missed out on some of the local support they could have gained, spent more time than necessary away from families at desolate locations, and received no credit in the personnel system for their remote tours.[34] This consequence increased stress, boredom, and family problems.

The problem got worse when President Kennedy directed SAC to a 50 percent alert rate after the Berlin crisis. Fighter brigadier general Alvan C. Gillem II, now a SAC division commander, complained to SAC headquarters of the morale problem and proposed to take one bomber or tanker off alert each day long enough to fly a training sortie. This would, he contended, increase proficiency (SAC crews only flew from two to three each month) and "do much to relieve the boredom."[35] Vice CINCSAC lieutenant general John P. McConnell replied that these actions can be taken only "if and when the world situation eases."[36] SAC did not receive increased manning levels to meet the increased alert commitment. As a result, aircrews served so much alert time that they often had to get their normal duties accomplished during free time or by working long hours when not on alert. The cumulative effect of an increased alert commitment was chronic stress, reduced flying proficiency, boredom, morale problems, and claustrophobia from insularity.

Insularity was not just personal, it was institutional. SAC's enduring focus on a single mission, single strategy, single weapon, and single enemy promoted monistic thinking and intense camaraderie. In return for their many sacrifices, some

141

SAC officers received spot promotions at a rate unavailable to others in the Air Force. Often a short-term advantage, spot promoting in the long run automatically placed many of these early promotees up for subsequent promotion against more senior officers who had more experience. This procedure resulted in some inadvertent promotion passovers for SAC's spot-promoted officers, especially aircrews. In part to avoid these unfair comparisons, but more likely because of insular pride, SAC favored "taking care of its own" by keeping its people within the command. A proud but indicting saying was prevalent: "Once in SAC always in SAC; once out of SAC never back."[37]

SAC generally kept its people within the command for an entire career. LeMay and later Power often did not let their top people go to graduate school or to Air Force professional military schools. LeMay exhorted that if they wanted to learn about airpower, the best place to be was in SAC.[38] SAC was too busy with its most important mission to heed many peripheral concerns. The result produced a growing disparity in education between SAC and other Air Force personnel.

Figure 11 offers evidence as to the lack of graduate and professional military schooling between fighter and bomber generals in the World War II generations.[39] Two wars interrupted the advanced schooling of these generations, but one can discern that the bomber generals from SAC had more difficulty getting released for graduate school and for intermediate service school than fighter generals.

SAC's proud insularity militated against the breadth of experience necessary to meet the challenges of Flexible Response and Capitol Hill. Figure 12 shows the relative lack of breadth in assignment among bomber generals. It also illustrates that more than 90 percent of the junior generation fighter generals had jobs with other services, allies, or civilians within government before they reached the rank of full general; at the same time, nearly 70 percent of the dominant bomber generals had little experience outside the Air Force.[40]

Furthermore, a survey of all 1,156 officers in the general ranks of the Air Force from 1953 to 1972 revealed that in 1953 more than 40 percent had at least one senior

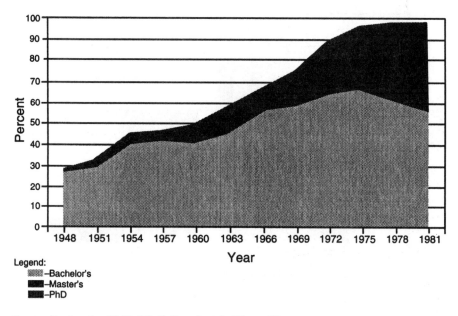

Legend:
▓▓▓ –Bachelor's
███ –Master's
███ –PhD

Source: Headquarters USAF, *U.S. Air Force Statistical Digest, FY 1948–1982.*

Figure 11. Air Force Officer Education Levels: Highest Degrees Achieved

assignment in an "outside community." By 1972 the percent had declined to less than 10 percent. The Air Force would pay deeply for its narrow experience base during the Vietnam War. After retirement, LeMay lamented that he wasn't "smart enough" to "have a [broadening] career plan" for his people.[41]

Adding to SAC's problems by the early 1960s was a low retention rate for aircrews. Many of the old warriors stayed on, but SAC was having difficulty retaining the four-to-seven-year group of young airmen who were just finishing their initial military commitment. This group comprised the post-Korean War generation. Many were disillusioned by the sight of "hump" officers—senior majors or lieutenant colonels—sitting alert in much the same job as the younger officers. One study listed "isolation from families, boredom from crew routine, lack of career motivation, and the demanding alert status" as the major complaints.[42] This word reached many students in pilot training, who, in a survey in 1965, overwhelmingly listed SAC at the bottom of their preference sheet.[43]

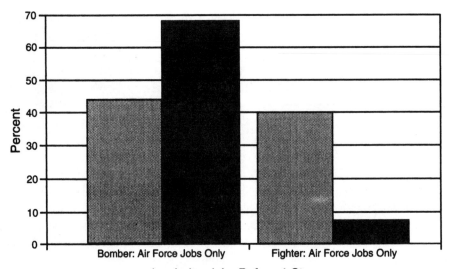

Insularity: Jobs Before 4-Stars

Legend:
▨—Senior WW2 Gen
■—Junior WW2 Gen

Source: Arnold Kanter, "The Career Patterns of Air Force Generals," *American Journal of Political Science* 21, no. 2 (May 1977): 362.

Figure 12. Fighter versus Bomber Generals: Job Breadth

SAC's proud insularity, coupled with its mission and budgetary precedence, caused much bitterness and divisiveness in the Air Force. Seemingly unaware of the costs of the limited vision and experience of many SAC officers, however, LeMay brought his favorites from SAC to Washington to do battle.

Secretary of the Air Force Zuckert remembered the Air Force of the early 1960s:

> One of the troubles was that they [McNamara's whiz kids] were bright as hell and they were articulate as hell. One of the great constant and losing fights that I fought was to try and make the Air Force more articulate. The Air Force was relatively inarticulate. A military requirement is a requirement because it is a military requirement. End of justification. To try to change that culture in the Air Force was a tremendous job. It almost made me quit in the first year because I could see we were not getting anywhere. . . . Eventually, we got better. But to try to change the culture of an organization that had been the dominant defense organization throughout the 1950s was not easy.[44]

The inability of the Air Force to convince the OSD, JCS, and to a lesser extent Congress to support its ideas and programs in the early 1960s resulted from many factors. The senior leaders of the air arm included warriors and operators who generally retained an absolute faith in strategic bombing. They had been so busy building SAC that they had allowed themselves to remain narrowly focused. Insular and relatively uneducated in political and economic affairs, as well as the affairs of their sister services, Air Force officers attached themselves to the independent doctrine that had ushered in such prominence for the past 10 to 15 years. The intense single-minded focus on their mission and their enemy advanced a monistic perspective in an increasingly pluralistic world. Ironically, the senior leaders had become steadfast conservatives in a service that professed to be always forward looking.

The capability and will to use SAC's nuclear arsenal formed the basis for the staunch absolutist belief in the decisiveness of airpower. SAC and its generals ardently retained both—even while the nation began to question both. The Air Force was slow to sense the winds of political and economic change. But it was easier for the Air Force to see it needed more than experience to forge its future. It had to improve its educational system.

In late 1961 the Air Force chief of staff mandated that more than 95 percent of all newly commissioned Air Force officers should have a bachelor's degree; by 1962 it became 100 percent.[45] LeMay terminated the aviation cadet program and used a more progressive officer training school to increase the proportion of college graduates in the Air Force.[46] By April 1963 even LeMay was complaining to the Air University that air staff officers could not competently perform their work.[47] He encouraged commands to send their best people to the Air Force Institute of Technology for advanced degrees in science, engineering, and management. "Project M" studies of 1955–62 indicated degrees in the sciences were increasing only slowly; social science degrees were decreasing.[48] But all the military services were experiencing similar problems. In 1964 a disappointed President Johnson directed McNamara to review the academic education and professional military education programs and to broaden and strengthen them. Education became a top priority, and the services would make great strides in this area (fig. 13). But raising the level of education within the senior military leadership could pay real dividends only in the future. For the present, Johnson had to work with the available manpower.

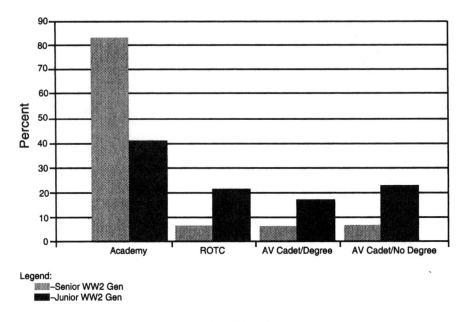

Source: Headquarters USAF, *US Air Force Statistical Digest FY 1948–1982.*

Figure 13. Undergraduate Education Commissioning Source

The problems of the Air Force in Washington did not stem from junior officers. The hump of aviation cadets had arrived in the senior ranks. The proportion of Air Force generals who had completed college declined during the 1960s.[49] Additionally, a large and growing gap existed between the more highly educated administrator and engineering generals on the one hand and the operations generals who increasingly dominated the key positions on the other.[50] The degrees obtained tended to reinforce specialization, and management degrees were lacking, particularly among operations generals.[51]

Professional military education (PME) also had failed the senior leadership of the early 1960s. Figure 11 showed how two wars had interrupted the PME of the World War II cohort. In 1962 the Air University Board of Visitors recommended that Air University increase contacts with the civilian community to "ensure accuracy and effectiveness of its analyses and assessments."[52] However, the ambitious 10-year plan drafted for 1963–1973 impressed the board. The plan sought to integrate civilian with military educational programs and outline goals for each. It also recommended an increase in PME quotas for resident programs and the successful accomplishment of PME as prerequisites for promotion. The plan also called for a more flexible curriculum and higher faculty qualifications.[53] The latter had been a constant and critical problem and would remain so. The 1963 BOV recommended upgrading the faculty's formal education and noted that the Air Force had greater difficulty than the other services in developing and presenting clear views on new doctrine.[54] A 1964 study found "the educational level of the faculty of both the Air Command and Staff College and the Air War College has been until recent date below that of the student bodies."[55] But events were improving. The mission statement of the Air War College in 1965 reads as follows:

> To prepare senior officers for high command and staff duty by developing in them a sound understanding of military strategy in support of national security policy in order to insure an intelligent contribution toward the effective deployment and employment of aerospace power.[56]

As Air University received the support required to right itself, another war would sap its resources.

That same summer of 1964 marked the near extinction of General LeMay's one-year extension as chief of staff. Concerned that a retired LeMay would speak out for Barry M. Goldwater in the approaching election, President Johnson extended LeMay's tenure for seven months, over the protests of McNamara and without telling Zuckert.[57] LeMay must have known he was a lame duck. Nevertheless, he continued to fight McNamara for what he considered were essential principles and programs for American security. But the unswerving and equally strong-willed defense secretary swept much of the "crude" military advice aside and began to determine military policy himself. A bitter LeMay recalled his feelings: "The Kennedy Administration came in and right from the start we got the back of the hand. Get out of our way. We think nothing of you and your opinions. We don't like you as people. We have no respect for you. Don't bother us." He went on to say McNamara was like a hospital administrator who insisted on doing brain surgery.[58] Zuckert recalled the intransigence of both parties: "Without a real reflective quality in the military . . . we butted our heads against a stone wall and just kept doing it and doing it and doing it."[59] Senior Air Force leaders couldn't convince their civilian bosses that business management principles sometimes were unsuited to defense policy—that the metaphysical and psychological dimensions of war were not quantifiable. But McNamara made the rules. In 1964 LeMay finally admitted his dilemma to Congress: "It is becoming more and more difficult to get experience and judgment ground into the solutions of problems," he testified. "We have to try to translate experience and judgment into cold hard facts to win a case. Sometimes this is very difficult to do."[60]

LeMay was not alone in his feelings. Many military personnel of the World War II generation, confident of past values and methods they felt had assured victory and subsequent US security, questioned the need for change. But their time was drawing to a close. One Korean War generation air staffer noted of the older group: "Their attitudes may range from belligerency to skepticism based on ignorance of the process, and antagonism toward the civilian analyst who has presumed to study military problems." The same observer was representative of many of the younger officers who noted the failures induced by such obstinacy. "The traditional ploy of the military man who limited his argument to an affirmation of his professional judgment has been generally discredited." He continued, "Instead of hostility, it would be more fruitful for the military strategist to learn more about the tools of analysis in order to apply them both to his own studies and in cooperation with the civilian analyst."[61] The fall of the World War II absolutists in the mid-1960s had a telling influence on future leadership.

LeMay's last seven months of active duty had a similarly telling effect on him, too. The stress of warring with McNamara weakened his health and influence. Nevertheless, the beleaguered chief finished his tenure as an ardent absolutist. Interviewed shortly before retirement, LeMay summarized his feelings on key issues. In reference to the conventional buildup, he asserted that "all conventional forces do is delay the inevitable nuclear confrontation. . . . We have gone too far with our conventional capability. . . . We don't want the 'beefing up' if you weaken our strategic capability." On the Vietnam conflict he advised, "The Communists are out for world domination and always have been." He advocated bombing North Vietnam and was not concerned about China, which was vulnerable to "a few well-placed nukes." Furthermore, "Maybe it would be a good thing if the Chinese came to the support of North Vietnam. We could set back the Chinese nuclear program, or knock it out for good." On the use of nuclear weapons he said, "I am a strong believer in the earliest possible use of tactical nuclear weapons to stop a fracas immediately. If aggression is promptly dealt with in force, it can be controlled and there is a good chance of avoiding a general nuclear exchange."[62] While the chief made sense to many in the military at the time, to the civilian defense analysts he had become "the most primitive thinker in the Kennedy and Johnson Administrations," who had lost influence and retired "rebuffed, frustrated, disgusted, and bitter."[63]

In truth, General LeMay had made tremendous contributions to his country. He was the outstanding operational commander for the Army Air Forces in World War II. After that war he took his methods and vision to Offut AFB, Nebraska, where he built an impressive Strategic Air Command. LeMay was an operational genius. While his operational credentials were respected in Congress, his lack of political judgment did not set well in Washington. He and many in his generation relied on "experience" and "military judgment" alone to determine military policy. Those skills were inadequate in the new era. In fact, most of the Air Force generals who watched him in Washington admitted that he was a poor chief of staff.[64] America's leading bomber general

149

did not like the political or social atmosphere and obligations of Washington.[65] He confessed the limitations of his expertise as well as his attitude much later: "I was in the operational and command end of the game most of the time except for the unpleasant tours I had in the Pentagon."[66]

The senior World War II generation of Air Force four-stars retired en masse in the mid-1960s. The extremist of absolutism and commander of SAC from 1957 to 1964, Thomas S. Power retired on 1 December 1964 and soon thereafter published *Design for Survival* (1965). Curtis LeMay retired with little fanfare on 1 February 1965 and subsequently published *America Is in Danger* (1968). They joined absolutist general Twining's *Neither Liberty Nor Safety* (1966) to form a trio of foreboding books that warned America of the dangers of abandoning absolutist teachings.

Though his civilian contemporaries perceived him to be an "unreconstructable" cold warrior, LeMay was an oracle to many in the Air Force. Many of the programs and methods he fashioned in SAC became Air Force methods and standards that would endure for decades. His imperative to focus on the mission and his call for dedicated action-oriented officers made an indelible imprint on the soul of the Air Force. Even many absolutist beliefs—most prominently LeMay's avid, unconditional belief in the efficacy of airpower through strategic bombing—would endure. Technological zeal also would continue. To his junior cohort, however, the bitterness and failure of his methods mandated a change of approach, at least in degree.

A few thought the message should change, too. "Prevailing" in nuclear war with overwhelming strategic superiority proved no longer economically practical—given escalating costs as well as other demands on the economy—and appeared increasingly dubious politically. Pragmatists were making headway by the mid-1960s. In the spring of 1963 Secretary Zuckert had established Project Forecast to provide a blueprint of technological and strategic possibilities in the 1965–75 time frame. Fighter major general Jerry D. Page headed the policy panel that sought to mate goals of the Air Force with national policy. In April 1963, after discussions with pragmatist major general Page, Maj Gen Dale O. Smith delivered a scathing indictment of "the deplorable condition of aerospace power today" that was "to a large extent the result of allowing Air Force doctrine to stagnate and become inapplicable to modern conditions." The Air Force, Smith argued, "was a victim of 'hardening of the categories' by avoiding full consideration of national military doctrine, national and foreign policy, as well as arms control philosophies." It had not "appropriately related or influenced developments in these fields to pure Air Force doctrine nor anticipated their impact."[67]

In February 1964 Page received permission from Secretary Zuckert to clarify Air Force basic doctrine. Most Air Force doctrinal manuals were nearly nine years old. The Air Force basic doctrine manual was almost four years old. It originated from a belated 1959 revision which hadn't revised much more than changing the term *air power* to *aerospace power*.[68] In contrast, Army basic doctrine was one year old and the naval equivalent one and one-half years old.[69]

The contrast between the old basic doctrinal manual and Page's new August 1964 manual revealed the shift in Air Force thinking. The old manuals had asserted, "Basic doctrine evolves from experience and from analysis of the continuing impact of new developments." The new manual stated, "Basic doctrine evolves through the continuing analysis and testing of military operations in the light of national objective and the changing military environment." Older manuals indicated that the Air Force was "the primary aerospace arm of the United States. . . . Of the various types of military forces, those which conduct operations in the aerospace are most capable of decisive results." The new manual cautioned that "Aerospace Forces are one part of a national military establishment maintained to support national policy objectives in our relations with foreign powers."[70] Secretary Zuckert believed the new manual revealed air leaders had abandoned their old belief that "there was [not] any war which couldn't be won by air power alone," but, according to Zuckert, the new AFM 1-1 rightly acclaimed airpower was "the supreme deterrent to general war" and "that there was no war which could be won without airpower." He was wrong on both counts.

151

Notes

1. Richard K. Betts, *Soldiers, Statesman, and Cold War Crises* (Cambridge, Mass.: Harvard University Press, 1977), 156–57.

2. Thomas M. Coffey, *Iron Eagle: The Turbulent Life of General Curtis LeMay* (New York: Crown Publishers, Inc., 1986), 391.

3. Richard H. Kohn and Joseph Harahan, eds., *Strategic Air Warfare* (Washington, D.C.: Office of Air Force History [OAFH], 1988), 119. Junior cohort bomber general David A. Burchinal recalled the Soviets "froze in place," and "we were never further from war than at the time of Cuba, never further" (p. 2).

4. Robert F. Kennedy, *Thirteen Days: A Memoir of the Cuban Missile Crisis* (New York: W. W. Norton and Company, 1969), 31. Kennedy also noted that one member of the JCS recommended using nuclear weapons, as the Soviets would. JFK supposedly responded that if he was wrong, there would be no one around in the end to know. See Kennedy, 48; Betts, 161; and Coffey, 391. Coffey suggests JFK was concerned that US military action in Cuba would spark another Soviet response in Berlin.

5. Kennedy, 31; and Betts, 156–57. Kennedy recalls that Sweeney at TAC informed him that there was only a 90 percent probability of getting all the missiles with a surgical strike.

6. Robert Frank Futrell, *Ideas, Concepts, Doctrine: Basic Thinking in the United States Air Force,1961–1984*, vol. 2 (Maxwell AFB, Ala.: Air University Press, 1989), 84; and Robert Frank Futrell, "The Influence of the Air Power Concept on Air Force Planning, 1945–1962," in *Military Planning in the Twentieth Century: Proceedings of the Eleventh Military History Symposium, USAF Academy, 1984* (Washington, D.C.: Government Printing Office [GPO]), 267–68.

7. Kohn and Harahan, 114.

8. Thomas S. Power, *Design for Survival* (New York: Coward-McCann, 1965), 22, 135.

9. Futrell, *Ideas*, 85.

10. Ibid., 83.

11. Betts, 108.

12. Ibid., 70–71. Betts claims LeMay's reappointment came over the objections of McNamara. See also Theodore C. Sorensen, *Kennedy* (New York: Harper and Row, 1965), 685; and Coffey, 424.

13. Robert Ginsburgh, *U.S. Military Strategy in the Sixties* (New York: W. W. Norton and Co., Inc., 1965), 100.

14. Ibid., 62.

15. Futrell, *Ideas*, 82.

16. Ibid., 105.

17. Ibid.

18. Power, 77.

19. Futrell, *Ideas*, 105; and Betts, 112–13.

20. Power, 79; and Futrell, *Ideas*, 93.

21. Futrell, *Ideas*, 104.

22. Power, 14–15.

23. House, *Department of Defense Appropriations for 1964*, 90th Congress, 1st sess., pt. 1, 111–12.

24. Futrell, *Ideas*, 93. "In other words, if we stop trying, we certainly are not going to succeed in defending ourselves."

25. L. Kraar, "Defense Strategy," *Wall Street Journal*, 16 February 1961; and History, Tactical Air Command, January–June 1961, 66–68.

26. Futrell, *Ideas*, 152.

27. Ibid., 48.

28. Ibid., 56–57.

29. Ibid., 181.

30. Mark Perry, *Four Stars: The Inside Story of the Forty-five Year Battle Between the Joints Chiefs of Staff and America's Civilian Leaders* (Boston: Houghton Mifflin Company, 1988), 142; and Alfred Steinberg, *Sam Johnson's Boy: A Close-up of the President From Texas* (New York: Macmillan, 1968), 108, 761.

31. Kohn and Harahan, 125–29. David A. Burchinal added, "We should have gone incendiary like we did in Japan: warned them to get our of the way, and then destroyed their means to exist. It wouldn't have cost anything in the way of casualties, really." LeMay responded, "If you destroy the capability to win war, then the will to wage war disappears also."

32. Ibid., 121–22.

33. Betts, 189. Betts argues this incentive contributed to intelligence and reporting distortions later in Vietnam. Gen David C. Jones, interviewed by author, 22 June 1992. General Jones reflected that the pressure of this intensely competitive climate created action-oriented officers and brought the best to the top, though it tempted some to cheat at the margins. Gen T. R. Milton, interviewed by author, 15 June 1992. General Milton asserted that the management control system fostered cheating: "Honest men didn't have a chance."

34. Alfred Goldberg, *History of the United States Air Force* (Washington, D.C.: OAFH, 1982), 121,127. Goldberg alleges SAC's aircrews averaged more than three months each year on alert overseas. He also characterizes SAC crews as proud but exasperated from long flights and constant alert, resulting in poor retention and a peacetime "combat fatigue."

35. Lt Col Morris E. Shiver, "Retention of Junior Officers in the Strategic Air Command," Air War College Report no. 3167 (Maxwell AFB, Ala.: Air University, January 1966), 38.

36. Ibid., 39.

37. Gen Horace M. Wade, transcript of oral history interview by Hugh N. Ahmann, 10–12 October 1978, Air Force Historical Research Agency (AFHRA), Maxwell AFB, Ala., 267.

38. Gen William V. McBride, transcript of oral history interview by Dr. James C. Hasdorff, 29–31 January 1980, AFHRA, Maxwell AFB, Ala., 210-12.

39. See figure 11. None of the four senior generation fighter pilots went to graduate school (figures were taken from a small sample size).

40. Secretary of the Air Force Zuckert grew frustrated with the narrowness of perspective, especially from the SAC community. He "retired" a good many lieutenant generals who "were not pulling their weight." Eugene M. Zuckert, transcript of oral history interview by Dr. George M. Watson, 3, 4, and 5, 9 December 1986, AFHRA, Maxwell AFB, Ala., 13. He also recommended that the "excess" air division commanders in SAC be transferred to the JCS and OSD to increase representation on those critical staffs. Watson, 28–29. The Air Staff said they would "research it."

41. Gen Curtis E. LeMay, transcript of oral history interview by Dr. Edgar F. Puryear Jr., 17 November 1976, AFHRA, Maxwell AFB, Ala., 40–41.

42. Shiver, 5.

43. Ibid., 33–34. Most listed TAC or ADC (Air Defense Command) as their top choice.

44. Eugene M. Zuckert, transcript of oral history interview by USAF, file number K239.0512-1763, 10–11; and Lt Gen Albert Clarke, transcript of oral history interview with author, 6 June 1992. As one general remembered, "McNamara's people were smart as hell and there were lots of them; we weren't smart enough, and they ate us up." Ginsburgh, 55–56. Ginsburgh, an air staff colonel, noted the services "simply did not have the required talent" to think strategically. There was an overemphasis on tactics and administration; most officers had neither the time nor inclination to refine strategy or doctrine. See Arthur T. Hadley, *A Report From the Field: The Straw Giant* (New York: Random House, 1986), 145. Hadley remembered, "Whiz kids did not move in a vacuum, but they didn't dash their heads up against any George Marshalls, Forest Shermans, or Tommy Whites, either."

45. Zuckert, interview with Watson, 34; Richard Stokes, *Preserving the Lambent Flame* (Maxwell AFB, Ala.: Air University Press, 1986), 53.

46. Officer Training School (OTS) generally admitted volunteer college graduates into a 90-day Air Force indoctrination program before commissioning them as officers. OTS methods appealed to reason more than the rigid discipline traditional in the aviation cadet program.

47. Richard L. Davis and Frank P. Donnini, *Professional Military Education for Air Force Officers: Comments and Criticisms* (Maxwell AFB, Ala.: Air University Press, 1991), 58.

48. Ludrew B. Grappe, Ray W. Alvord, and James V. Poland, *Air Force Officer Performance Evaluation: Rating Trends and Relationships from 1954 through 1965* (Lackland AFB, Tex.: Personnel Research Laboratory, October 1967), 157–58.

49. Arnold Kanter, "The Career Patterns of Air Force Generals," *Journal of Political Science*, May 1977, 367.

50. Ibid., 361; and Arnold Kanter, "Managerial Careers of Air Force Generals: A Test of the Janowitz Convergence Hypothesis," *Journal of Political and Military Sociology*, vol. 4 (Spring 1976): 125.

51. Kanter, "Career Patterns," 360–61.

52. Davis and Donnini, 57.

53. Ibid., 7.

54. Ibid., 56.

55. Ibid., 53–54.

56. O. Mitchell, "The First Generation: A Policy History of the Air Force Officer Corps, 1944–1973," OAFH, Washington, D.C., May 1991, 605.

57. Gen George S. Brown, transcript of oral history interview by Dr. Edgar F. Puryear Jr., 14 September 1977, AFHRA, Maxwell AFB, Ala., 7; and Betts, 70–71.

58. Coffey, 370; and Kohn and Harahan, 121. Bomber general Burchinal added that the whiz kids thought they could use airpower "like a scalpel in a bloody hospital operation, where as in truth, military force is a pretty damn blunt instrument. You use it for maximum shock effect—hard, fast, and continuous—and get the job done."

59. Eugene Zuckert, transcript of oral history interview by Lawrence E. McQuade, 2 May 1964, AFHRA, Maxwell AFB, Ala., 11–12, 18; and Eugene M. Zuckert, transcript of oral history interview by Dr. Edgar F. Puryear Jr., 28 September 1977, AFHRA, Maxwell AFB, Ala., 34. Zuckert longed for a General White who was five years younger to handle the McNamara "tradition."

60. *DOD Appropriations 1964*, pt. 4, 512–13.

61. Ginsburgh, 10–11; Hadley cites Henry Kissinger's comment on the "new generation" of officers in the 1960s: "A new breed of military officer emerged; men who had learned the new jargon, who could present the systems analysis arguments so much in vogue, more articulate than the older generation and more skillful in bureaucratic maneuvering. On some levels it eased civilian-military relationships; on a deeper level it deprived the policy process of the simpler, cruder, but perhaps more relevant assessments which in the final analysis are needed when issues are reduced to a test of arms." See Hadley, 170.

62. Gen Curtis E. LeMay, transcript of oral history interview by USAF, January 1965, AFHRA, Maxwell AFB, Ala., 10–11.

63. Betts, 178.

64. Gen George S. Brown, transcript of oral history interview by USAF, file number K239.0512-1383, 7–12; Gen Jacob E. Smart, transcript of oral history interview by Dr. Edgar F. Puryear Jr., 10 June 1980, AFHRA, Maxwell AFB, Ala., 2; and Gen John W. Vogt Jr., transcript of oral history interview by Dr. Edgar F. Puryear Jr., AFHRA, Maxwell AFB, Ala., 10.

65. Gen Leon Johnson, transcript of oral history interview by Dr. Edgar F. Puryear Jr., 12 July 1978, AFHRA, Maxwell AFB, Ala., 14.

66. Alfred E. Hurley and Robert C. Ehrhart, eds., "The Perceptions of Three Makers of Air Power History," *Air Power and Warfare: Proceedings of the Military History Symposium, United States Air Force Academy* (Washington, D.C.: OAFH, 1979), 198.

67. Futrell, 172–73.

68. Ibid., 9.

69. Ibid., 192.

70. Ibid., 235.

71. Ibid.

Chapter 6

Absolutists and the Frustration of Airpower in Vietnam (1964–69)

There seems to be a trend toward viewing all national questions in the context of the frustrating struggle against aggression in Vietnam. . . . But there is no doubt that, however frustrated we are with the conflict in Vietnam, the cost of failure to provide adequate forces for our security could be infinitely higher than the cost of Southeast Asia.

—Secretary of the Air Force Robert C. Seamans Jr., March 1969

The retirement of Curtis E. LeMay in 1965 placed the junior World War II generals in charge of an air force that faced the twin challenges of a spiraling arms race and the prospect of outright American involvement in the conflict in Southeast Asia. In the wake of the Cuban missile crisis, the Soviet Union engaged in a massive strategic arms buildup as well as continued support for "wars of national liberation." The United States, in turn, found itself reversing the illusory "missile gap" and confidently building its military to fulfill Kennedy's war doctrine. The new national defense policy of Flexible Response fed on a steady increase in the defense budget. It was more generous than previously to "general purpose forces" of the long-neglected Army and Navy than to its strategic-minded sister service. By 1965 the Air Force claimed it was hard pressed fiscally to maintain strategic superiority over the growing Soviet strategic threat and to build a credible force for conventional war at the same time.

The air arm found it difficult to adjust doctrinally to the challenge rising in Vietnam. The dominant absolutists continued to argue that airpower was indivisible and that the more important general (nuclear) war forces would be adequate for fighting limited war. However, as early as 1960 TAC had confessed that the Air Force was unprepared for a limited war using conventional weapons.[1] The 1964 Air Force doctrinal manual signaled change, but only as a modest shift, which had yet to be digested widely. Doctrinal and budgetary emphasis remained on strategic nuclear warfare.[2]

The tools at hand mirrored this doctrine. Strategic bombers concentrated on single-ship, low-altitude, high-speed penetration tactics to avoid SAMs and interceptors. Air refueling capability had expanded to increase the global reach of airpower. Propellered aircraft had vanished from speed-conscious SAC and TAC by 1961.[3] The Air Force produced long-range and standardized radios to enhance control and coordination of its assets. But the air arm neglected electronic countermeasures (ECM) as well as conventional munitions and delivery systems until the early 1960s.[4]

With limited budgets, a growing strategic threat, and the inertia of a long-held doctrine and force structure, the Air Force stood understandably reluctant to get involved in counterinsurgency warfare in a distant land during the Kennedy presidency. Nevertheless, pressured by Washington, Air Force Chief of Staff LeMay, whose concern over losing close air support to the Army exceeded his supreme confidence in airpower, ordered the establishment of the 4400th Combat Crew Training Squadron in April 1961. Funding came out of TAC's meager budget, and deployment to Vietnam occurred eight months later.[5]

From the beginning, many senior Air Force leaders felt the conflict resembled a conventional war worthy of jet aircraft and a strategic bombing campaign. Junior cohort fighter major general Momyer recalled that by 1961, "while we considered the merits of various approaches to counterinsurgency warfare, the fighting in parts of Southeast Asia had already passed through that stage of conflict."[6] Assessments from the field reflected similar beliefs in the need for jets—even against guerrillas. Lt Col Charles E. Trumbo Jr., director of plans in the 2d Air Division (Air Force headquarters) in South Vietnam, expressed a "commonly held opinion" in mid-1963 when he claimed "a squadron of F-100s [jets] over here could puncture the balloon of skeptics."[7] Momyer and fellow cohort bomber lieutenant general David A. Burchinal visited Vietnam in early 1963 and recommended "augmentation of United States tactical aviation [jet] units."[8]

Uncomfortable with the intricacies of counterinsurgency warfare and implicit Army domination in that realm, the Air Force sought a contribution more in concert with its doctrine and weaponry. As one analyst noted, "Many . . . hoped escalation would clarify and simplify the conflict."[9]

Before they retired, senior World War II absolutists persistently advocated a massive strategic bombing campaign against "instigative" North Vietnam. General LeMay summarized,

> All along I said that if we were going to get anywhere in Vietnam, we'd have to attack the North. But voices have been saying repeatedly: "No we must recognize a stable government down there in the South before we dare carry the war to the North." I don't believe that. If you carry the war to the North and really carry it there, you'll get your stable government. The military task confronting us is to make it so expensive for the North Vietnamese that they will stop their aggression against South Vietnam and Laos. If we make it too expensive for them, they will stop. They don't want to lose everything they have. There came a time when the Nazis threw their towel into the ring. Same way with the Japanese. We didn't bring that happy day about by sparring with 16-ounce gloves.[10]

Momyer noted, "All of [LeMay's] experience had taught him that such a campaign would end the war."[11] The absolutists' swift strategic bombing campaign would extract "an economic penalty" that should decide the issue quicker and ultimately save lives by averting a commitment of ground forces. At least it would determine whether the United States really wanted to make that ground commitment.

Others noticed that the Air Force absolutists tried to mold the war to fit their doctrine and equipment. Army general Bruce Palmer Jr., who had a ringside seat at JCS deliberations and later served as deputy commander of US forces in Vietnam, noted that the Air Force senior leaders were "unwavering in their beliefs, [they] believed that an all out air offensive not only could make North Vietnam incapable of further fighting, but could also compel its leaders to cease and desist in the South."[12] Defense civilians failed to share the beliefs of the Air Force. Secretary of Defense McNamara recalled the "strong school of thought in the Air Force that you could win the war in Vietnam with air power; a constant exaggeration of the potential use of air power in Vietnam, with a constant overstatement of the results of air power."[13]

Air absolutists saw a counterinsurgency war in the South as defensive, long, and agonizing. The initiative could be seized best with a vigorous application of airpower against North Vietnam. Despite the November 1964 JCS endorsement of LeMay's strategic air campaign against 94 targets in North Vietnam, McNamara rejected it, saying there was insufficient provocation for it and the focus should be on South Vietnam. As the months went by, the rest of the Johnson administration (including the chairman of the joint chiefs, Army general Maxwell D. Taylor) did not believe airpower could achieve its goals. Nonetheless, they came to regard it as useful in signaling resolve.[14] Until retirement the senior absolutists continued to advocate LeMay's Sunday punch. Yet they lost political influence with each predictable recommendation.

Little did the junior World War II generation realize as they received the mantle of Air Force leadership that this pesky little conflict in Southeast Asia soon would consume them. The Air Force would spend more time fighting in Southeast Asia and spend more money there than any of the other services. Airmen would fly more than twice the combat missions and drop twice the tonnage in Southeast Asia than they did in World War II. The Air Force would deploy more than one-third of its entire inventory to Southeast Asia and lose 2,257 aircraft and more than 2,700 personnel. Ultimately, US airpower dropped 500 pounds of bombs for every person in country or 70 tons per square mile.[15] Besides being absorbed and frustrated in Vietnam, the junior generation failed to realize the extent to which the senior cohort had lost the ear of the administration.

Bomber general John P. McConnell succeeded LeMay as chief of staff. Sensing his alienation from Secretary of Defense McNamara and Secretary of the Air Force Zuckert, LeMay had been careful not to recommend a successor, as it might cause adverse prejudice against that nominee.[16] During SAC's domination of the Air Force in the early 1960s, LeMay sent SAC bomber generals Walter C. Sweeney Jr. to command TAC (October 1961) and McConnell (September 1962) to the

European Command. This "broadening" experience factored into Zuckert's nomination of McConnell.[17] But McConnell's selection had more to do with his relationship with President Lyndon B. Johnson than with his breadth of experience. In 1957 McConnell had visited then Senator Johnson's ranch in Texas to give him a two-day briefing on SAC. He subsequently returned to the ranch on several other occasions, and the two became friends, both comfortable in homespun deal making.[18] In 1964 President Johnson recalled McConnell from Europe to ask if he wished to become chief of staff, and if so, how he would behave. McConnell responded that he would provide professional advice but would remain loyal and support the president if there were disagreement.[19] The new chief exhibited strong characteristics from his SAC background— described as "intensely competitive, aggressive, operationally oriented, hard-driving, ambitious, ruthless, brash," and as one secretary of the Air Force recalled, "A pretty salty character . . . certainly of the old school."[20] While this junior cohort of the bomber school lacked LeMay's "incisiveness," he had other dimensions that made him more effective on Capitol Hill— he was "wily, plotting, opportunistic, politically charming, compromising," and he had a "reputation for knowing his way around Washington."[21]

In the mid-1960s the new chief and his peers attempted to handle the challenges of Flexible Response better than their highly respected yet politically disenfranchised seniors. While the junior cohort was not as steeped in the memories of the long struggle for service independence and the management of the tremendous air effort in World War II, they generally remained believers in the absolutist vision of the decisiveness of airpower through strategic bombing. As squadron and group leaders in World War II and as apprentices of the seniors, the junior cohort remembered the value of using supreme means to attain decisive ends. But they suffered from inherent difficulties that would limit their ability to contend with the challenges of the Vietnam era.[22] This generation had fewer college graduates than the senior generation; in large measure because of their membership in the largest "aviation cadet" population bulge, one-half of them never received a college degree (fig. 14). Besides undergraduate education, the World War II and the Korean War generations had interrupted opportunities for graduate education and professional military education (figs. 15 and 16). A survey of all Air Force general officers from 1953 to 1972 shows that the annual proportions of generals holding advanced degrees increased steadily throughout the period. But there occurred a "large and growing gap between the more highly educated administrators and technologists, and those generals whose careers were in operations and staff work"; that is, those running the Air Force.[23]

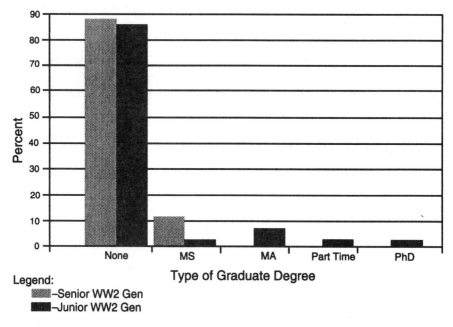

Legend:
▨–Senior WW2 Gen
■–Junior WW2 Gen

Figure 14. Graduate Education of Air Force Four-Star Generals

The junior generation also emanated from the insularity of the senior generation in the 1950s and early 1960s. Figure 17 reflects the distribution by area of formative experience of four-star generals in the World War II generations. Although a slight decrease from senior to junior generations occurred in bomber pilot dominance (no doubt, in part from the demands of Vietnam), the large decrease in the number of generalists made the effect of insularity apparent. An analyst noted that in 1953 more than 40 percent of the generals on active duty

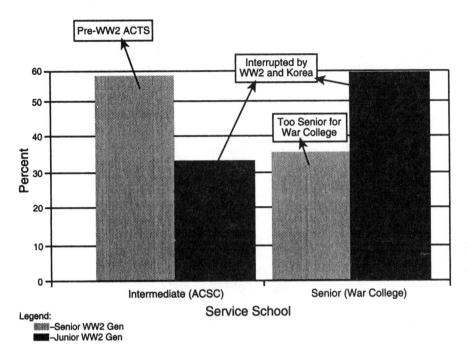

Figure 15. Professional Military Education of Air Force Four-Star Generals

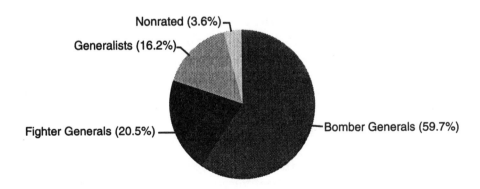

Figure 16. Distribution of Full Generals: Senior World War II Generation

had at least one senior assignment in an outside community. By 1972 the figure had decreased to less than 10 percent.[24] The insularity of the fighter and bomber communities was breeding members of the junior cohort who were narrow in experience in an environment that demanded breadth of experience and knowledge. In sum, the junior cohort too were field marshals, busy building their sword and shield for the emergent national security state, more than they were sophisticated soldier-statesmen.

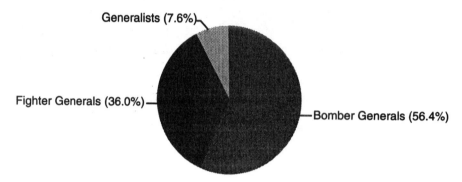

Generalists (7.6%)

Fighter Generals (36.0%)

Bomber Generals (56.4%)

Figure 17. Distribution of Full Generals: Junior World War II Generation

As Air Force vice chief of staff during LeMay's last six months, McConnell witnessed a steady erosion of Air Force influence over defense policy. The new chief hoped his friendship with the president, as well as his political acumen, would serve the interests of the Air Force better. He realized that divisiveness and some archaic methods had to change if the Air Force were to regain its sway. The top junior cohort desired to widen the perspective of the Air Force without destroying the pride and preeminence of SAC.[25] Broadening and reunification became a top priority; the challenges of Vietnam would provide the opportunity.

The Vietnam crisis flared in McConnell's first week as chief. On 7 February 1965 the Vietcong struck American forces at the Pleiku Air Base (AB), and the United States responded the following day with reprisal air strikes, code named Flaming Dart I. Two days later enemy forces struck American billets at

164

Qui Nhon, which provoked Flaming Dart II. As the US government searched for a course of action, the JCS recommended an 11-week strategic bombing plan to destroy most of the "94" strategic targets.[26] McConnell, in the tradition of LeMay, favored an even more intense 28-day strategic bombing campaign.[27]

Like LeMay, McConnell was now anxious to demonstrate the efficacy of airpower against the only worthy target, the war-making capacity of North Vietnam, and by inference, North Vietnamese will. As in World War II, it must be a supreme, compressed effort against the enemy's economy (rather than his deployed forces) that, as one analyst noted, "could not help but have significant results."[28] McConnell insisted airpower must be exercised before deciding to commit ground troops. Nevertheless, in March, without approval for their strategic bombing campaign, the JCS agreed to commit troops over McConnell's objections.[29]

The junior cohort's failure to influence the president was not surprising. Johnson had been suspicious of the military for some time. He had warned LeMay not to do to him on Capitol Hill what LeMay had done earlier for Johnson as senator: prime members to ask questions that when answered would be critical of the administration.[30] The president retained the Kennedy administration's dismay over the narrowness of military advice. Johnson lamented in 1965:

> And those generals. Oh, they'd love the war, too. It's hard to be a hero without a war. Heroes need battles and bombs and bullets in order to be heroic. That's why I am suspicious of the military. They're always so narrow in their appraisal of everything. They see everything in military terms.[31]

The consistency of JCS advice for an aggressive bombing campaign disturbed both the domestically focused president and his business-oriented defense secretary. Both recalled the "frightful" behavior of some in the JCS during the Cuban missile crisis and desired to keep a close rein on the military. As the Vietnam War progressed, Johnson began to chide his generals. All he heard from them was "bomb, bomb, bomb. . . . Well, I want to know why there's nothing else. You generals have all been educated at taxpayers' expense, and you're not giving me any ideas. . . . I want some solutions. I want some answers."[32]

What the perplexed commander in chief and his ineffectual minister of war failed to appreciate was the nature of American military traditions. Historian Russell F. Weigley has characterized the "American way of war" as being aimed "at carrying the war to the enemy, and at winning victory by the means sanctioned by the most deeply rooted historical American conceptions of strategy, the destruction of the enemy's armed forces and of his ability to wage war."[33] The desire to use maximum available means to seize the initiative and end the war with overwhelming force ran deep in the veins of the World War II generations. To them even the Korean War had been a conventional experience against an identifiable enemy. Now they faced an elusive enemy who was difficult to identify. Most in the military considered Kennedy's recent call for counterinsurgency capability as "romantic." Conventional experience and a cold war focus on Europe circumscribed the American military's ability to respond. The Air Force leadership had neither the education nor breadth of experience to challenge the emerging civilian solution, at least to the satisfaction of their superiors.

That solution, limited war theory, was embraced by the administration. Academically in vogue at the time, it espoused the notion that the principal aim of strategy was not to destroy the enemy but to deter, compel, or coerce him (usually towards a negotiated settlement) by the threat or use of carefully calibrated force.[34] The theory appealed to the president because it was a cheap, low-risk answer to what became an increasingly difficult problem. Johnson believed airpower would be the chief instrument of this coercive diplomacy:

> I saw our bombs as my political resources for negotiating a peace. On the one hand, our planes and our bombs could be used as carrots for the South, strengthening the morale of the South Vietnamese and pushing them to clean up their corrupt house, by demonstrating the depth of our commitment to the war. On the other hand, our bombs could be used as sticks against the North, pressuring North Vietnam to stop its aggression against the South. By keeping a lid on all the designated targets, I knew I could keep the control of the war in my own hands. If China reacted to our slow escalation by threatening to

retaliate, we'd have plenty of time to ease off the bombing. But this control—so essential for preventing World War III—would be lost the moment we unleashed a total assault on the North—for that would be rape rather than seduction—and then there would be no turning back. The Chinese reaction would be instant and total.[35]

But the assumptions implicit in limited war theory were invalid in revolutionary war. Johnson's civilian advisors' rationale assumed a North Vietnamese economic motivation, mechanistic concern over costs and benefits, and a sensible threshold of pain. But North Vietnam did not fit the mold of rational systems analysis. Vietnamese reunification was an absolute value more than a relative one.[36] The failure to realize this conclusion resulted, in large measure, from American arrogance. Neither the JCS nor the Johnson administration would ever dream that, in Johnson's words, "this raggedy-ass little fourth-rate country" would be able to resist the threat or use of American military power.[37] Both the military and the civilian leadership preferred to accommodate events to fit their notion of strategy. The civilians believed, then hoped, that the enemy would break at the next increment of force. For the military, operational successes took precedence over political signaling. The military sought maximum acceptable force; the civilians desired minimum practical force. Arrogance of American military might, coupled with poor civil-military relations, fostered pursuit of two disparate notions of means at the cost of rigorous scrutiny of assumptions, objectives, costs, and strategy.

McConnell had failed to escape Johnson's stereotype or to resurrect influence of the Air Force over the conduct of the war. By July 1965 the administration viewed the war in the south as primary, and the Rolling Thunder campaign of selected bombing against North Vietnam that had begun in February 1965 was an adjunct—a tool for Johnson's diplomacy of violence.[38] Publicly, the Air Force chief supported what he termed Johnson's strategy of "strategic persuasion," which McConnell claimed "gives the President a highly flexible tool in inducing North Vietnam eventually to accept his offer of unconditional discussions."[39] Privately, he told his field commanders only airpower could defeat the guerrillas in the south, and the air commanders were to support

Gen William C. Westmoreland in his first phase of operations. McConnell predicted that things would "rock along" for a few months, and if the situation continued to deteriorate, there would be a change. Furthermore, he continued, forceful action against the north scheduled for next year, could check Westmoreland's second phase.[40]

At home, General McConnell now realized that challenges of the new era taxed his institution. Growing involvement of tactical air forces in Southeast Asia necessitated a rebuilding of TAC. However, McConnell inherited a bomber-dominated senior leadership and a long-subordinated minority of fighter generals. The only fighter general who stood in a key operational four-star position was Gen Gabriel P. Disosway. He had "escaped" the SAC-dominated Air Staff to command the United States Air Forces in Europe. In August 1965 McConnell took action to provide more tactical (fighter) experience in key senior positions. The retirement of bomber general Sweeney that month opened command of TAC to Disosway. The widely respected fighter general Bruce K. Holloway replaced Disosway at USAFE. Two months earlier, McConnell had promoted fighter major general Joseph H. Moore, the in-country Air Force commander in South Vietnam (2d Air Division), to lieutenant general.[41] Still, the senior theater commander, the commander of PACAF, would remain a bomber position—where future candidates for chief would get their "tactical experience" and supervise fighter subordinates who waged war.

McConnell remained optimistic for most of 1966. Like his romantic predecessors, he continued to praise the capabilities and relevance of airpower in Vietnam. In a January speech he concluded,

> Above all . . . it must be recognized that, in this day and age, wars of any kind cannot be won without airpower and without exploiting its almost limitless potential to the fullest. . . . Whoever proves his superiority in the air will prevail in all other dimensions. We have that superiority in Vietnam, and that is why I have no doubt that we will achieve our stated objectives. . . . I assure you that airpower in Vietnam is accomplishing and will accomplish every task assigned to it, within whatever limits are or may be established.[42]

168

What the chief had believed would be a temporary policy governing the air war—strictly controlled political signaling by way of slow gradualism—continued indefinitely. The JCS had learned to act with unanimity to avoid exploitation of any divisiveness by McNamara. They continued to recommend faster escalation but publicly remained loyal to the president. Johnson gave them just enough hope for the future to prevent revolt but not enough to lose sight of who was boss. As one historian observed, "His consensus-oriented modus operandi effectively stifled debate [and] by making concessions to each side without giving any what it wanted, he managed to keep dissent and controversy under control."[43] As the war progressed, Johnson grew more fearful of public military dissent. In February 1966 he asked General Westmoreland not to "pull a MacArthur" on him.[44] By late 1966 the president and his military advisors dealt with each other by "stealth and indirection." As tensions heightened, the chairman of the JCS, Army general Earle G. Wheeler, alerted commanders to the "absolute necessity for every military man to keep his mouth shut and get on with the war."[45]

The disillusionment of McConnell with both limited war theorists and the performance of airpower became apparent in his speeches beginning in early 1967. Hindered by inadequate technologies for limited war, ineffective strategies, and the lack of adequate intelligence and bomb damage assessment, the performance of airpower failed to live up to romantic expectations.[46] McConnell began to qualify the capabilities of airpower more often. At a Pentagon press conference in February 1967, the Air Force chief answered that "airpower alone cannot bring the enemy to the conference table, but it has reduced his fighting capability and morale . . . to the point where he can no longer rely on his tactics to offset the advantages which superior personnel, efficient organization, and modern equipment provides [sic] to us."[47] Indeed, massive doses of airpower helped to forestall an enemy victory and altered the calculus of land warfare. But airpower failed to achieve the decisiveness that enthusiasts had hoped for. Privately, absolutists rationalized limited efficacy as a product of civilian interference.

169

Part of the frustration stemmed from the confusion that limited war theory conveyed to the World War II generations. The military saw policy as the independent variable from which strategy and tactics were derived; the limited war theorists viewed policy as a dependent variable reevaluated in light of strategic and tactical results.[48] The latter was perplexing, especially to Air Force absolutists, and many could not fathom the continued limits placed on airpower.[49] Even air leaders who better understood limited war expressed disbelief. Seventh Air Force commander fighter general Momyer witnessed a boomerang effect of the theory: "To wait until [the enemy] has disseminated his supplies among thousands of trucks, sampans, rafts, and bicycles, and then to send our multi-million dollar aircraft after those individual vehicles—this is how to maximize our cost, not his."[50] McConnell himself reportedly lamented after a 1967 Rolling Thunder briefing: "I can't tell you how I feel. . . . I'm so sick of it. . . . I have never been so godd––– frustrated by it all."[51] Traditional notions of victory emerged subordinated to mere denial of enemy victory. The differing perspectives espoused by the absolutists and by the limited war theorists created an artificial incongruity between methods of military and political victory. This development confused McConnell throughout his tenure. He concluded upon retirement:

> If you want to achieve military victory, then you fight a war a lot different than we're fighting this one. You don't circumscribe the commanders in the field; you tell them what the job to do is and let them go do it. If you're attempting to use the military to achieve a political decision, then that's an *entirely different* proposition. So I wouldn't say that the military has been misused in terms of attempting to achieve a political decision, but it certainly has not been properly used for the purpose of achieving a military decision. (Emphasis added)[52]

The junior cohort faced exacerbated civil-military relations and pressure from the retired senior cohort by the fall of 1967.[53] The Senate Preparedness Subcommittee Hearings on the Air War in North Vietnam (Stennis hearings) in August provided a forum for the tight-lipped generals to vent their frustrations and endorse escalation. As historian George Herring notes, in response Johnson "kicked the now obviously dissident McNamara downstairs to the World Bank and tossed the JCS a bone by authorizing a handful of new bombing targets. But he refused to confront head on the larger issues of either the air or ground war."[54] One researcher uncovered evidence that the JCS nearly resigned en masse on 25 August.[55]

Tension increased in the new year as the US Marine base at Khe Sanh came under siege by the communists. The president feared that the loss of Khe Sanh would have the same fatal effects that the loss of Dien Bien Phu had on the French in 1954. Johnson transformed his White House situation room into a military command post and closely supervised details of the unfolding operation. Reports emanated that the worried president demanded guarantees from each chief that Khe Sanh would not fall.[56]

Khe Sanh did not fall, in part because McConnell by 1968 had moved generals with more tactical experience into key leadership positions. General Momyer, then commander of Air Training Command (ATC), assisted General Disosway at TAC in increasing and improving pilot training to meet the demands of Vietnam. In July 1966 Momyer received a promotion to full general and became commander of Seventh Air Force, the senior Air Force position in South Vietnam. In August 1968 he succeeded Disosway as commander of TAC. Momyer was followed by generalist general George S. Brown at Seventh Air Force in August 1968. In September 1966 fighter general James Ferguson became commander of Air Force Systems Command, a critical position for developing new technologies and weapons systems.

McConnell had realized also the need to broaden and nurture a few generals he considered capable of succeeding him.[57] In February 1967 he relieved bomber general Hunter Harris Jr. as PACAF commander and replaced him with former SAC commander bomber general John D. Ryan.[58] In August 1966 McConnell had brought fighter general Holloway from USAFE to be his vice chief of staff. Holloway gave the fighter community intimate access to McConnell. In July 1968 the Air Force chief demonstrated his resolve to "reunify the Air Force" when he moved fighter general Holloway to take command of SAC. Holloway vacated the vice chief's position to make room for bomber general Ryan, who returned from his broadening experience in PACAF to build experience in Washington before succeeding McConnell. Bomber general Joseph J. Nazzaro followed Ryan from SAC to PACAF. The bomber generals still held most of the top Air Force positions, and a chosen few gained experience in limited war. Meanwhile, more fighter generals were gaining critical combat command experience and slowly breaking into the top echelon.

The arrival of more tactical aviators in positions of command did not alleviate the Air Force's problems in fighting against an elusive, strong-willed enemy while shackled with close civilian control of air strikes. Johnson's nine "cease-fires" and 10 "bombing halts" seemed to earn only enemy contempt. Problems with the efficacy of airpower were becoming clear to McConnell in his last year. In late October 1967 absolutist McConnell advocated attacks on the enemy's rice crop to suppress the "enemy's will to wage war."[59] By August 1969, a few weeks after retirement, McConnell admitted that attacks on the dikes would have been a pretty fruitless operation.[60] Limits of airpower were becoming apparent, even to the chief.

At home, a demand for B-52s in Southeast Asia complicated the Air Force's primary mission of contending with the Soviet strategic threat. Ironically, the appearance of many ICBMs as the new centerpiece of strategic deterrence in part had opened the venerable bombers for consideration as a viable weapon in limited war. Still, strategic forces maintained budgetary preeminence within the Air Force until 1966 (fig. 18). SAC's alert posture formed the cornerstone of its mission of deterrence. In the late 1960s clear strategic superiority proved too costly and yielded to what ultimately became known as strategic sufficiency. President Kennedy had directed 50 percent of SAC's bomber crews to serve alert at dispersed sites on the heels of the Berlin crisis. A reduced insistence on strategic superiority and a growing reliance on the cheaper and more plentiful ICBM systems relieved the hard-pressed bomber crews.[61] But requests for B-52s in Southeast Asia offset this reduction in the demands on the now shrinking bomber force.

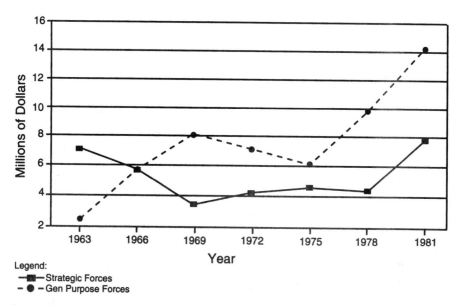

Source: Department of Defense Budget Office, Washington, D.C. This chart appeared in the annual *Air Force Almanac* issue of *Air Force Magazine.*

Figure 18. Air Force Budget Allocation (1963–81) in 1994 Dollars

SAC had refined its centralization and control, so vital in its high-stakes mission conducted from dispersed bases. This approach proved helpful in the Cuban missile crisis and was in consonance with close control of military means emerging from the White House. But constant alert encouraged the dominance of routine and stifled innovation. Shortly before retirement, General White had warned of "a static, nondynamic frame of mind" that might result from extensive alert duty.[62] The monistic focus on general war against the Soviet Union and the cultivation of control and routine left SAC somewhat less prepared in mind and body for limited war in Southeast Asia.

SAC's institutional imperative for nuclear war was amplified by the senior absolutists dominating SAC who strongly resisted committing resources to Southeast Asia in the early 1960s. SAC commander general Power told the Air Staff not to "talk to me about that; that's not our life. That's not our business. We don't want to get in the business of dropping any conventional bombs. We are in the nuclear business, and we want to stay there."[63] The feeling permeated the SAC staff.

SAC's deputy director of plans, bomber major general Howard A. Davis, told a study group later that "he would have put anyone in a straight jacket who had told him a few weeks before that he would be using B-52s to drop iron bombs on guerrillas in Vietnam."[64] Power also resisted the commitment of SAC air-refueling tankers to Southeast Asia. SAC had three major objections: first, it would detract from its SIOP and alert commitment; second, it would take too much time to reconfigure the aircraft and resume control for strategic operations, if needed; and third, the B-52's systems could be compromised in Southeast Asia, which would reduce its deterrent credibility in general war.[65] Besides, of what use could B-52s be in a counterinsurgency war? Nevertheless, a growing minority in SAC, especially in lower echelons, became "bored with alert" and excited about joining Military Airlift Command (MAC) and TAC in action in Southeast Asia.[66]

Junior cohort bomber general Ryan replaced Power at SAC in December 1964 and was more willing to deploy B-52s to Southeast Asia. In response to Vietcong attacks on Pleiku and Qui Nhon, SAC deployed 30 B-52s to Guam on 17 February 1965 to conduct "strategic aerospace warfare on a limited or global scale using conventional and/or nuclear weapons."[67] Conventional training in SAC had resumed only in late 1963, and the B-52 fleet was slowly converting to a conventional capability. But Ryan accelerated the process. Initially, most of the crews on temporary duty (TDY) at Guam had "little or no experience" in formation flying and pattern bombing.[68] Many were older pilots who had grown accustomed to years of disciplined procedural adherence inherent in executing the SIOP. SAC was having problems with adapting bomb bays for conventional operations. They also needed navigational and aiming aids for Southeast Asia. The lack of radar return data from Vietnam for radar aiming stymied early employment. On 23 May the B-52s began flying a few unarmed missions over South Vietnam to take radar pictures and later to test bombing with the assistance of ground beacons.[69]

Finally, on 16 June the B-52s received tasking for their first Arc Light mission—missions to carpet-bomb a target area in South Vietnam. Commander of Military Assistance Command, Vietnam (MACV), Army general Westmoreland, reserved for himself targeting decisions and approval of requests for the B-52s: "Such an important weapon system was worthy of his personal attention."[70] Each request required the approval of the JCS and the White House before SAC received tasking. According to the vice commander of SAC, bomber general Nazarro, the first B-52 bombing mission in Vietnam was planned well in advance, but as the order to execute was being transmitted from SAC to Guam, Nazarro found problems with it and took 15 minutes to change it; spacing between the three-ship formations had been based entirely on the use of onboard radars.

Next, the US ambassador to Vietnam, Army general Taylor, directed an Air Force general to be airborne in the area to ensure that the ground beacon used as an aiming reference was properly coordinated with the bombers.[71] The World War II-like 30-plane bomber stream of three-ship elements (cells) flew in trail from Guam to their night rendezvous with the tankers. A typhoon put the first element at the rendezvous point nine minutes early, so the cell leader decided to make a 360-degree turn to lose time. As he neared completion of the turn, he ran one of his cell mates into the formation behind him. Two B-52s caught fire and plunged into the dark Pacific. One frustrated fighter general assigned to SAC at that time mourned, "How in the hell we ever lived with it [rendezvous plan], I'll never know."[72] PACAF commander, bomber general Harris, simply blamed the accident on bad weather.[73] It was an unfortunate beginning; SAC would have to innovate and show flexibility in this different war.

The centralization and control of the Pacific bombers rivaled that of the Twentieth Air Force in the same region in World War II. The Army-dominated MACV staff nominated targets for preplanned Arc Light missions, which were then validated by the JCS and authorized by the administration. Mission planning was accomplished at various SAC headquarters with "all details approved by at least six separate planners; all must agree on all phases of the strike."[74] Mission orders were dispatched normally 24 hours prior to time over target (TOT) but sometimes as late as 18 hours prior (though changes could be made up to 12 hours before TOT). Missions began as 30-plane raids for the first two months before smaller formations were flown.[75] SAC closely supervised all sorties and by regulation demanded that cockpit transmissions be recorded. This procedure resulted in aircrews passing notes "ankle deep" in the cockpit so as not to indict themselves.[76]

But the greatest difficulty was that SAC violated the Air Force's chief doctrinal commandment of *indivisibility*—which inferred the centralized management of airpower. A SAC liaison was set up in MACV in March 1965 to coordinate tankers and, later, Arc Light missions. It reported to SAC and not to the theater air commander, the commander of 2d Air Division (after April 1966 commander of Seventh Air Force). In most of World War II and the Korean War, the theater air commander controlled air force assets. SAC chose to take its heritage from the Twentieth Air Force experience and refused to relinquish control over its aircraft. SAC still "took care of its own," fearing that if needed, it would not be able to resume control of its assets from Seventh Air Force promptly in a crisis.

Additionally, if the president approved the long-sought massive bombing campaign of the North, SAC's commander, bomber general Ryan, insisted on running the strategic bombing effort.[77] After repeated pleas from the fighter generals at Seventh Air Force and (in 1967) Westmoreland for control of the "tactical" Arc Light missions, McConnell convinced the JCS to move the SAC liaison office to Seventh Air Force Headquarters, call it the SAC advanced echelon (SACADVON), and attach it to the new MACV air deputy (Seventh Air Force commander).[78] In short, little changed but organizational titles and office locations. If the fighter generals in South Vietnam could not get another blue-suiter to integrate airpower, how could they convince the Navy to agree to cooperate under a single theater air commander?

The Vietnam challenge slowly eroded the traditional insularity and rigidity of SAC. Fighter cohort, SAC Lt Gen Alvan C. Gillem II, 3d Air Division and later Eighth Air Force commander at Guam from June 1968 to July 1970, saw the Vietnam War as a great escape from the static routine at SAC. Gillem set up a popular rotation out of Guam, Okinawa, and Thailand for his TDY SAC personnel to "see the world." He called the Arc Light missions "the greatest training we ever had"; they revitalized the bomber fleet, helped boost morale, provided much flying training and a strong learning curve, and enhanced aircrew opportunities to mature into positions of flight leadership and instructor status.[79] SAC personnel responded well to the challenge. Maintenance crews performed admirably with an average of only eight cancellations for maintenance deficiencies out of up to 1,800 sorties each month.[80] Aircrews and staffs reduced reaction time, anticipated diverts and mission changes, increased flexibility, and refined bombing accuracy.[81]

As B-52 bombings provided an awesome display of firepower truly feared by enemy forces, they increased MACV's appetite. Sortie rates climbed from 300 a month in 1965 to a surge capability of 1,800 each month in 1968.[82] In 1968 the new SAC commander, fighter general Holloway, expressed concern with the stress that alert requirements and rising sortie demands in Southeast Asia generated on his aircrews and aircraft.

Increasingly willing to liberate aircrews and aircraft from the routine of alert, Holloway sent aircrews to Southeast Asia on TDY orders for up to 180 days at a time. Many aircrews began to average 14 months of TDY every three years, without credit for a remote tour or a campaign ribbon. To meet demands of B-52 pilots, SAC established a special training unit by 1968. Holloway cried for relief for his crews and planes; he tried unsuccessfully to reduce B-52 sortie requirements through a more creative use of formations and tactics. He also attempted, with only marginal success, to get pilots from other weapons systems—the airlift and especially fighter forces needed pilots, too.[83]

Notes

1. History, Tactical Air Command, January–June 1961, vol. 1, 66, 68. TAC commander Gen Frank Everest's speech at a commander's conference in February 1960 was the first of many admissions from TAC that the Air Force was unprepared for limited war. See History, Tactical Air Command, June–December 1959, vol. 1, 26. The Air Force informed all subordinated commands that development of nonnuclear weapons was to be terminated; the Air Force would monitor naval programs and weapons.

2. Col Dennis M. Drew, "Rolling Thunder 1965: Anatomy of a Failure," Research Report no. AU-ARI-CP-86-3 (Maxwell AFB, Ala.: Air University Press, 1986), 26. Drew notes that the new doctrinal edition recognized the possibility of limited wars, but the *emphasis* remained as before. "The manual devoted 11 pages of discussion to air operations in general and tactical nuclear warfare and a scant two pages to a discussion of conventional air operations. Under the heading of conventional air operations, strategic operations were not included, indicating there was no provision for strategic bombardment using nonnuclear weapons."

3. William W. Momyer, *Airpower in Three Wars: WWII, Korea, Vietnam* (Washington, D.C.: Government Printing Office, [GPO] 1978), 249.

4. Robert Frank Futrell, *Ideas, Concepts, Doctrine: Basic Thinking in the United States Air Force, 1961–1984*, vol. 2 (Maxwell AFB, Ala.: Air University Press, 1989), 288.

5. Ibid. TAC was a small training force in the early 1960s comprising approximately 12 percent of the Air Force. Gen Horace M. Wade, transcript of oral history interview by Hugh N. Ahmann, 10–12 October 1978, 357, Air Force Historical Research Agency (cited hereafter as AFHRA), Maxwell AFB, Ala.; and Donald J. Mrozek, *Airpower and the Ground War in Vietnam: Ideas and Actions* (Maxwell AFB, Ala.: Air University Press, 1988), 36, 55. Army general William Westmoreland recalls LeMay's warning against trying to usurp the Air Force role in close air support in late 1964 and admonishing fighter major general Joseph H. Moore, then the ranking Air Force officer in Vietnam, for "failure to uphold Air Force doctrine." Earl H. Tilford Jr., *Setup: What the Air Force Did in Vietnam and Why* (Maxwell AFB, Ala.: Air University Press, 1991), 50, 62.

6. Momyer, 10.

7. Lt Col Charles E. Trumbo Jr., transcript of oral history interview by Joseph W. Grainger, 13 July 1963, AFHRA, cited in Tilford, 79.

8. Ibid.

9. Mrozek, 62.

10. Curtis E. LeMay with MacKinlay Kantor, *Mission with LeMay: My Story* (Garden City, N.Y.: Doubleday, 1965), 565; Thomas M. Coffey, *Iron Eagle: The Turbulent Life of General Curtis LeMay* (New York: Crown Publishers, 1986), 489. In his preface Coffey argues that LeMay never claimed to want to bomb North Vietnam "back into the stone age" and that the citation in his memoir was an editorial oversight.

11. Momyer, 13.

12. Bruce Palmer Jr., *The 25-Year War: America's Military Role in Vietnam* (Lexington, Ky.: University Press of Kentucky, 1984), 34.

13. Edgar F. Puryear Jr., *Stars in Flight: A Study in Air Force Character and Leadership* (San Rafael, Calif.: Presidio Press, 1981), 120.

14. Mark Clodfelter, *The Limits of Air Power: The American Bombing of North Vietnam* (New York: Free Press, 1989), 51–71.

15. Thomas C. Thayer, *War Without Fronts: The American Experience in Vietnam* (Boulder, Colo.: Westview Press, 1985), 26, 37; Tilford, xvii, 282; and Futrell, 34.

16. Puryear, 12.

17. Eugene M. Zuckert, transcript of oral history interview by Dr. Edgar F. Puryear Jr., 28 September 1977, 39–40, AFHRA. General Sweeney suffered from ill health.

18. Gen John P. McConnell, transcript of oral history interview by Dr. Edgar F. Puryear Jr., 1975, 28, AFHRA; also, Gen John P. McConnell, transcript of oral history interview by Dorothy Pierce McSweeny, Lyndon Johnson Library, 28 August 1969, AFHRA.

19. McConnell, interviewed by Puryear; and McConnell, interviewed by McSweeny.

20. Gen Russell E. Dougherty, transcript of oral history interview by Dr. Edgar F. Puryear Jr., 27 March 1979, 3, AFHRA; Gen Bruce K. Holloway, transcript of oral history interview by Dr. Edgar F. Puryear Jr., 7 July 1978, 15, AFHRA; Gen Leon W. Johnson, transcript of oral history interview by Dr. Edgar F. Puryear Jr., 12 July 1978, 24, AFHRA; and Dr. Robert C. Seamans Jr., transcript of oral history interview by Lt Col Lynn R. Officer and Hugh N. Ahmann, 24–27 September, 27 November 1973, and 24 March 1974, 38, AFHRA.

21. Holloway, interviewed by Puryear; Gen Gabriel Disosway, transcript of oral history interview by Dr. Edgar F. Puryear Jr., 17 January 1979, 11, AFHRA; Gen Jacob E. Smart, transcript of oral history interview by Dr. Edgar F. Puryear Jr., 17 July 1979, 15, AFHRA; and Gen John W. Vogt Jr., interviewed by author, 23 April 1992.

22. This observation was perhaps true of the World War II generation in the other services as well as many in civilian leadership positions.

23. Arnold Kanter, "Managerial Careers of Air Force Generals: A Test of the Janowitz Convergence Hypothesis," *Journal of Political and Military Sociology*, Spring 1976, 125.

24. Arnold Kanter, "The Career Patterns of Air Force Generals," *American Journal of Political Science* 21, no. 2 (May 1977): 362.

25. Gen Joseph J. Nazarro, transcript of oral history interview by Dr. Edgar Puryear Jr., 4 May 1979, 121, AFHRA.

26. Momyer, 13. The 94 strategic targets developed by the Defense Intelligence Agency (DIA) at the request of the JCS "were considered to have a most direct relationship to the North Vietnamese war-making capacity and will to fight."

27. Drew, 33.

28. Robert W. Komer, *Bureaucracy at War: U.S. Performance in the Vietnam Conflict* (Boulder, Colo.: Westview Press, 1986), 54–55, 161.

29. John Schlight, *The War in South Vietnam: The Years of the Offensive, 1965–1968* (Washington, D.C.: Office of Air Force History [OAFH], 1988), 23; and Momyer, 21.

30. Richard K. Betts, *Soldiers, Statesmen, and Cold War Crises* (Cambridge, Mass.: Harvard University Press, 1977), 45.

31. Doris Kearns Goodwin, *Lyndon Johnson and the American Dream* (New York: Harper and Row, 1976), 252.

32. Betts, 179.

33. Russell Frank Weigley, *The American Way of War: A History of the United States Military Strategy and Policy* (New York: Macmillan, 1973), 464.

34. Thomas C. Schelling, *The Strategy of Conflict* (Cambridge, Mass.: Harvard University Press, 1960); and Thomas C. Schelling, *Arms and Influence* (New Haven, Conn.: Yale University Press, 1966) are credited sources for this limited war theory. Schelling discusses force as a coercive means of political signaling. Robert Endicott Osgood, *Limited War: The Challenge to American Strategy* (Chicago: University of Chicago Press, 1957) warns of the dangers of allowing limited war to escalate to irrational world war.

35. Goodwin, 264–65.

36. Peter Braestrup, ed., *Vietnam as History: Ten Years After the Paris Peace Accords*, Wilson Center Conference Report Series 2108 (Washington, D.C.: University Press of America, 1984), 80.

37. George C. Herring, "'Cold Blood': LBJ's Conduct of Limited War in Vietnam," *The Harmon Memorial Lectures in Military History* (Colorado Springs, Colo.: USAF Academy, 1990), 2.

38. Clodfelter, 71.

39. Futrell, 303.

40. Schlight, 76.

41. Gen Joseph H. Moore had replaced bomber major general Rollen H. Anthis as commander of 2d Air Division.

42. Headquarters PACAF, *The Effects of U.S. Air Operations in Southeast Asia: 1965–1968*, Headquarters PACAF, November 1969, 1-1. General McConnell made similar remarks in a 24 March speech to the Air Force Association at Carswell AFB, Texas. See also Tilford, 121. Tilford cites a September 1966 McConnell statement in *Air Force and Space Digest* (later *Air Force Magazine*): "In assessing the Air Force's achievements in Southeast Asia, there is one factor that stands out: that is the impressive margin by which air power has exceeded many early estimates of its usefulness in limited conflicts."

43. Herring, 8.

44. Ibid.

45. Ibid., 9.

46. Mark Clodfelter, "Of Demons, Storms, and Thunder: A Preliminary Look at Vietnam's Impact on the Persian Gulf Air Campaign," *Airpower Journal* 5, no. 4 (Winter 1991): 22. Clodfelter concludes, "The multitude of political, military, and operational restrictions on bombing, multiplied by the guerrilla nature of the ground war in the South, emasculated the air campaign, enabling North Vietnamese leaders to use it to create popular support for the war at a minimum cost."

47. Headquarters PACAF, *Effects of U.S. Air Operations*, 1-7.

48. Betts, 24.

49. Clodfelter, *The Limits of Air Power*, 144–45. For the "hands tied" perspective, see Jack Broughton, *Thud Ridge* (New York: Bantam Books,

1969); and Jack Broughton, *Going Downtown: The War Against Hanoi and Washington* (New York: Orion Books, 1988).

50. Nick Kotz, *Wild Blue Yonder: Money, Politics, and the B-1 Bomber* (New York: Pantheon Books, 1988), 82.

51. David Halberstam, *The Best and The Brightest* (New York: Random House, 1969), 646–67.

52. McConnell, interviewed by McSweeny. For a good summary of the absolutist McConnell's views on airpower in Vietnam, see Futrell, 478.

53. McConnell, interviewed by McSweeny. On 6 September 1967 McConnell attempted to allay the concerns of senior cohorts at a past commanders' dinner at Kelly AFB, Texas: "I can assure you that we are given every opportunity to convey our opinions and recommendations to the proper authorities [but] it is our job to carry out the decisions to the best of our ability."

54. Herring, 11.

55. Mark Perry, *Four Stars: The Inside Story of the Forty-five Year Battle Between the Joint Chiefs of Staff and America's Civilian Leaders* (Boston: Houghton Mifflin, 1989), 164–65.

56. Bernard C. Nalty, *Air Power and the Fight for Khe Sanh* (Washington, D.C.: OAFH, 1986), 17; and Betts, 45.

57. Wade, interviewed by Ahmann, 429. As deputy chief of staff for Personnel from August 1966 to July 1968, Wade was directed by McConnell to broaden the Air Force.

58. Gen Theodore R. Milton, transcript of oral history interview by Dr. Edgar F. Puryear Jr., 9 April 1976, 24–26, AFHRA; and Disosway, interviewed by Puryear. Harris, an obstinate absolutist, had difficulty with Admiral Sharp, commander in chief of the Pacific Command, as well as some of the Air Force generals (mostly fighter) on the staffs in the Pacific region. Disosway claims he was offered the PACAF job but declined (he was six months from retirement). He convinced McConnell to send General Ryan to get "broadening and tactical experience." Gen Theodore R. Milton interviewed by author, 15 June 1992.

59. Clodfelter, *Limits of Air Power*, 110. Clodfelter cites *Pentagon Papers*, Gravel edition, vol. 4: 233.

60. McConnell, interviewed by McSweeny. McConnell sensed both the strong will of the enemy and rising adverse public opinion by 1969.

61. In 1960 SAC had 1,716 heavy bombers and 12 Atlas ICBMs; and in 1966 SAC had 591 heavy bombers and 968 ICBMs.

62. Futrell, 33. White was referring to missile crews, but the same inference could be extended to bombers. Extensive alert duty meant reduced flying time and experience.

63. Wade, interviewed by Ahmann, 395; and Vogt interview. When fighter brigadier general John W. Vogt flew to SAC headquarters to convince Power to explore possibilities for the conventional use of B-52s, Power banished him from Offutt AFB and directed SAC not to allow Vogt to return to any SAC base.

64. Gen Alvan C. Gillem II, transcript of oral history interview by Lt Col Arthur W. McCants Jr. and Maj Scottie S. Thompson, 13–15 February 1979, 153, AFHRA.

65. Ibid.; Wade, interviewed by Ahmann, 398; Momyer, 182, 284; and Thomas A. Keaney, *Strategic Bombers and Conventional Weapons: Airpower Options* (Fort Lesley J. McNair, Washington, D.C.: National Defense University Press, 1984), 20.

66. Gillem, interviewed by McCants and Thompson, 165.

67. Dale R. Funk, "Study of the Use of B-52 Bombers in War in Vietnam," Air War College Report no. 3350 (Maxwell AFB, Ala., Air War College, May 1967), 11. Found in SAC OPPLAN 52–65.

68. Ibid., 4; Drew Drenkowski, "Operation Linebacker II," *Soldier of Fortune* 2, no. 3 (September 1977): 24; and Keaney, 22, 29. B-52 crews had a two-week course on conventional operations, then they went on a six-month rotation to Guam. They went "with only the barest introduction to conventional tactics" and used modified nuclear bombing procedures. They lacked institutional innovation.

69. Drenkowski, 15–20.

70. Schlight, 51.

71. Nazarro, interviewed by Puryear, 118.

72. Gillem, interviewed by McCants and Thompson, 140.

73. Gen Hunter Harris Jr., transcript of oral history interview by Arthur K. Marmor, 8 February 1967, 39; and Schlight, 54, 82. Many on the Air Staff advised against any more strikes for General Westmoreland in the South. They suspected he would demand too much costly airpower in the South and provide only meager efforts at bomb damage assessment. McConnell overruled their objections on grounds that the Air Force must "prevent Westmoreland from trying to fight the war solely with ground troops and helicopters."

74. Kenneth E. Wehrman, End of Tour Report, 26 March 1968–20 May 1969 (Maxwell AFB, Ala., 1969). Wehrman was SACADVON commander at MACV. See Keaney, 21. Keaney alleges the centralized control from SAC was a holdover from World War II and the SIOP and that in Vietnam it "became an impediment to close coordination of strikes."

75. Schlight, 82.

76. Wade, interviewed by Ahmann, 409.

77. Gillem, interviewed by McCants and Thompson, 157.

78. Nazarro, interviewed by Puryear, 133; Schlight, 149–50; Momyer, 101; Gordon M. Graham, End of Tour Report, August 1966–July 1967 (Maxwell AFB, Ala., 1967), 3; and Gilbert L. Meyers, End of Tour Report, April 1965–August 1966 (Maxwell AFB, Ala., 1967), 2.

79. Gillem, interviewed by McCants and Thompson, 165–66, 191. Gillem remarked that if he'd had to do it over again, he would have given control to Seventh Air Force (p. 152).

80. Ibid., 159.

81. Ibid., 142, 149. Innovation and tactical refinement came from various sources. Gillem and his older crews with World War II experience knew of the necessity to plan for diverts. Gillem also fought systemic stereotyping of tactics and timing; maintenance limitations and distance encouraged predictable operational tempos with strikes occurring every two hours and 20 minutes and with three sets of bombs falling two to three minutes apart. Captured Vietcong confessed to taking shelter every two hours and 20 minutes or so and knowing precisely when the coast would be clear. The opening of the closer U-Tapao Royal Thai Air Force Base in Thailand (April 1967) could reduce predictability, though its shorter sortie duration (4 hours) often rushed the aircrews. See also Funk, 40; Palmer, 37; Schlight, 256; and HQ PACAF, Directorate of Tactical Evaluation, Contemporary Historical Evaluation of Combat Operations (CHECO) Project Division, *Arc Light, June 1967–December 1968* (Maxwell AFB, Ala., August 1969), 10. See also Gen George S. Brown, transcript of oral history interview by Maj Richard B. Clement and Capt R. G. Swenston, at Corona Harvest, 19–20 October 1970, 41, AFHRA, Maxwell AFB, Ala.; and Contemporary Historical Evaluation of Combat Operations (CHECO) Project, 13. Seventh Air Force worked with SAC crews and field commanders (with support from SAC headquarters) to reduce response times and divert capability. They ultimately got divert capability down to 90 minutes. Generalist general Brown (Seventh Air Force commander, August 1968–August 1970) and fighter cohort general Holloway (SAC commander, July 1968–April 1972) both claimed to have a role in adjusting SAC's formations and tactics to enhance flexibility. See also Schlight, 135–36, 150, 163. The refinement of bombing accuracy required support of technologies and support systems. Such SAC derivative systems as beacon bombing and Combat Skyspot (ground radar directed deliveries) supplanted radar deliveries, providing an all-weather delivery system accurate from 1,500 to 700 feet.

82. CHECO, 8. Costs ran to $911 million each year.

83. Gen Bruce K. Holloway, interviewed by author, January 1992; and Tilford, 278–79. Tilford also cites SAC histories on problems with morale and hindered promotions because of TDY jostling which precluded officer effectiveness reports—annual reports at home station and critical for promotion—and retention problems. Gen Bruce K. Holloway, interviewed by author, 4 February 1993. Holloway claims promotion boards were understanding of the TDY commitment. See also Robert L. Chappelle, "Replacement Training Within SAC a Result of U.S. Involvement in Southeast Asia," Air War College Report (Maxwell AFB, Ala.: Air War College, 1971); and Gen Alvan C. Gillem II, interviewed by author, 4 February 1993. Gillem recalls only a few fighter pilots came to SAC and to tankers because they didn't want to be copilots in B-52s. More SAC pilots went to tactical air forces but usually in aircraft like the EB-66 or light forward air control (FAC) aircraft (fewer to fighters).

Chapter 7

The Vindication of Airpower and the Rise of the Fighter Community (1965–72)

Airmen came increasingly to believe that airpower, in its own right, could produce decisive results. The validity of such a view was suggested by results of the Allies' combined bomber offensive in Europe and by the surrender of Japan in the 1940s. Additional evidence came from the skies over Hanoi in December 1972. In a concentrated 11-day test, our air strategy persuaded a determined adversary with a remarkably elaborate air defense system that overt aggression could not be sustained in the presence of unrestricted U.S. airpower.

—Gen William W. Momyer, USAF, Retired

Officers who excel at the use of tactical weapons must show mental flexibility, inventiveness, and broad teamwork. Fighter pilot officers, therefore, tended to be more at home with complexity than their bomber brethren. By denying fighter officers an appropriate voice in positions of power, the Air Force found itself often backing rather simplistic defense policies that alienated the other services.

—Arthur T. Hadley
A Report from the Field

The insatiable demand for pilots in Vietnam provided the perfect opportunity for John McConnell to "reunite the Air Force."[1] The air service decided to spread the burden evenly. While SAC crews flew to Southeast Asia for up to six months at a time, the fighter pilots engaged in 100 missions over North Vietnam for one year.[2] The Air Force went to Vietnam for one year 10 times over; SAC for six months 20 times over. While that policy did little for institutional memory, it did facilitate exchange between SAC and TAC. Combat losses, retirement of the World War II and Korean pilot bulge, expansion of forces and sorties, explosive requirement for forward air controllers, and short tour lengths contributed to a demand for pilots that far exceeded supply. The Air Force cut tour lengths in Europe and TAC, replaced pilots with navigators in the rear cockpits of two-seat fighters, and shortened training to meet the demands.[3] As a result, many in SAC found it possible to join the tactical air forces during the war.

SAC pilots who entered fighter units had to break into a tough, insular culture that, as Thomas Wolfe observed, followed "a rigid set of beliefs I called the 'code of the right stuff,'" where "everyone, friend or foe, was judged by four standards: courage, skill, coolness, and eagerness for combat."[4] Many such pilots found it difficult to make the transition to the aggressive, individualistic ethos that valued flying skills in a more dynamic arena than they had been used to as the first measure of acceptance. Most of them suffered from minimal transitional training; a few did extremely well, but many did not fare as well and remained somewhat alienated within the fighter community.

What some lower echelon fighter commanders perceived as oversupervision and control, lack of empathy, flexibility, or understanding of "tactical airpower [which had been] subordinated to the prejudices[5] of the SAC pilots and the bomber generals" exacerbated the clash of cultures. Many of the higher echelon fighter commanders in Vietnam voiced similar concerns, especially with oversupervision and massive reporting requirements.[6] Fighter culture favored decentralization and delegation. As the war dragged on, bomber cohort PACAF commanders eventually loosened their grip.

Until December 1972 the fighter culture had conducted most of the dangerous bombing in North Vietnam.[7] Though SAC performed well in the relatively benign environment of Arc Light, it was understandably reluctant to risk its great bombers against the SAM and MiG threat up North. From April 1966 on, the B-52s occasionally ventured into the North, and even had SAMs fired at them as early as September 1967. These strikes always received top priority for protection by the tactical forces of the Seventh Air Force.[8] But SAC followed a "no sweat" procedure that, if there were any active enemy SAMs or MiGs in the area, the B-52s generally aborted their mission. Battle-hardened fighter crews, who ironically conducted most of the strategic bombing, noted this timidity.

If the Vietnam War split SAC between nuclear and conventional commitments, it rejuvenated the tactical air forces. Budget preeminence shifted to tactical (general purpose) forces by 1966. The fighter force doubled in size by FY 1965.[9] Flexible Response, and especially the Vietnam War, fostered the growth of tactical wings and the reduction of SAC wings (fig. 19).

The force structure shift manifested itself in the number of fighters and especially the shrinking number of bombers available to fly (fig. 20).

The types of cockpits available signaled a shift in the flying population (fig. 21).

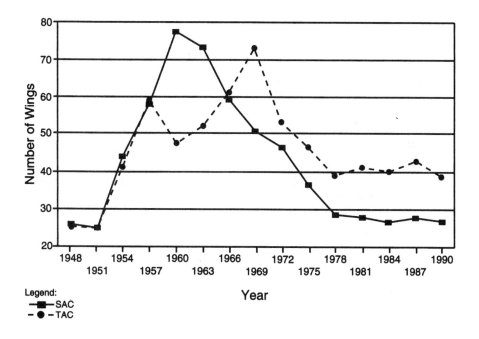

Source: Headquarters USAF, *U.S. Air Force Statistical Digest, FY 1948–1990.* On file at Air Force Office of History, Bolling AFB, Washington, D.C.

Figure 19. Number and Distribution of Air Force Wings (both airlift and overseas wings)

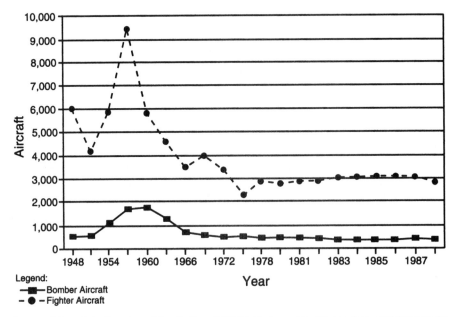

Source: Office of the Secretary of the Air Force/FMBMP, Pentagon, Washington, D.C.; and Strategic Air Command Histories, 1948–1990.

Figure 20. Bomber versus Fighter Aircraft Total Active Inventory

More fighters meant more fighter pilots who manned more fighter wings and provided additional opportunities for leadership and command. The fighter community gained increased combat experience and exposure and tapped into the traditional frontline Air Force mission of strategic bombing. By 1969 the ratio of Tactical Air Force (TAF) generals to SAC generals had increased from 1.3 to 1 in 1963 to 2 to 1.[10]

When fighter general Gabriel Disosway returned from Europe to command TAC in August 1965, he faced two problems. First, he had to gain intraservice bureaucratic leverage to offset the dominance of the "monolithic, solid, and global" commands—SAC and MAC. Disosway conceived of "12-Star" letters. He would meet with PACAF and USAFE (theater) commanders to discuss needs and proposals. He would subsequently initiate proposals under the combined signatures of the three four-star generals. As one general on the Air Staff recalled: "It was effective and unprecedented. We

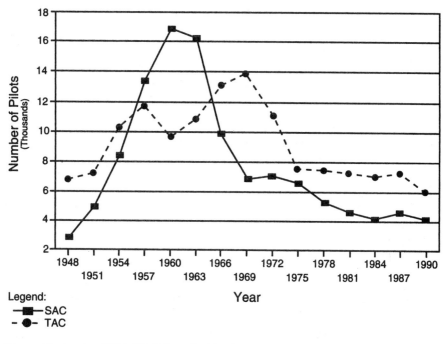

Legend:
—■—SAC
- ●- TAC

Year

Source: Headquarters USAF, *U.S. Air Force Statistical Digest, FY 1948–1990.*

Figure 21. Number and Distribution of Pilots (1948–90)

[TAC] never got anything before that."[11] Second, Disosway sought to build and support a force to fight the air war in Vietnam. The new TAC commander reinvigorated his staff with fighter pilots and worked closely with fighter major general William W. Momyer at Air Training Command and fighter general James Ferguson, who took over at Systems Command in 1966.[12] For the remainder of the war, TAC worked closely with the Seventh Air Force to meet the tactical and technical needs of the air war. TAC also worked closely with Systems Command to develop cluster-bomb munitions (CBU), precision-guided munitions (PGM), radar warning systems, fixed-wing gunships, F-4E Gatling guns, electronic warfare aircraft, forward air control aircraft, and long-range aid to navigation (LORAN) systems.[13] To improve tactical prowess, TAC sent selected pilots through a resurgent fighter weapons school at Nellis AFB, Nevada.[14]

Upon assuming command from Sweeney at TAC, Disosway immediately did as he had in USAFE and removed SAC's centralized system of maintenance, as well as its management control system in his new command.[15] Disosway saw SAC as too systemized and centralized. He wanted to decentralize planning and execution and push authority downward. On the one hand, Disosway agreed with his mentor, General Everest, who observed that SAC needed centralization given the demands of the SIOP, with the penalty that "SAC crews have major decisions made for them in Omaha." On the other hand, he noted, "TAC crews must make major decisions every time they fly. . . . TAC can afford to delegate."[16] TAC's decentralized solution helped to alleviate the significant saturation at depots and continual delays of centralized maintenance, supply, and reporting during the rapid 1966 buildup in Vietnam. Officially endorsed "maximum base self-sufficiency" programs led to greater capability and responsibility for the fighter wings blossoming in Southeast Asia. They also broadened the skills of fighter pilots who were often required—many for the first time—to get involved in administrative and additional duties around the base.[17]

This broadening and delegation was inculcated also in the flying experience. As in previous wars, fighter pilots flew close-air-support missions in direct contact and coordination with the US and allied armies. Fighter pilots who served as ground and airborne forward air controllers lived and worked daily with ground forces. They continued to fly their traditional array of missions and added search and rescue, defense suppression, and strategic bombing. They flew far more missions than the bomber cohort and more missions over North Vietnam (fig. 22).

This greater variety and quantity of combat experience provided fighter pilots with a significant advantage over the bomber cohort in competing for future leadership positions in a military that prized combat and command experience. The fighter culture also took pride in rewarding innovation and delegating flight leadership and other responsibilities to those worthy recipients, regardless of rank and age. This trend nurtured the accomplished pilots; that is, those who had

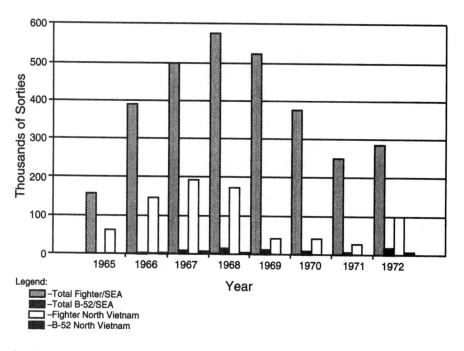

Legend:
▨ –Total Fighter/SEA
■ –Total B-52/SEA
▢ –Fighter North Vietnam
■ –B-52 North Vietnam

Source: Thomas C. Thayer, *War Without Fronts: The American Experience in Vietnam* (Boulder, Colo.: Westview Press, 1985), 80, 82, and 84.

Figure 22. Combat Sortie Comparison of B-52 versus Fighter/RECCE

received experience in leadership and responsibility at an earlier age than most bomber pilots.

Greater involvement offered more opportunities for fighter leaders to conceive and direct innovative tactics in a war that demanded creativity. Seventh Air Force commander, General Momyer, and his staff played key roles in directing and coordinating American and allied soldiers, marines, sailors, and airmen who participated in Operations Neutralize and Niagara.[18] Junior fighter leaders also had increasing opportunities over time to innovate under the Seventh Air Force.[19] The result provided a growing community of fighter pilots with a broader and more creative experience base than their SAC peers.

Technology also played a strong role in shifting power from the bomber to the fighter communities. Air refueling gave fighters the range; technology gave them the payload, accuracy, and survivability to deliver more weapons, and to deliver them farther, more precisely, and with greater flexibility than before.[20] The atomic bomb had created the ascendancy of strategic bombers; now, precision-guided munitions offered preeminence to the fighters. Previously constrained to lesser missions, fighters with air refueling and PGM were gaining access to the "decisive" and sacred mission of strategic bombing.

Requests from Southeast Asia and the 12-Star letters began to make serious inroads into the Air Force research and development budget, which was previously dominated by SAC programs. Formal proposals came forward for an all-purpose and later all-weather aircraft (TFX) beginning in 1961, an air-superiority fighter (FX) in February 1966, a close-air-support aircraft (AX) in September 1966, and an airborne lookdown radar system in 1967. With the exception of the TFX (F-111), which saw service in Vietnam, these aircraft would evolve eventually into fielded weapons systems after the war.[21] McConnell despaired over the costs of the Vietnam War: "We have fought the war to a considerable extent at the expense of modernization." He reached the "sobering conclusion" that he was leaving the Air Force with the same budget in FY 1970 that he had in FY 1964 but with "less airpower than when I became Chief of Staff 4½ years ago."[22] Only the tactical air forces relatively inexpensive future weapons systems received funding (fig. 23).

Technological zeal, astronomical costs, and ICBM capability undermined SAC's ability to procure a future strategic bomber—a factor which a former SAC commander believed "started SAC's downfall."[23] Fiscal realities grounded romantic hopes for high-performance capabilities. The absolutists pushed technology (primarily with overly ambitious performance specifications) to achieve the elusive doctrinal *decisiveness* which always seemed to be just around the corner. McConnell agreed with Secretary of the Air Force Harold Brown (and Defense Secretary McNamara) that the B-70 had "pushed the state of the art" too far for an affordable capability whose survivability at high altitude against SAMs was problematic.[24] LeMay's effort at a low-altitude replacement called the "advanced manned precision strike

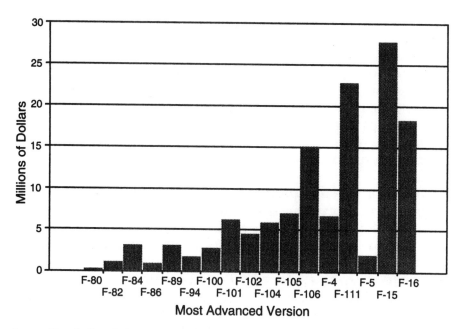

Source: Marcelle Knaack, *Encyclopedia of USAF Aircraft and Missile Systems*, vol. 1, *Post-World War II Fighters* (Washington, D.C.: Office of Air Force History, 1978).

Figure 23. Major Fighter Flyaway Costs in 1994 Dollars

system" (AMPSS) and later the "advanced manned strategic aircraft" (AMSA) was not precise, nonnuclear-capable (originally), or affordable.[25] At the end of 1964, DOD decided to phase out manned bombers completely by 1970.[26] A retiring LeMay admonished his Washington staff to continue to fight for a new strategic bomber. He reminded them that "it takes a long time here to get things done; however, water wears away the stone."[27]

McConnell held a determined commitment to AMSA and saw its indefinite delay as his primary failing.[28] Faced with the inevitable retirement of aging B-52s with no prospect of funding AMSA, McConnell accepted DOD's proposal, in the ultimate irony, that F-111 fighters, upgraded as FB-111s, replace the fragile B-52C/Fs. The Nixon administration reduced to 76 FB-111s the chief's April 1965 proposal for 210 FB-111s to replace 345 B-52s.[29] By the end of the war, the gold-plated AMSA (now B-1) program had little production support. According to the new secretary of the Air Force, John M. McLucas, the program provided an "insurance in case there might be a need, so we wanted to pay as small a premium for that insurance as we could."[30] Sophisticated Air Force strategic bombers had priced themselves out of the market, especially during a war where sparse research and development funds focused more on immediate concerns of munitions and avionics development and while larger production funds kept current lines open with adequate spare parts.

The Nixon era accepted a reduction in American goals and expectations. Accepting the parity of Soviet strategic systems, Nixon endorsed "strategic sufficiency," brought American policy more in line with capabilities, and attempted to reestablish credibility with a policy of "realistic deterrence." At the same time, he exploited the rift between the Soviet Union and Red China to regain some diplomatic initiative. The new president also opened arms limitation negotiations with the Soviets. Assured by an onset of détente, Nixon reduced the Kennedy administration's two-and-a-half war capability to a one-and-a-half capability, with the United States meeting its treaty obligations and showing a willingness to fight for "vital interests." In what came to be known as the Nixon Doctrine, Americans would contribute air and sea power but expected affected allies to provide the bulk of the land forces.[31]

If Nixon were to fulfill his campaign promise to pull US forces from Vietnam with honor, he first had to patch up civil-military relations. Nixon began to get rid of McNamara's hold-over "whiz kids," and his secretary of defense, Melvin R. Laird, worked to regain the confidence of the military. Laird instructed his uniformed leadership: "Live within your budgets, support me on Vietnam [withdrawal], and you can do what you want with your money."[32] Withdrawal from Vietnam would proceed under the protective umbrella of airpower.

Six months after Nixon took office, a frustrated McConnell passed his mantle of responsibility on to his choice as successor, junior generation bomber general John D. Ryan, a SAC general who had recently been broadened in PACAF. Ryan also personified the SAC mold—a terse, no-nonsense, aggressive field commander who eschewed the social and political atmosphere of Washington. For that matter, this ardent proponent of strategic airpower had "little use for the art of compromise" and disliked the diplomacy inherent in joint, allied, and congressional obligations. But the new chief was blunt and always honest and generally respected the tactical competency of his field commanders—though he despaired that Vietnam was "ruining SAC." Ryan stood anxious to end the war.[33]

Ryan recognized the value of his "broadening" experience and expanded the program begun by McConnell. He kept the PACAF commander position occupied by the bomber cohort but sent the most promising generals to the Seventh Air Force to get combat leadership experience. Furthermore, he pushed career-broadening assignments down to talented younger generals. The result illuminated a growing number of Korean War generation "generalists," whose extensive experience fostered understanding and skills more conducive to effective high command in the coming era.[34] Still, Ryan's junior World War II generation would have to extricate US forces from Vietnam "with honor." As US airpower prevented enemy forces from massing in significant numbers to ruin the "Vietnamization" process within South Vietnam, intelligence sources warned of a massive enemy buildup in sanctuaries adjacent to South Vietnam. Nixon responded with a redeployment of US air and naval forces to Southeast Asia. On 30 March 1972 the North Vietnamese launched a massive conventional invasion of South Vietnam. Nixon's recent diplomacy with the Soviets and Chinese gave him confidence that he could respond forcefully to the invasion. The allies responded with large doses of airpower and began to double their air strength. By early May, Nixon decided that the air campaign should be expanded to provide North Vietnam with "a warning that things might get out of hand if the offensive did not stop."[35] The president drafted orders for Linebacker I and directed the air forces to conduct an extensive air campaign against the enemy's transportation and supply system.[36] Determined to "stop at nothing to bring the enemy to his knees," Nixon removed many of Washington's constraints on airpower to provide the military with its long-sought latitude to employ its doctrine "properly."[37]

For the Air Force the burden of planning and conducting Linebacker I fell upon the Seventh Air Force and its newly arrived commander, fighter general John W. Vogt. This former combat fighter squadron commander and ace from World War II had an unusually broad career. He graduated from Yale and later received a master's degree in international affairs at Columbia. He topped his academic education off as a fellow at the Harvard School of International Affairs. Additionally, he had extensive experience on the Joint Staff, the staff of the secretary of defense, the Air Staff, and the PACAF staff. Having halted the initial enemy onslaught with airpower, Vogt now was given the "responsibility to pick the targets and run the campaign." This responsibility included permission to mine Haiphong Harbor, cut rail links from China, and conduct a massive air campaign against a vast JCS list of validated targets.[38]

Given a more favorable political and technological climate, Vogt and his staff performed their mission with extraordinary skill. They waged the air campaign systematically and with a flexibility of execution that shifted to avoid bad weather and unnecessary exposure to threats. The Seventh Air Force also provided air cover, electronic warfare and air rescue assets, and anti-SAM forces to support its noticeably younger aircrews.[39] Vogt took advantage of new technologies to increase effectiveness. Against critical targets he used recently upgraded F-4s and their precise navigational and bombing system known as LORAN.[40] The Seventh Air Force employed tactical reconnaissance aircraft and remotely piloted vehicles extensively to assess the damage and status of enemy defenses and targets. In September F-111s returned to Southeast Asia to provide an all-weather, day-or-night, low-altitude capability. Vogt's staff also developed an effective early warning system known as "Teaball," which warned aircraft of enemy threats. By August it contributed significantly to improving the Air Force kill ratio from less than one to one, to four to one. The Seventh Air Force also employed "hunter-killer" teams of F-4 and F-105 "wild weasel" aircraft to find and destroy enemy radars. Vogt's staff disseminated relevant lessons from flight debriefings throughout the command to facilitate the learning rate of his young pilots. But his most important weapon was the PGM that gave Air Force fighters a lethality and "an estimated 100-fold increase in accuracy and effectiveness."[41] Vogt waged his intensive air campaign in coordination with the Navy and SAC.

While Vogt preferred to have control of the B-52s, he had to receive targeting authority for B-52 strikes from the commander of Pacific Command or the JCS. SAC retained exclusive control over the timing and weight of the B-52 strikes. SAC also used such strategic reconnaissance aircraft as the SR-71 independently to contribute to the targeting process from afar, sometimes without consultation with the Seventh Air Force.[42] B-52 strikes always received top priority for protection by the tactical forces of the Seventh Air Force. B-52s flew many successful sorties against North Vietnam, but the pilots aborted too many missions under the no-sweat policy. Consequently, SAC reversed the concept of operations in the second week of November 1972 to "press on" missions, actions many in the Seventh Air Force considered overdue.[43] In late October the Guam crews began to experiment with more complex multiformation attacks to put more ordnance on targets. This plan complicated supporting aircraft requirements. When SAC pilots failed to inform tactical escort aircraft of timing, routing, or target changes, they received less-than-adequate support.

B-52s were also vulnerable to SAMs fired in a "track-on-jam" mode, a mode in which the missile was guided to the source of airborne jamming. The pilots could defeat SAMs launched in this mode by maintaining good formation to enhance intraflight complementary jamming that, coupled with jamming from escorting EB-66 aircraft, increased SAM miss distances. Unfortunately, on 22 November a "press on" B-52 was lost to a "track-on-jam" SAM and crashed near the Thai border. High winds had blown the protective chaff corridor sown by escorting fighter aircraft from the path of the hapless B-52. The coming months would provide this kind of problem with greater consequences.[44]

All in all, Linebacker I helped to persuade North Vietnam to abandon its goal of an immediate military takeover of the South and contributed to concessions at the negotiation table.

Reports indicated logistics flow had been reduced by 80 percent and significant damage had been done to most military targets in the North.[45] Vogt's liberal interdiction campaign worked because of Nixon's diplomatic isolation of the enemy, relatively good weather, severance of the port at Haiphong and the two rail links to China, and the vulnerability of a conventional army exposed to airpower while consuming supplies far faster than they could be replenished. Unshackled from previous restrictions, Vogt used the new precision of his fighter force as the key weapon in a broad interdiction campaign that destroyed many strategic targets while keeping civilian casualties to a minimum. It marked the beginning of a new era.

Linebacker I ground to a halt in anticipation of a peace accord. However, in December the North Vietnamese reneged on their October agreements. The bombing pause allowed the North to rebuild and rearm; they brought in more than 2,300 SAMs to the Red River valley alone.[46] Anticipating further constraints on his Vietnam policy from the next month's new Congress, Nixon seized a fleeting opportunity to act and asserted to his confidants:

> [The enemy] has now gone over the brink and so have we. We have the power to destroy his war-making capability. The only question is whether we have the will to use that power. What distinguishes me from Johnson is that I have the will in spades.[47]

Finally, Nixon gave the absolutists their chance. He warned the chairman of the JCS, Adm Thomas M. Moorer, "This is your chance to use military power effectively to win this war, and if you don't I'll consider you personally responsible."[48] Moorer, in turn, told the commander of SAC, fighter general John C. Meyer, that he wanted the people of Hanoi to hear the bombs around the clock, but he cautioned Meyer to minimize damage to the civilian populace and third world shipping.[49]

Finally, the B-52s had been summoned to conduct a strategic bombing campaign against the war-making capacity and will of the North Vietnamese. Using B-52s extensively demonstrated Nixon's resolve, and massive bombers offered an all-weather capability and huge cargo of bombs that would intensify the air war to an unprecedented level. Though SAC had been planning sporadically to do so since 1965, it intensified preparations in August 1972 for a large B-52 offensive against the North. Eighth Air Force pored over the expansive target list and submitted its proposal. On 15 December SAC received official notification to plan and execute, for three days minimum, a strategic bombing campaign using all available assets (more than 50 percent of SAC's B-52s were in theater) to commence on the eighteenth. The object was "maximum destruction of selected military targets in the vicinity of Hanoi/Haiphong."[50]

The field commander assigned to execute this campaign was Eighth Air Force commander, fighter cohort lieutenant general Gerald W. Johnson. Johnson "blew his cork" when he saw how little resemblance SAC's detailed Linebacker II execute order bore to what he had submitted. The field commander was particularly upset about the repetitive routing that his staff calculated would result in losses considerably higher than SAC's 3 percent prediction. One Eighth Air Force staff officer recalled: "When I saw the map [showing the routing], I realized two things: that the weight of effort would be very large, and that it was not going to be a turkey shoot—unless you were on the ground up there."[51] SAC headquarters selected targets, determined weight of effort, and prescribed all routing north of the 20th parallel. The heavily staffed SAC headquarters had war-gamed similar operations and probably felt the Eighth Air Force staff had their hands full coordinating with the tankers and fighters and determining routing to and from the base.[52] Vogt and the Navy were reportedly "furious that the B-52s had taken over the primary role and that SAC was selecting its own targets."[53] Theater familiarity and experience gave way to the "experts" in strategic bombing.[54]

Vogt had a legitimate concern over the feasibility of an operation planned from a headquarters 10 time zones away. It put SAC's global command and control system to the test. First, SAC had to receive targeting approval from the JCS. Second, SAC's target area planning had to be accomplished and the operations order written, approved, and disseminated. Once Eighth Air Force staffers received this order, they had to plan the en route portion and coordinate it with tankers and fighters thousands of miles away. Upon completion of this coordination, the Eighth Air Force fashioned a finished product for distribution to its crews (some of whom flew out of distant Thailand). The aircraft commanders then needed sufficient time to brief their cells and aircrews before proceeding to their aircraft. Time from takeoff at Guam to target varied from six to seven hours. Considering the above, SAC calculated that its plan needed to be completed 42 hours prior to the first takeoff. Inevitably, crews received last-minute changes on every mission and on some occasions waited at the end of the runway with engines running for their mission packets.[55]

This time factor played heavily into the rigidity of the early campaign. SAC commander Meyer expressed concern about the inexperience of his crews, the dangers of mid-air collisions, the SAM threat, and the need for utmost accuracy. Consequently, SAC advanced a simple plan. The B-52s would fly at night in three bomber streams of approximately 48 bombers spaced four to five hours apart.[56] They would fly in cells of three, with the following cell from three to 10 minutes behind along the same route. Aircrews were instructed to maintain good formation for ECM integrity and to beware of mid-air collisions. They were to take no evasive maneuvers and to maintain steady course and altitude approximately four minutes prior to bomb release to ensure accuracy.

The first night, 18 December, three B-52s were lost and two more suffered damage. Meyer was concerned, but he considered the losses acceptable. Besides, the second night's crews had begun to start their engines as the first night's last aircraft were landing at Guam.[57] The 42-hour planning cycle would preclude significant changes for night two. Concerned that initial losses came from a breakdown in ECM (jamming) cross-coverage, 43d Strategic Wing commander James R. McCarthy warned his crews that they faced court-martial if they "knowingly disrupted cell integrity to evade SAMs."[58] McCarthy accompanied the second night's raid as the "airborne mission commander." After releasing bombs, the aircraft commander of McCarthy's B-52 put the bomber into a steep turn, "and a second later, a SAM exploded where the right wing had been."[59] McCarthy rescinded his earlier threat and advised waves two and three that he authorized SAM evasive measures as long as "they maintained cell formation and were straight and level prior to bomb release."[60]

Faced again with the time compression factor at Offutt AFB and just receiving word that night that two produced no losses, Meyer disregarded the growing concerns of some of the crews concerning the dangers of continuing stereotyped tactics. Night three's routing, altitudes, and times mirrored those of nights one and two.[61] When the enemy downed three B-52s in the first wave, Vogt's anti-SAM wild weasel pilots radioed General Vogt to divert the following waves. SAC had not planned for any alternate targets. Vogt pleaded with his friend Johnson on the phone from Saigon to Guam. Johnson recommended that the more vulnerable B-52Gs (those with unmodified ECM devices) in the second wave should return to Guam, but he informed Vogt that SAC had to make the decision. Concerned about implications of a mission cancellation—an American bomber attack had never been turned back by enemy action—Meyer consulted with his staff, Ryan, and JCS. SAC's reputation was at stake; Ryan, Meyer, and the SAC staff agreed that waves two and three must "press on." As they relayed the decision, Johnson already had canceled the vulnerable B-52Gs in wave two, but two B-52Gs and one B-52D were lost in wave three, and another B-52D suffered serious damage.[62]

It was SAC's darkest hour. Nixon was furious and "raised holy hell about the fact that they [B-52s] kept going over the same targets at the same times."[63] Adm Noel Gayler, the new commander of Pacific Command (CINCPAC), insisted that SAC share targeting responsibility with Pacific Command (PACOM).[64] Meyer, who knew on the second night that Nixon wanted the campaign to continue beyond three days, revamped Linebacker after the unacceptable losses on the night of the twentieth. He sent only 30 B-52Ds, mostly out of U-Tapao Air Base, Thailand, each night with double the fighter protection, compressed time over target, and varied routing and altitudes; Meyer abandoned the psychological strategy of bombing Hanoi all night. After losing two more B-52s on the fourth night, he prohibited attacks in the Hanoi area. Concerned with SAM effectiveness, Meyer began to target SAM sites and storage areas. The campaign was falling away from its stated objectives. Nevertheless, he lost no B-52s between 22 and 24 December.

Nixon ordered a 36-hour bombing halt for Christmas and hoped the North Vietnamese would return to negotiate. Instead, they rearmed, and the president ordered a massive raid against Hanoi and Haiphong for the twenty-sixth. Over the Christmas break, Meyer, at Johnson's suggestion, delegated planning responsibility to the Eighth Air Force.[65] After the Christmas recess, Admiral Gayler "took sole responsibility for air operations over North Vietnam, and SAC, the Seventh Air Force, and Task Force 77 (Navy) nominated targets for CINCPAC approval."[66] These actions mitigated the problems of conducting a campaign from SAC headquarters on the other side of the globe at a time when communication technologies and unity of command proved inadequate to implement a truly global doctrine.

The Eighth Air Force planned the 26 December raid as its most ambitious and complex one to date. Johnson's staff was glad to dictate its own prospects for survival: The staff had 120 B-52s strike 10 different targets in 15 minutes. Four waves of bombers struck Hanoi from four different directions, and two waves struck Haiphong from two different directions. The staff carefully choreographed flight paths and turns to provide maximum mutual support and to confuse the enemy. General Johnson expressed more confidence in his crews and delegated intracell and intercell tactics to the wings. Decentralized planning and the recess ensured operations orders in the hands of all supporting units on time. The attack proved extremely successful; only two B-52s were lost—both members of two-ship cells with weakened ECM coverage.[67]

The next morning Hanoi notified Nixon it wanted to talk. The president continued the bombings for three more nights at a lower level until the communists agreed to all his negotiating conditions. Sixty bombers flew each of the last three nights, and by the twenty-eighth they met only feeble resistance. One crewman recollected, "By the tenth day [28 December] there were no missiles, there were no MiGs, there was no AAA [antiaircraft artillery]—there was no threat. It was easy pickings."[68] As the aircrews prepared for what they thought would be the knockout blows, Nixon notified General Johnson to halt the bombings.

The intensity and persistence of Linebacker II shocked the North Vietnamese and dislocated their population. Threats to continue convinced them to sign a peace accord that closely resembled the October agreements they had abandoned. Henry A. Kissinger and Nixon both felt the effort was successful in bringing about the "honorable" extraction of the United States from the conflict.[69] Little attention focused on the fighters who had assaulted North Vietnam day and night, had supported the B-52 strikes at night, and had taken out the most difficult targets with LORAN or with PGM during the brief periods of workable weather. For example, on one occasion SAC had difficulty getting JCS approval to hit a critical SAM missile assembly area because of the likelihood of unacceptable damage to the civilian populace. Vogt, however, got approval to bomb the target with LORAN-equipped F-4s. The next day, 16 F-4 fighter-bombers flew in close formation at high altitude despite the firing of 48 SAMs, and bombed the target accurately through the clouds.[70] F-4s also destroyed such previously untouchable targets as the Hanoi AM transmitter and the Hanoi thermal power plant with laser-guided bombs and kept the rail lines to China closed.[71]

Instead, most attention highlighted the intensive B-52 raids in the battle of wills that characterized the tradition of strategic bombing. SAC wavered after the disaster of the third night, but it recovered by adjusting tactics and decentralizing planning and execution of the operation. The perceived success of the relentless bomber offensive managed by airmen revived the beliefs of the absolutists in the decisiveness of strategic bombing. Sen. Barry Goldwater claimed on the Senate floor in February 1973:

> Let us hope that the strategic bombing lesson of the 12 days in December does not escape us as we plan for the future. Airpower, specifically strategic airpower, can be decisive when applied against strategic targets—industrial and military—in the heartland of the enemy regardless of the size of the nation.[72]

Admirals Sharp and Moorer, SAC Generals Meyer and Johnson, fighter generals Momyer and Vogt all smiled on the efficacy of airpower. The more avid absolutists claimed strategic bombing could have won the war in 1965.[73] It became a firmly held conviction that vindicated their World War II experience and the validity of their doctrine. It served an institutional consolation particularly appealing in the aftermath of a bitter and divisive war. Hardly anyone realized the real lesson for the future of strategic bombing had been exhibited by the fighter-bombers. They had demonstrated greater versatility, survivability, and the ability finally to achieve that long-elusive "precision" strategic bombing—a capability particularly relevant to limited war.[74]

Notes

1. Gen Joseph J. Nazarro, transcript of oral history interview by Dr. Edgar F. Puryear Jr., 4 May 1979, Air Force Historical Research Agency (hereafter cited as AFHRA), Maxwell AFB, Alabama, 121; and Gen Horace M. Wade, transcript of oral history interview by Hugh N. Ahmann, 10–12 October 1978, AFHRA, 429.

2. Fighter pilots did receive campaign ribbons, remote tour credit, and favorable (combat) officer effectiveness reports.

3. John Schlight, *The War in South Vietnam—The Years of the Offensive, 1965–1968* (Washington, D. C.: Office of Air Force History [OAFH], 1988), 163; Gen John Shaud, transcript of oral history interview by author, 23 April 1992. Shaud recalled that many of SAC's finest young officers left SAC at this time and did not return.

4. Jack Broughton, *Going Downtown: The War Against Hanoi and Washington* (New York: Orion Books, 1988), x. Thomas Wolfe wrote Broughton's preface. Wolfe captures the essence of the "right stuff" in his classic *The Right Stuff* (New York: Farrar, Straus, Giroux, 1979).

5. Broughton, 141; Jack Broughton, *Thud Ridge* (New York: Bantam Books, 1969), 143; and Robert F. Dorr, *Air War Hanoi* (London: Blandford Press, 1988), 72.

6. Broughton, *Going Downtown*, 96,104–5, 194, 233–38, 265, 280; Broughton, *Thud Ridge*, xv, 18, 95; and Frederick C. Blesse, *Check Six: A Fighter Pilot Looks Back* (New York: Ivy Books, 1987), 192–93; Dorr, 53; Lt Gen Alvan C. Gillem II, transcript of oral history interview by Arthur W. McCants Jr. and Scottie Thompson, 13–15 February 1979.

7. Robert Frank Futrell, *Ideas, Concepts, Doctrine: Basic Thinking in the United States Air Force, 1961–1984*, vol. 2 (Maxwell AFB, Ala.: Air University Press, 1989), 288. The tactical air force also had its teething problems. Air-to-air combat skills had atrophied. Early bombing raids in Rolling Thunder were noticeably inaccurate, and it took a while for pilots to reduce their average accuracy from 750 feet to 365 feet. Additionally, fighter pilots began the war using such outdated tactics as level high-altitude bombing.

8. William W. Momyer, *Airpower in Three Wars: WW II, Korea, Vietnam* (Washington, D.C.: Government Printing Office [GPO], 1978), 283.

9. Futrell, 46, 121

10. Headquarters USAF, *U.S. Air Force Statistical Digest FY 1957–1978* (Washington, D.C.: Directorate of Data Systems and Statistics, Comptroller of the Air Force, Headquarters USAF), on file at OAFH, Bolling AFB, Washington, D.C.

11. Lt Gen Albert P. Clarke, transcript of oral history interview by Jacob Neufeld, 2 May 1973, AFHRA, 6.

12. Gen Theodore R. Milton, transcript of oral history interview by author, 15 June 1992.

13. Ibid., 7; Futrell, 288–92; Donald J. Mrozek, *Airpower and the Ground War in Vietnam: Ideas and Actions* (Maxwell AFB, Ala.: Air University Press, 1988), 123–26. Mrozek points out how LeMay and Sweeney were reluctant to endorse the gunship conceived by two young fighter pilots; McConnell approved it only for counterinsurgency. Schlight, 90, 230–34; Carl Berger, ed., *The United States Air Force in Southeast Asia, 1961–1973: An Illustrated Account* (Washington, D.C.: OAFH, 1984), 47, 75, 118; Dorr, 107; and Blesse, 148–52.

14. Futrell, 295.

15. Gen Gabriel Disosway, transcript of oral history interview by Dr. Edgar F. Puryear Jr., 17 January 1979, AFHRA, 6, 11.

16. Gen Frank F. Everest, transcript of oral history interview by Dr. Edgar F. Puryear Jr., 16 July 1979, AFHRA, 5.

17. Schlight, 168, 181. Schlight rightfully notes that these duties did little to enhance the combat flying skills of pilots.

18. Berger, 51, 156; Momyer, 303–5; Bernard C. Nalty, *Air Power and the Fight for Khe Sanh* (Washington, D. C.: OAFH, 1986); and Mrozek, 79. Operation Neutralize combined allied air forces to bomb North Vietnamese troops and artillery positions along the demilitarized zone in late 1967. Operation Niagara combined the effort to provide air support for the siege at Khe Sanh.

19. Berger, 81–82. Fighter wing commander Col Robin Olds conceived and led Operation Bolo to surprise enemy MiGs; Maj Gen Otis C. Moore, transcript of oral history interview by Dr. Edgar F. Puryear Jr., 1 July 1979, AFHRA, 15. Fighter brigadier general James R. Allen planned the Son Tay raid to free US prisoners of war in North Vietnam.

20. Vietnam's jet fighters could exceed most World War II bombers in all these features.

21. Futrell, 470–80.

22. Ibid., 478; Gen John P. McConnell, transcript of oral history interview by Dorothy Pierce McSweeny, 28 August 1969, AFHRA, 31.

23. Gen Bruce K. Holloway, transcript of oral history interview by Lt Col Vaughn H. Gallacher, 16–18 August 1977, AFHRA, 352.

24. Futrell, 391.

25. Ibid., 394. The Air Force reluctantly pursued a nonnuclear capability in late 1966 after insistence of Secretary of the Air Force Harold Brown. Nick Kotz, *Wild Blue Yonder: Money, Politics, and the B-1 Bomber* (New York: Pantheon Books, 1988), 73, 79–80.

26. Futrell, 124.

27. Kotz, 84.

28. McConnell, interviewed by McSweeny.

29. Futrell, 393–96; Kotz, 85.

30. Futrell, 397; Kotz, 112–17. A 1973 General Accounting Office (GAO) report showed cost overruns and performance reductions. It encouraged mounting congressional criticism. The Air Force clung to the speed requirement and the "disastrous escape capsule." Fighter cohort general Larry D. Welch recalled that the fight to "beat down the B-1 design requirements into something more buildable, affordable, and practical" was very difficult.

31. Futrell, 264, 477–78; Russell Frank Weigley, *The American Way of War: A History of the United States Military Strategy and Policy* (New York: Macmillan, 1973), 469.

32. Kotz, 95.

33. Gen Theodore R. Milton, transcript of oral history interview by Dr. Edgar F. Puryear Jr., 9 April 1976, AFHRA, 9, 11; Moore, interviewed by Puryear, 15; Gen William W. Momyer, transcript of oral history interview by Dr. Edgar F. Puryear Jr., 7 September 1981, AFHRA, 7–8; Gen Bruce K. Holloway, transcript of oral history interview by Dr. Edgar F. Puryear Jr., 7 July 1978, AFHRA, 22; Gen Russell E. Dougherty, transcript of oral history interview by Dr. Edgar F. Puryear Jr., 27 March 1979, AFHRA, 6–19; Gen George S. Brown, transcript of oral history interview by Dr. Edgar F. Puryear Jr., 14 September 1977, AFHRA, 13; and Bruce Palmer Jr., *The 25-Year War: America's Military Role in Vietnam* (Lexington, Ky.: University Press of Kentucky, 1984), 92.

34. Two of these generalists were former bomber pilots George S. Brown and David C. Jones, who each had commanded fighter wings before being assigned to the Seventh Air Force. They both would become chiefs of staff of the Air Force and subsequently chairmen of the Joint Chiefs of Staff.

35. Henry A. Kissinger, *The White House Years* (Boston: Little, Brown and Company, 1979), 1118.

36. See Headquarters PACAF, Directorate of Tactical Evaluation, CHECO Division, *USAF Air Operations Against North Vietnam, 1 July 1971–30 June 1972*, 3, at Maxwell AFB, Ala., for verbatim JCS directive.

37. Richard M. Nixon, *RN: The Memoirs of Richard Nixon*, 2 vols. (New York: Warner Books, 1978), 85. The term *properly* implied the desire of airmen to wage a systematic, relentless, air campaign with minimal political interference.

38. Headquarters PACAF, Directorate of Operations Analysis, CHECO Division, *Linebacker: An Overview of the First 120 Days* (27 September 1973), 61.

39. Most of the World War II and Korean War "hump" of pilots had retired. Headquarters USAF, *First 120 Days*, 49–51. Gen John W. Vogt launched weather sorties first to determine whether primary or alternate targets should be hit and second whether the raids should be delayed (note the delegation of authority to these aircrews).

40. Ibid., 52, 64–65. Vogt had special fusing on the bombs dropped by the LORAN F-4s so their bomb craters could be discerned from others. This strategy was necessary to iron out any "time differential" errors in bombing accuracy for the critical regions in North Vietnam that might merit future attacks. Vogt always tagged at least one LORAN mission per day to bomb while level at high altitude. He knew he would need an all-weather precision bombing capability as the monsoon season approached. It was a prescient decision, and accuracies improved to within 200 meters. See also Karl J. Eschmann, *Linebacker: The Untold Story of the Air Raids Over North Vietnam* (New York: Ivy Books, 1989), 36.

41. Ibid., 25, 32. For example, the Thanh Hoa bridge, first attacked on 3 April 1965, was never disabled despite repeated assault by Air Force and Navy fighters. The Air Force sent 79 F-105s that dropped 638, 750-lb. bombs, fired 32 Bullpup air-to-ground missiles, and launched 266, 2.75 inch rockets to no avail. The target became known as the "Dragon's Jaw" as its defenders shot down four of the attackers. Finally, on 13 May 1972 Vogt sent three flights of F-4s with laser-guided bombs and dropped the bridge with no losses. The Paul Doumer Bridge had earned a similar reputation, but it was dropped by fighters employing laser-guided bombs on 10 May. Vogt commented, "As fast as they could repair bridges, we could drop them . . . [the enemy] was beginning to dry up." See also A. J. C. Lavalle, ed., *The Tale of Two Bridges and the Battle for the Skies Over North Vietnam* (Washington, D.C.: GPO, 1976).

42. Richard H. Kohn and Joseph Harahan, eds., *Air Interdiction in World War II, Korea, and Vietnam* (Washington, D.C.: OAFH, 1986), 78. On one occasion a SAC SR-71 spotted some 50 tanks "descending on Quang Tri," and SAC forwarded an urgent message to the Joint Chiefs of Staff which came to the Pacific Command directing the Seventh Air Force to "take under attack these tanks which constitute a major threat." Vogt knew for some time that they had been friendly M-48 tanks abandoned by the Army of the Republic of Vietnam (ARVN).

43. James R. McCarthy and George B. Allison, *Linebacker II: A View From the Rock* (Maxwell AFB, Ala.: Airpower Research Institute, 1979), 30; Mark Clodfelter, *The Limits of Air Power: The American Bombing of North Vietnam* (New York: Free Press, 1989), 165; and Headquarters PACAF, *First 120 Days*, 6. Vogt and others in Seventh Air Force became frustrated at how sometimes "over half" of the B-52s would abort if a SAM signal came up or a SAM was fired in the vicinity.

44. Eschmann, 66–67.

45. Ibid., 57; Earl H. Tilford Jr., *Setup: What the Air Force Did in Vietnam and Why* (Maxwell AFB, Ala.: Air University Press, 1991), 234; and Clodfelter, 167–70.

46. Drew Drenkowski, "Operation Linebacker II," *Soldier of Fortune* 2, no. 3 (September 1977): 24; and Eschmann, 77.

47. Nixon, 60.

48. Ibid., 242; and Clodfelter, 184.

49. Leonard D. G. Teixeira, "Linebacker II: A Strategic and Tactical Case Study" (Maxwell AFB, Ala., April 1990), 7; and Clodfelter, 184.

50. McCarthy and Allison, 26–27; and Eschmann, 74.

51. Teixeira, 8; and Clodfelter, 185. One member of the Eighth Air Force staff recalled: "As far as we were concerned it was a new plan." See also George B. Allison, "Bombers Go to Bullseye," *Aerospace Historian*, Winter 1982, 231.

52. Gen Gerald W. Johnson, transcript of oral history interview by author, 5 February 1993.

53. Clodfelter, 192.

54. In fairness, the SAC advanced echelon had kept SAC abreast of Linebacker I operations. Additionally, SAC had access to SR-71 reconnaissance aircraft information and other intelligence sources. SAC did not enter the fray cold. More important, fellow fighter pilots Vogt and Johnson had developed a good working relationship during Linebacker I.

55. Johnson interview; Clodfelter, 186; McCarthy and Allison, 50, 79; and Eschmann, 156.

56. McCarthy and Allison, 31; Teixeira, 10; Clodfelter, 186; and Charles K. Hopkins, "Linebacker II: A Firsthand View," *Aerospace Historian*, Fall 1976, 134.

57. McCarthy and Allison, 65.

58. Ibid., 67–70.

59. Ibid., 75.

60. Ibid., 73.

61. Ibid., 77.

62. Ibid., 79–89; Gen John W. Vogt, transcript of oral history interview by author, 23 April 1992; and Johnson.

63. Nixon, 246; and Clodfelter, 187.

64. Momyer, 107; and Futrell, 286.

65. Allison, 231. Lt Gen Glen W. Martin, vice CINCSAC at the time, recalled that "the operational planning and tactical analysis were incredibly complex with very little time available in the 24-hour kaleidoscope to take advantage of all crossfeed and potential improvements."

66. Ibid.

67. McCarthy and Allison, 126–44; Clodfelter, 188; Eschmann, 163–79; Teixeira, 21; and Bill Yenne, *SAC: A Primer of Modern Strategic Airpower* (Novato, Calif.: Presidio Press, 1985), 112–16.

68. Clodfelter, 189.

69. Kissinger, 1461, 1467; Nixon, 259; Teixeira, 28; and Momyer, 243.

70. Tilford, 261; and Vogt.

71. Eschmann, 163, 181; Headquarters PACAF, *Air Operations*,154–59, 174, 201. CHECO assessed that eight F-4s with laser-guided bombs had the "equivalent level of destruction" of more than 2,000 sorties with unguided munitions. Precision-guided munitions opened many new targets to strike within populated areas.

72. Clodfelter, 201.

73. Ibid.

74. One can nevertheless argue legitimately that it took the mass and intensity of the B-52s to induce the signing of the peace accords.

Chapter 8

Changing of the Guard: The Rise of the Fighter Generals (1973–82)

The only thing harder than getting a new idea into the military mind is to get the old one out.

—Sir Basil H. Liddell Hart
Innovations in the Strategic Air Command

The other side of the coin is that the Twinings, the LeMays, and the Powers belong to a passing generation. The new generation of officers is growing up in a different environment—well, somewhat different.

—Bernard Brodie
War and Politics

Air Force Chief of Staff John D. Ryan, glad to be done with Vietnam, surveyed the state of his service and consoled his staff by commenting that "at least we got rid of the warlords."[1] But the junior World War II generation's attempt to reunify the Air Force proved short-lived. After the humiliation of the Cuban missile crisis, the Soviets had begun a massive strategic and conventional force buildup that by the early 1970s threatened to place the United States at what conservatives termed a "decided disadvantage." Though strategic parity was becoming an accepted concept of the Nixon administration, strategic inferiority was not. In Ryan's eyes, extraction from Vietnam permitted the Air Force to resume without distraction its top cold war obligation— strategic deterrence. The race to "catch" the Soviets refocused both SAC and the TAF on this now larger menace. Dialogue and intercourse between the communities receded again as SAC resumed the nuclear watch, and the TAF concentrated primarily on the challenge of conventional war with the Soviets. Moreover, as aircraft became more sophisticated, they became more difficult and costly to transfer between bombers and fighters.[2]

While the Nixon administration negotiated for a strategic arms limitation treaty (SALT), the junior air generation saw superiority as the best deterrent. The politicians' responsibility was to ensure deterrence did not fail; the military's responsibility was to be prepared, if it did fail, to limit damage and try to "win" the unthinkable nuclear conflict. Naturally, the military concentrated again on refining the means of war— a task which often conflicted with principles of arms control and détente. For example, despite considerable political opposition within the administration and Congress, General Ryan and the commander of SAC, Gen Bruce K. Holloway, lobbied stubbornly for increased accuracy in the Minuteman intercontinental ballistic missile in the early 1970s.[3] Civilian leaders opposed that initiative because they thought it might raise the specter of a first-strike capability, which would destabilize détente and fuel the arms race unnecessarily. The Air Force also continued to pursue costly performance requirements (often for only marginal performance enhancement) in its new strategic bomber, the B-1, despite post-Vietnam defense budget cuts. The military professionals sought superiority through clear qualitative advantages to offset eroding numerical comparisons with the Soviets. But again, at what cost? Hardly anyone in the World War II generation understood that only détente could salvage US security in the face of swelling domestic opposition to defense spending and intervention. Many of the junior cohort had much to understand about détente, politics, and economics in the new age.

Anxious to reassert strategic credibility, the Air Force insisted on maintaining superiority in strategic bombers and multiple independently targeted reentry vehicle (MIRV) ICBMs. The United States should not, Air Force officials argued, barter away this advantage and key strategic modernization provisions in the SALT I negotiations in early 1972.[4] While a few air absolutists decried SALT and its sacrifice of US strategic superiority, many of the new Korean War generation, just breaking into the general officer ranks, accepted the notion of strategic parity.[5] Young air leaders began to embrace the need for an assured second-strike capability as adequate and to consider as necessary mutual restraint of a spiraling arms race. With the signing of the Antiballistic Missile (ABM) Treaty in May 1972 and the interim agreement on strategic arms limitations, followed in November 1974 by the Vladivostok Accords, the United States and the Soviet Union indeed had entered an era of détente.

Complexities of deterrence, détente, strategic sufficiency, arms limits, limited war, and peacekeeping proved more comprehensible to pragmatists than they did to absolutists. In a sociological analysis of Air Force leaders and future leaders in the mid-1970s, observers noted the twilight of "the upper echelons of the US military . . . dominated by a generation of general officers recruited and socialized during the trauma and urgency of World War II." The study perceived a "markedly different [and] less authoritarian" emerging elite "struggling to redefine its profession," accommodate change, and move "toward a more pragmatic outlook."[6] The members of the new generation had received more education but were "less authoritarian" than their predecessors. The analysis concluded that "the crucial difference between 'absolutists' and 'pragmatists' rests in the degree to which the professional military man has internalized the implications of deterrent strategy and has modified the 'killing business' as the organizing principle of the profession."[7] Furthermore, the same researchers discovered in a 1974 survey of Air War College and Air Command and Staff College students (Korean War generation) the presence of more pluralistic and pragmatic views than had existed in the 1960s.[8] Critically different formative experiences of the old and new generation shaped adaptability.

Besides the indelible impact of early years, the Korean War generation—those commissioned too late to participate in World War II yet able to participate in the Korean War—had a greater opportunity to seek professional military and graduate school education during their careers than their senior and junior predecessors. Figure 24 shows the context.

Samuel Huntington, a distinguished scholar on the American military, noted after the Vietnam War that

> the older generation officers were often less than completely receptive to the new ideas and approaches which the civilian strategists were developing. Now, however, there is a younger generation of

213

professional military officers, the products of the war colleges, civilian universities, and research institutes, who have the intellectual and academic background and interests to play a role in developing strategic doctrines and ideas.[9]

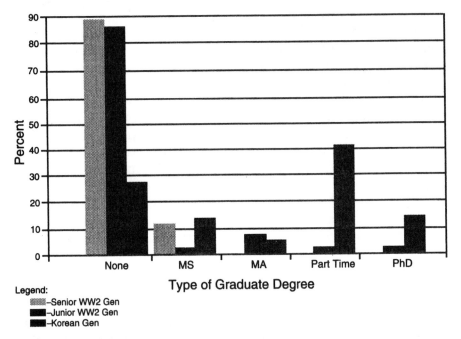

Legend:
▨ –Senior WW2 Gen
█ –Junior WW2 Gen
█ –Korean Gen

Source: Samuel Huntingdon, "After Containment: The Functions of the Military Establishment," *Annals of the American Academy of Political and Social Science: The Military and American Society,* March 1973, 3–15.

Figure 24. Advanced Education of Air Force Four-Star Generals

Nixon's secretary of defense, Melvin R. Laird, also observed the difference. Laird pressured General Ryan and Secretary of the Air Force Robert C. Seamans to bring young people into the four-star ranks.[10] Secretary Seamans broke the air service's traditions of using command of SAC and the vice chief's position as required proving grounds for future chiefs by nominating the popular, bright, and young general George S. Brown to succeed Ryan as chief of staff in 1973.[11]

Brown had an unusually diverse and deliberately broadened career, which exposed him to command challenges in many areas of the Air Force.[12] Brown had flown in World War II as a bomber squadron commander and had led the surviving bombers back from the infamous raid on the Ploesti oil refineries. He then served in Air Training Command and Air Defense Command and commanded a troop carrier group early in the Korean War. Next, he commanded a fighter wing and served as director of operations for Fifth Air Force in the last year of the Korean War. After that war, he commanded a pilot training wing, went to the National War College, and served as executive officer to the Air Force chief of staff. He later served as military assistant to Secretary of Defense McNamara, followed by a stint as commander of a transport numbered air force and of the joint weapons testing center. After serving as assistant to the chairman of the JCS, Brown went to Vietnam to command the Seventh Air Force, followed by command of Air Force Systems Command. The selection of this "generalist" broke SAC's domination of the top position. Peers characterized Brown as "smoother" and "more sophisticated" than Ryan, and he was well liked and respected both within his service and on Capitol Hill.[13] One month after selection as chief, this pragmatist anticipated the need for reinforcement of the Israelis in October of 1973 and, without orders, stockpiled equipment at points of embarkation for rapid shipment to Israel. Brown's timely actions did much to help save Israel when the presidential order to resupply finally came.[14]

President Nixon and new defense secretary James R. Schlesinger selected Brown as the new chairman of the JCS less than one year after he had become Air Force chief of staff. A *New York Times* editorial in June 1974 perceived winds of change:

> In selecting General Brown as Chairman, Mr. Schlesinger was hoping not only to install a professional with an outlook similar to his, but also to invigorate the intellectual calibre of the Joint Chiefs, which by common Pentagon judgment has deteriorated over the last decade.[15]

Secretary Schlesinger replaced General Brown with Gen David C. Jones as the new Air Force chief. Jones had been selected over the capable Gen John Vogt who, instead, left his Pacific command to replace Jones in the increasingly important position of commander of USAFE. Colleagues described the new chief as intelligent, hardworking, and a confident, independent thinker.[16]

Jones had a diverse background that rivaled the background of Brown and Vogt. He had been a flying training instructor and an air rescue pilot, and then he had flown in combat as a bomber squadron commander in the Korean War. He then commanded an air refueling squadron and served as General LeMay's aide. Next, he became an aircraft maintenance commander before attending the National War College and subsequently working on the Air Staff. In the mid-1960s he commanded a tactical fighter wing and then served on the USAFE staff. In 1969 he went to Vietnam as the vice commander of Seventh Air Force before returning to become a SAC numbered Air Force commander. After that, General Jones returned to Europe where he became commander in chief of USAFE. At USAFE Jones had successfully unified the NATO air forces, centralized targeting, and debunked the myth of Soviet invincibility. Like his predecessor, Jones was a junior cohort pragmatist who had witnessed firsthand the complexities of the limited wars in Korea and Vietnam.

Conventional conflicts proved more likely and merited more attention. From 1974 to 1978 Brown and Jones presided over crises in Cyprus, Lebanon, Cambodia, and Korea that required limited, pragmatic responses. The broadened junior cohort also proved influential in negotiations for SALT I, the Vladivostok Accords, SALT II, and the Panama Canal Treaty.[17] The 1975 air doctrine manual still recognized the primary role of strategic deterrence, but envisioned other important roles for conventional airpower in deterrence, persuasion, and coercion and accepted the notion of sufficiency.[18] Strategic arms limitations reduced the cost of arming SAC, and they offered pragmatists more opportunities to secure funding and to contend with other threats. Under the new leadership, JCS and Air Force staff papers improved, were well argued and detailed, and were commended by congressional staffers.[19] An analyst of the period provided the following summary:

> The lag between the change in conditions and the change in attitudes was evident in the fact that more realistic and prudent Air Force officers emerged predominantly in the lower ranks, where the fight for autonomy had not been a formative generational experience. . . . These officers did not begin to take over the leadership of the service

until after 1970. Recent Chiefs such as George Brown and David Jones have had backgrounds more diverse and balanced than did their predecessors [and even began to give] advice more conservative than some of the principal civilians.[20]

The Air Force chiefs had learned much since their days in the Pentagon with General LeMay.

Nevertheless, even the new Air Force leadership fought hard to preserve the centerpiece of its tradition and doctrine—the strategic bomber. By the 1970s TAC was procuring new fighters and MAC new transports, but SAC was still having difficulty buying the B-1. Little money had been available for procurement during the costly Vietnam War. In the interim, ICBMs and SLBMs rose to become the preeminent legs of the Triad. Additionally, one SAC commander recalled the period when Congress, resolved to cut defense spending, questioned the purchase of the ultraexpensive and sinister-looking strategic bomber in the wake of the unpopular Vietnam War, with inflated images of the death and destruction of innocent lives in Hanoi still lingering.[21] Furthermore, with characteristic technological zeal, the Air Force undermined its cause by chasing performance specifications that proved exceedingly expensive and yielded only a marginal return—a phenomenon known as "gold-plating."[22]

Feeling the budget pinch, General Jones reportedly gathered 10 of his 12 four-star generals (minus General Vogt) in December 1974 to discuss the impact of procuring 240 B-1s on the likely budget of the Air Force. The new chief insisted that the B-1 not go forward unless the Air Force commanders united in unequivocal support. The most optimistic initial assessment determined the $24 billion B-1 program would consume most of the Air Force budget and would preclude fighter procurement. Upon reexamination, the leadership reduced some gold-plating and concluded the Air Force should procure the B-1. The air arm also would procure top priority fighters but would sacrifice some airlift and close-air-support programs, as well as training, supply, and maintenance funds.[23]

The Air Force simply could not control B-1 costs to the satisfaction of many in Congress, despite an aggressive lobbying campaign on Capitol Hill. In 1976 the Brookings

217

Institute published a study that concluded a standoff B-52 force equipped with air-launched cruise missiles (ALCM) was far more cost effective than a fleet of B-1s. The study also concluded manned bombers should be only an insurance policy in case ICBMs and SLBMs failed.[24] Amidst rising congressional concern and considering the cost of the B-1 program to the Air Force, Jones directed the Air Force not to lobby for the B-1 in the Carter administration.[25]

Meanwhile, the cruise missile had crept into Air Force programs. Former secretary of defense Laird liked the program, but he placed it initially under the more receptive US Navy.[26] President Jimmy Carter noted that the cruise missile seemed to cause the Soviets more consternation than the B-1.[27] Anxious to demonstrate decisiveness and cognizant of new stealth technology, the new president weighed the cost effectiveness and deterrent value of the B-52/cruise missile combination versus the B-1 penetrating bomber and decided to cut the B-1 in June 1977—against the advice of his Air Force chief. Fulfilling his campaign promise, Carter hoped that killing the B-1 would free moneys for such programs as the MX and cruise missiles, which he hoped would develop into more meaningful bargaining chips in SALT II.[28] He preferred to wait for the stealth bomber.

Unlike his mentor LeMay, Jones remained loyal to the president's decision and did not attempt an end run to Congress. In congressional testimony Jones asserted he was "more concerned with our overall strategic posture than with any single weapons system" and that the B-1 controversy was "diverting attention from our broader strategic needs."[29] Long-time supporters of the Air Force— Senate Armed Services Committee chairman John C. Stennis and House Appropriations Committee chairman George H. Mahon—agreed. Mahon stated in 1978:

> We are looking at national defense through a little knothole as though the bomber was everything that was going to save us from war or win the war if war should come. Does not everybody in the House know that the weapon of the future is the intercontinental missile? Do we not know that the only purpose of the bomber is to do the cleanup job? And after the atomic exchange, we could probably do the cleanup job in an oxcart.[30]

Would a conventional (nonnuclear) capability enhance the utility and marketing of the strategic bomber? In early 1974 Sen. John H. Glenn Jr. pushed for a conventional capability in the B-1. One author noted that the "SAC-dominated leadership scorned the notion; their $100 million superbomber" in a conventional role "would be like hitching a thoroughbred to a milk wagon." Furthermore, one air general reportedly said, "There was no damn way we were going to risk losing a $100 million strategic asset in some conventional shoot-out. But if the senator wanted us to say we'd do that, we were ready to oblige him."[31] On the heels of the frustrating Vietnam experience, the renewed determination of SAC to contend with the greater Soviet strategic threat allowed it to return to the pride and single-minded focus that had been its founding essence. Strategic airpower refocused on a method of war it perceived as more inclined to decisiveness—nuclear warfare. Indeed, SAC had made only limited and belated attempts to make the B-1 a capable conventional bomber. The new SAC commander, Gen Russell E. Dougherty, took over in late 1974 and noted the conventional capability demonstrated in Linebacker II had all but evaporated in his command. Dougherty tried to resurrect a conventional capability in his strategic bombers, but he failed to change the mind-set.[32] The Soviet strategic menace absorbed the full attention and budget of SAC again; interest in conventional warfare atrophied.

Budget cuts added to the neglect of conventional capabilities and increased hardships in SAC. The bomber and missile command received a lesser share of a shrinking defense budget. Flying hours for bomber crews fell to three to four times each month and averaged three to four hours' duration. The Soviet SLBM threat increased dispersal and tightened the readiness of SAC alert forces (without adequate additional funding). Crews often averaged 12 to 13 days of alert each month.[33] In desperation, SAC imported a few jet T-38s from Air Training Command to bolster the morale and flying skills of its pilots.

SAC's future as a dynamic command also appeared bleak. Few pilot training graduates wanted to go to the cold and remote five "northern tier" SAC bases to sit alert in old aircraft when they could fly more often in newer fighter and airlift aircraft at more appealing locations. SAC continued to receive generally the bottom graduates of undergraduate pilot training. Concerned over "equitable distribution of talent" and implications for the future, the Air Force revised its long-standing policy that permitted pilot training students to select aircraft based upon class standing. Beginning in 1972 all commands received graduates from all sections of the class. In 1976 pilot graduates had at least to meet "fighter and reconnaissance" minimum standards of flying proficiency for admission into TAC. By 1978 the top 10 percent received guarantee of their choice of aircraft type, if available.[34]

Job attitudes in SAC reflected more difficulties. Air Force personnel surveys and studies in the mid-1970s and early 1980s indicated that SAC aircrews and missilemen thought they suffered longer hours, boredom with alert, and work repetition. During this time they lacked the prestige, job satisfaction, job motivation, and task autonomy found in other commands. Only one-half of these SAC officers came from the ranks of volunteers, and though they exhibited a high sense of job importance, unit cohesion, and maintenance of high standards, they didn't consider their jobs as intrinsically rewarding as other jobs in the Air Force. They displayed a preference for easy and repetitive jobs, and "they did not believe they needed to apply a variety of skills to complete their tasks."[35] Always feeling and meeting the pressure and demands of strategic deterrence, SAC saw that its fundamental nature and methodology had changed little from LeMay's time.

No such status quo pervaded the TAF as it packed up its forces from Southeast Asia and moved to Europe in support of the new defense policy embodied in MC 14/3, which endorsed a conventional buildup in NATO to repel significant Warsaw Pact conventional forces in kind, without necessarily resorting to an immediate nuclear response.[36] An easing of tensions with China and a desire to assure European allies that the United States had not forgotten its primary commitment to NATO encouraged the move. The ferocity and nature of the tactical air war in the October 1973 Yom Kippur War seemed more relevant to the TAF than did Vietnam. In a high-stakes NATO confrontation, the TAF needed more forces to withstand the kind of attrition experienced on both sides in this most recent clash of modern American and

Soviet arms in conventional warfare. To contend with proliferating Soviet SAM systems, TAC increased requirements for anti-SAM Wild Weasel aircraft and improved its electronic countermeasures, high-speed aircraft, computer-aided aiming systems to ensure single-pass accuracy, precision-guided munitions and armored close-air-support aircraft.[37] Budget realities accelerated a discussion of a low-cost fighter to augment the new F-15 and replace the F-4. The Air Force insisted on qualitative advantage, but it could not afford to neglect that quantity had a quality of its own—vast numbers could eventually overwhelm fewer technologically superior forces. Fortunately for the TAF, SALT I and delays in the B-1, coupled with the top priority of NATO in the Nixon, Ford, Carter, and Reagan administrations, provided increased funding for TAF programs. Figure 25 shows the shift in budget emphasis. By FY 1975 Secretary of Defense Schlesinger testified that general forces (as opposed to strategic forces) received more than 70 percent of defense expenditures. The largest segment (25 percent) of the total expenditures went to procure tactical fighters.[38]

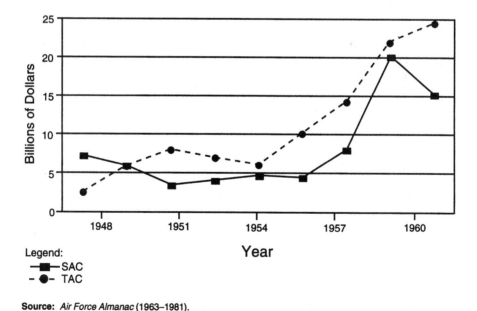

Legend:
—■—SAC
- ●- TAC

Source: *Air Force Almanac* (1963–1981).

Figure 25. Air Force Budget Allocation in 1994 Dollars

Reemphasizing a conventional NATO strategy (ensured by US nuclear capability) encouraged more cooperation with the Army. In late 1973 General Brown instructed fighter general Robert J. Dixon, new commander of TAC, to abide by previous agreements and continue the close working relationship that Brown had established with Gen Creighton Abrams (now the Army chief of staff) while serving with him in Vietnam. Brown and Abrams directed Dixon and Gen William Dupuy, commander of Army Training and Doctrine Command, to carry the "commonality of purpose . . . into the entire fabric of relationships between the two Services."[39] Dixon and Dupuy labored on what Dixon termed "an Air Force-Army air-land battle team [to] get the most capability out of what we have and provide the most precise, analytical and coordinated information possible on our needs for added capabilities."[40]

Spurred by the need to fight outnumbered and win on the NATO front, the two services had formed in 1975 a formal joint air-land forces application team to work out joint combat issues.[41] General Jones and General Vogt believed as commanders of United States Air Forces in Europe that airpower had to be devoted to the land battle as it had in the 1973 Middle East war.[42] An axiom floated around NATO air forces that a Soviet T-72 tank parked in front of your officer's club could not be prevented from getting there by the finest of air superiority or strategic bombing campaigns. The Army admitted the criticality of the tactical air war. Its July 1976 doctrinal manual, FM 100-5, *Operations,* stated that "the Army cannot win the land battle without the Air Force."[43] By 1982 the wedding between the Army and tactical airpower was codified in the "AirLand Battle" doctrine in FM 100-5 that "meant to convey the interaction between all aspects of air and ground power in a firepower and maneuver context."[44] The importance of improving Air Force/Army relations called for more fighter experience and resources within the Air Force.

Doctrinal, procurement, and budgetary shifts towards tactical airpower in the 1970s manifested themselves proportionally in greater numbers of fighter wings, aircraft, and pilots retained during defense cutbacks through the mid-1970s and also greater numbers during defense growth beginning in the late 1970s (documented in figures in chapter

7). From 1971 to 1982 fighter pilots on average outnumbered bomber pilots by four to one.[45] Figure 26 reveals distribution of manpower shifts within the Air Force.

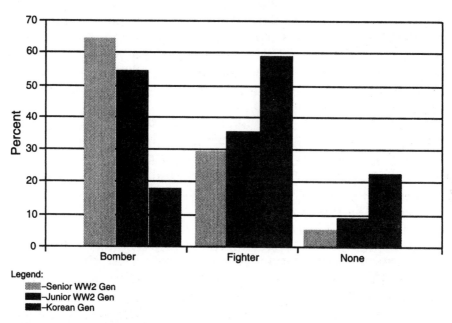

Legend:
▨ —Senior WW2 Gen
■ —Junior WW2 Gen
■ —Korean Gen

Source: *DOD Authorizations for Appropriations FY 1979.*

Figure 26. Type of Combat Experience of Air Force Four-Star Generals

The growing proportion of fighter force structure within the Air Force placed a greater demand on flag officers with fighter backgrounds. The results of a study in all grades of Air Force general officers from 1953 to 1972 indicate that the fundamental change began to take effect as early as 1968.

Secretary of Defense Laird's successful attempt to bring "youth" (and new thinking) into the upper echelons of the military on the heels of the Vietnam War corroborates data. Immediately upon becoming chief of staff in 1973, generalist general Brown directed his chief of personnel, fighter general Dixon, to ensure that his office identify people beforehand for early promotion to facilitate the youth movement that would eclipse the bomber-dominant junior World War II generation.[46] Observers regarded Dixon as a competent personnel chief, but he had only one month to implement the policy before becoming TAC commander. He met the rising need for flag officers with fighter experience by promoting officers with fighter backgrounds earlier ("below the zone") than their competitors; this meant they were young enough to compete in greater proportion for the higher flag officer ranks before reaching mandatory retirement at 35 years of service. In the 1970s fighter wing commanders tended to be younger than bomber wing commanders—fighter wings were generally smaller in base population than bomber wings. SAC valued seniority more than TAC did. In each year of the 1970s, a greater number and percentage of fighter pilots received promotions below the zone than bomber pilots.[47] Korean War generation four-stars with fighter backgrounds reached four-star rank on average more than one year earlier than their bomber peers.[48]

Combat experience continued as a highly valued commodity for promotion in the air arm. The disparity between SAC's and TAC's combat experience deeply concerned the bomber command, even before the Vietnam War ended. Fighter general Holloway, commander of SAC, had complained to chief of staff General Ryan in 1970 regarding SAC's low promotion rates to colonel, primarily because "a) they do not receive Southeast Asia tour credit, and b) their opportunity to obtain a college degree [or an advanced degree] has been severely restricted."[49] The distribution of combat experience then shifted to generals with fighter backgrounds. Additionally, the Korean War generation had 10 percent fewer generals with "Air Force only" experience than did the junior World War II generation. Fighter four stars in the Korean War generation assumed 15 percent less insularity than the bomber generals. In short, the fighter community had a broader career experience base and more combat experience. More importantly, strategic arms limits compressed the SAC budget and force structure, while the TAF enjoyed growing support for its cooperation with the Army in the crucial conventional buildup in Europe.

TAF also met (better than SAC) Secretary Laird's desire to reduce centralization and increase innovation in the military.[50] TAF's success in decentralized operations during

Vietnam expanded in the 1970s. Under the lengthy and resolute command of Generals Momyer (1968–73), Dixon (1973-78), and Wilbur L. Creech (1978–84), decentralized operations pushed responsibility and aggressive competence down the hierarchy.[51] TAF trained intensively in sophisticated "flag" series (Red Flag and Green Flag) mock wars in realistic scenarios versus aggressor forces. Proficiency, not rank, determined mission leaders; often captains commanded dozens of aircraft—opportunities on a scale unavailable in SAC. The tactical air warfare center exploited a flurry of innovative technologies. The fighter weapons schools raised competencies in the perfection of technique. Many of TAC's policies began to be adopted Air Force wide.[52] A survey conducted by the Air Force Leadership and Management Development Center in 1982 concluded that TAC scored higher than other commands in potential for combat effectiveness.[53] TAF led efforts to return *decisiveness* to airpower primarily through refinement of technique and a more affordable and diverse technological effort that sought lethality.

By the early 1980s TAF had its hands in virtually every mission. Fighters around the periphery of Eurasia remained on air defense and nuclear alert, for example, and could perform every war-fighting mission. The long-range capability of modern fighters, increased by air refueling, approached the range capabilities of strategic bombers. Precision-guided munitions, computer navigation, and aiming systems redefined traditional norms of mass and lethality. Fighters could now put each bomb precisely on target. The preference to minimize collateral damage in an era of limited war made fighters even more attractive. Fighters continued to become more flexible, versatile, survivable, accurate, and cost effective than bombers. Strategic bombers remained more efficient than fighters only in carpet bombing and deep strikes into the heartland of the Soviet Union—though many questioned their survivability in these roles against modern defenses.

By 1978 the fighter-laden Korean War generation had seized the mantle of senior leadership in the Air Force. As aggressive Soviet behavior shattered the Carter administration's cautious defense spending, TAF received in 1979 even more money than previously. Still hesitant to fund the B-1, MX, and naval programs, Carter bolstered spending on the Army and TAF.[54] His defense policy, force structure, technology, and internal institutional dynamics clearly favored the TAF community. In 1975 bomber generals outnumbered fighter generals on the Air Staff by two to one, and in the major (four-star) command positions by four to three.[55] By 1982 there were no bomber generals in key Air Staff positions, and fighter generals outnumbered bomber generals in the major commands by five to four.[56]

The selection of fighter Korean War cohort general Charles A. Gabriel as chief of staff in 1982 capped the ascendancy of TAF within the Air Force. Sen. Barry Goldwater, a longtime supporter of the Air Force, apparently summarized what the country wanted and the Air Force now produced in General Gabriel. At Gabriel's confirmation hearings Goldwater testified,

> As you might expect from this recitation of his distinguished background, General Gabriel is a highly decorated combat veteran. He has had broad exposure to our NATO allies, and he has held staff positions which involved thorough involvement with Air Force commands other than the Tactical Air Command.

> For several years, Mr. Chairman, I have encouraged succeeding Administrations, the Department of Defense, and the Air Force leadership to name a fighter pilot as the Chief of Staff. I remember Secretary Kissinger asked me once, "Why do you want a fighter pilot to be Chief of Staff?" I said, "Well, they have to sit up in that cockpit all by themselves with no one to tell them what to do, where to go, how to do it, and when to quit." Now we finally have one up there, and I think we will get that kind of thinking from this gentleman. As far as I am concerned, they could not have picked a better man.[57]

The influence of the ascendant fighter generals could be felt by the early years of the Reagan presidency. The procurement of fighters increased. Water had even vitiated the stone that prevented the procurement of a new strategic bomber. But the Air Force reintroduced the B-1 in 1979 as the broader based "long-range combat aircraft," one capable of carrying out its nuclear mission with or without cruise missiles and simultaneously enjoying a role in naval surveillance, mine laying, interdiction, and even antisubmarine warfare. The new B-1 would provide a force that, as the Air Force deputy chief of

226

staff for Research and Development proudly noted, "might provide our only means for adding mass firepower at the right spot and at the right time to blunt the massive armored spearhead attack which is a key element of Soviet theatre-warfighting doctrine."[58] It was a marketing technique in stark contrast to the past.

The ascendance of the tactical community did not mean that Air Force educational problems had been solved. Certainly, the formal educational levels of the average officer had improved dramatically since the early 1960s. Nevertheless, critics had accused Air Force base educational programs of being "diploma mills," and the quality of the degrees came under scrutiny.[59] Furthermore, studies at Air University indicated that the Vietnam War had interrupted professional military education enrollments by up to 30 percent.[60]

Doctrinal progress also was found wanting. Many in the Air Force (particularly in SAC) thought that, after the anomaly of Vietnam, the Air Force should return to its primary focus on the Soviet Union and general war, much as it had done after Korea.[61] Many would neglect Vietnam as they had Korea. From 1974 to 1979 the Air War College spent only two and one-half hours on the Vietnam War—the time it spent on the 1967 Arab-Israeli War.[62] Several analysts have since assessed the 1970s as a "nadir" in the development of Air Force doctrine.[63]

A tactical or theater flavor began to color the fighter-dominated Air Force's pursuit of its doctrinal trinity: *globalism, indivisibility,* and *decisiveness.* Theater concerns flowing from theater experiences and theater challenges overshadowed traditional *globalism.* The pendulum of comprehending airpower in the broadest sense may have swung to the opposite end from where it had been more than two decades before. If a dominant SAC had tunnel vision on nuclear strategic warfare then, by the late 1970s a dominant TAF risked absorption into the provincial realm of "AirLand battle."[64] *Indivisibility* remained difficult, with SAC again focused solely on strategic nuclear warfare and the TAF on war at the battlefront. As one Air Force general recently confessed, "The doctrinal paradigm since the 1950s has been an air force that separated strategic and tactical applications of air power institutionally, organizationally, intellectually, and culturally."[65]

The ascendant TAF sought *decisiveness* against a formidable enemy through cooperation with the Army and through the traditional refinement of technique and technology. At risk stood a balanced and holistic concept of airpower. It remained to be determined if the TAF emphasis was any better than the previous SAC emphasis.

Notes

1. Lt Gen Alvan Gillem, USAF, Retired, interviewed by author, 5 February 1993.

2. Office of the Secretary of the Air Force, Air Force Manpower Statistical Analysis, computer run (Washington, D.C.: SAF/FMBMP), July 1992; and Nick Kotz, *Wild Blue Yonder: Money, Politics, and the B-1 Bomber* (New York: Pantheon Books, 1988), 11. A statistical analysis revealed five in 18 pilot training graduates in the decade after Vietnam were initially assigned to fighter or reconnaissance units, and 95 percent of those pilots stayed in their weapons system. Gen Russell E. Dougherty pointed out that the computerization of the assignment process in the early 1970s identified people with specialty codes and as "SAC or TAC resources. One could seldom cross between the two." See Gen Russell E. Dougherty, interviewed by author, 22 June 1992.

3. Robert Frank Futrell, *Ideas, Concepts, Doctrine: Basic Thinking in the Air Force, 1961–1984*, vol. 2 (Maxwell AFB, Ala.: Air University Press, 1989), 343–44; Donald A. MacKenzie, *Inventing Accuracy: A Historical Sociology of Nuclear Missile Guidance* (Cambridge, Mass.: MIT Press, 1990).

4. Kotz, 105. Kotz claims Secretary of Defense Laird said the Joint Chiefs of Staff wouldn't support SALT unless strategic modernization with the B-1 and Trident submarine was protected.

5. Donald F. Bletz, *The Role of the Military Professional in U.S. Foreign Policy* (New York: Praeger Publishers, 1972), 212. Bletz observed in a survey of the National War College classes of 1968–1970 that the vast majority of students rejected the spate of absolutist books published by retiring senior World War II generals (see chap. 5), 12, 273–74, 277. Furthermore, the new generation rejected the notion of unconditional surrender (and total victory) as invalid in the contemporary international environment. Richard K. Betts, *Soldiers, Statesmen, and Cold War Crises* (Cambridge, Mass.: Harvard University Press, 1977), 114. During SALT negotiations "younger military men tended to be less obdurate and less distinct in their attitudes from civilian strategists." Seventy percent of Air Force officers now favored arms control.

6. Franklin D. Margiotta, "A Military Elite in Transition: Air Force Leaders in the 1980s," *Armed Forces and Society* 2, no. 2 (Winter 1976): 155–56, 159, 163, 281. The analysis studied 351 (90 percent) of all line Air Force general officers as of 1 January 1974. Additionally, they sampled all line officers (1,971) serving as early promotees to the grades of major, lieutenant colonel, and colonel as well as students in service schools.

7. Ibid., 179; Arnold Kanter, "Managerial Careers of Air Force Generals: A Test of the Janowitz Convergence Hypothesis," *Journal of Political and Military Sociology*, Spring 1976, 131. "There is a growing gap between senior officers' images of their professional role—which emphasize combat-related skills and performance—and the predominant managerial tasks which they increasingly are called upon to perform." These conclusions came from research on all Air Force general officers who served from 1953 to 1972. Kanter uses Janowitz's definitions of "absolutist" and "pragmatist." See Morris Janowitz, *The Professional Soldier: A Social and Political Portrait* (Glencoe, Ill.: Free Press, 1960).

8. Margiotta, 179.

9. Samuel Huntington, "After Containment: The Functions of the Military Establishment," *The Annals of the American Academy of Political and Social Science: The Military and American Society*, March 1973, 15.

10. Secretary of the Air Force Robert C. Seamans Jr., transcript of oral history interview by Lt Col Lynn R. Officer and Hugh N. Ahmann, 27 November 1973 and 24 March 1974, 40, 49, and 51, Air Force Historical Research Agency (cited hereafter as AFHRA), Maxwell AFB, Ala. Laird also pressured the other services for youth and promoted young four-stars such as Elmo Zumwalt and Alexander Haig.

11. Edgar F. Puryear Jr., *George S. Brown, General USAF: Destined for Stars* (Novato, Calif.: Presidio Press, 1983), 123, 235. McNamara recommended Brown be considered for chief in the future; Gen Thomas White reportedly told his aide, while the ailing chief lay on his death bed in 1964, to wire Brown a congratulations from White when Brown became chairman of the JCS. Gen George S. Brown, transcript of oral history interview by Dr. Edgar F. Puryear Jr., 14 September 1977, 3, AFHRA. Brown "knew" four years in advance (from Ryan in 1969 [pressure from Laird?]) he would become chief.

12. Gen Horace M. Wade, transcript of oral history interview by Dr. Edgar F. Puryear Jr., 17 November 1970, AFHRA; Gen Robert C. Mathis, transcript of oral history interview by Dr. Edgar F. Puryear Jr., 8 April 1980, 5, AFHRA. Brown was "the most uniquely, broadly prepared man ever to become Chief or even to become chairman because his experience was quite unusual too. So it was clearly by design."

13. Gen Russell E. Doughtery, transcript of oral history interview by Dr. Edgar F. Puryear Jr., 27 March 1979, 2, AFHRA; Mark Perry, *Four Stars: The Inside Story of the Forty-five Year Battle Between the Joint Chiefs of Staff and America's Civilian Leaders* (Boston: Houghton Mifflin, 1989), 251; Gen Lucius D. Clay, transcript of oral history interview by Dr. Edgar F.

Puryear Jr., 19 September 1981, 32, AFHRA; Gen T. R. Milton, transcript of oral history interview by Dr. Edgar F. Puryear Jr., 28 June 1979, 2, AFHRA; Gen Jack J. Catton, transcript of oral history interview by Dr. Edgar F. Puryear Jr., 18 September 1981, 14, AFHRA; and Gen Jerome O'Malley, transcript of oral history interview by Dr. Edgar F. Puryear Jr., 10 August 1981, 7, AFHRA. Brown had his slipups: comments about Jews (at Duke University) and run-ins with the press.

14. Willard J. Webb and Ronald H. Cole, *The Chairmen of the Joint Chiefs of Staff* (Washington, D.C.: Government Printing Office, 1989), 91; Puryear, *George S. Brown*, 222–23.

15. Cited in Puryear, *George S. Brown*, 236; Betts, 62; and Perry, 251. Perry and Puryear commented on how James R. Schlesinger was impressed with Brown's intellect and wanted to get away from Vietnam and onto strategic issues.

16. Maj Gen Otis C. Moore, transcript of oral history interview by Dr. Edgar F. Puryear Jr., 1 July 1979, 17, AFHRA; Gen Russell E. Dougherty, transcript of oral history interview by Dr. Edgar F. Puryear Jr., 15 March 1979, 14, AFHRA; Gen John W. Vogt, transcript of oral history interview by Dr. Edgar F. Puryear Jr., 9 September 1981, 44, AFHRA. On Schlesinger's fondness for Jones, see Gen Gabriel Disosway, transcript of oral history interview by Dr. Edgar F. Puryear Jr., 17 January 1979, 6, AFHRA; Gen Bruce K. Holloway, transcript of oral history interview by Dr. Edgar F. Puryear Jr., 7 July 1978, 6, AFHRA; Gen Jacob E. Smart, transcript of oral history interview by Dr. Edgar F. Puryear Jr., 17 July 1979, 21, AFHRA; Catton, interviewed by Puryear, 14; Clay, interviewed by Puryear, 32; O'Malley, interviewed by Puryear, 7; Milton, interviewed by Puryear, 8; and Perry, 260–61. See also Gen William W. Momyer, transcript of oral history interview by Dr. Edgar F. Puryear Jr., 9 September 1981, 6, AFHRA; Gen John Vogt, interviewed by author, 23 April 1992; and Gen David C. Jones, interviewed by author, 23 June 1992.

17. Webb and Cole, 93–95, 100.

18. Futrell, 725.

19. Perry, 260–61.

20. Betts, 117; and Vance O. Mitchell, "The First Generation: A Policy History of the Air Force Officer Corps, 1944–1973," unpublished manuscript, Office of Air Force History (OAFH), May 1991, 613. Mitchell shows a table that outlines growth in proportion of "generalist" generals in 1970.

21. Dougherty, interviewed by author. Dougherty, commander of SAC from 1974 to 1977, recalled resentment building in SAC when the other major commands received new aircraft while SAC hadn't had a new one in 25 years. Dougherty also lamented that Congress and much of the public thought the B-1 looked hostile and complex, and they disliked the idea that it represented indiscriminate strategic bombing.

22. See Kotz for extensive discussion of gold-plating of Air Force strategic bombers.

23. Ibid., 118–20.

24. Alton H. Quanbeck and Archie L. Wood, *Modernizing the Strategic Bomber Force: Why and How* (Washington, D.C.: Brookings Institute, 1976); Futrell, 403; and Kotz, 17.

25. Kotz, 160.

26. Ibid., 163; and Futrell, 412–13.

27. Kotz, 167.

28. Ibid., 170–72; Futrell, 354; and Dougherty, interviewed by author, 22 June 1992.

29. Kotz, 173; and Futrell, 419.

30. Kotz, 179.

31. Ibid., 131–32.

32. Gen Russell E. Dougherty, transcript of oral history interview by John T. Bohn, 13 December 1977, 3, AFHRA; and Dougherty, interviewed by author, 22 June 1992. Dougherty complained SAC had no conventional capability when he visited B-1 units in 1988. Gen T. R. Milton, interviewed by author, 15 June 1992. Milton lamented the B-1 still had no credible conventional capability. See D. D. Karle and J. B. Hall, "Integrating Strategic and Tactical Airpower in Conventional Warfare: B-52 Employment" (Maxwell AFB, Ala.: Air University, May 1988).

33. David A. Anderton, *Strategic Air Command: Two Thirds of the Triad* (New York: Scribner's, 1976), 90; Gen Bruce K. Holloway, transcript of oral history interview by Lt Col Vaughn H. Gallacher, 16–18 August 1977, 352, AFHRA.

34. Briefing, Air Training Command, subject: UPT Assignment System, 1991. In 1974 the top 10 percent of graduates got their choice. This procedure was rescinded in 1976 and returned in 1978. Many top performers in pilot training who did not receive their choice were disillusioned and left the Air Force after serving their commitment. Flying skill is *not* directly related to leadership potential.

35. Stephen D. Bull, "Job Attitudes—How SAC Personnel Compare With the Rest of the Air Force" (Maxwell AFB, Ala.: Air University, April 1986), 11, 13, 29–30, 47–49. By the early 1980s SAC attitude scores were "significantly different from those of other Air Force personnel in 54 of 63 comparisons." See also J. K. Kennedy, "Job Attitudes of SAC Pilots Compared" (Maxwell AFB, Ala.: Air University, April 1986).

36. Vogt, interviewed by Puryear; and Futrell, 499, 721. The Air Force doctrinal manual (AFM 1-1) of 1971 admitted that strategic forces alone were insufficient to deter war; they needed to be augmented by strong conventional forces.

37. Futrell, 486.

38. David T. Johnson and Barry R. Schneider, eds., *Current Issues in U.S. Defense Policy* (Washington, D.C.: Center for Defense Information, 1991), 217.

39. Futrell, 530–31, 539–40; and Richard G. Davis, *The 31 Initiatives: A Study in Air Force-Army Cooperation* (Washington, D.C.: OAFH, 1987), 26.

40. Futrell, 540.

41. Ibid.; and Davis, 27.

42. Futrell, 494, 501.

43. US Army Field Manual (FM) 100-5, *Operations*, 1 July 1976, 8-1.

44. Davis, 32.

45. Statistics provided by Defense Manpower Data Center, Monterey, Calif., 4 March 1992.

46. Brown, oral history interview by Puryear, 11; and Gen Robert Kelley interviewed by author, July 1993. After Curtis LeMay retired, Secretary of the Air Force Zuckert formed a working group to establish a process for the promotion of general officers. Though still subject to influence by networks, this system endured through the mid-1980s.

47. Statistics, Defense Manpower Data Center.

48. Author spreadsheet; Gen Russell E. Dougherty, interviewed by author, 21 June 1992; and Gen John Shaud, interviewed by author, 11 April 1992. The Air Force was having a hard time finding jobs for SAC generals by the early 1980s. The power of a four-star general in large measure resulted from the number of general officers he got promoted; these usually remained loyal to their sponsor. Kelley, interviewed by author, July 1993.

49. Gen John D. Ryan's personal papers, on file at AFHRA, Maxwell AFB, Alabama, 11.

50. J. K. Turnipseed, "Analysis of Crystal Shield 86: The First SAC Innovation Task Force" (Maxwell AFB, Ala.: Air University, April 1987); and Lt Col Clarence O. Herrington Jr., *Innovation in the Strategic Air Command* (Maxwell AFB, Ala.: Air University Press, December 1987), 44. Both authors claimed that an obstinate SAC staff stonewalled efforts of the task force to recommend innovations in SAC in 1986.

51. This is not to say that the TAC commanders were any less authoritarian than SAC predecessors; it is merely to suggest that they elevated the fighter "ethos" to preeminence within the Air Force. Gen Wilbur L. Creech was perhaps most successful in this, though he did enjoy more financial and Air Staff support during his tenure. Kelley, interviewed by author.

52. A. D. Solis, "Strategy for Leading" (Maxwell AFB, Ala.: Air University, April 1988), labels Creech "visionary."

53. Mark K. Holmes, "Potential for Combat Effectiveness of Tactical Air Command Personnel" (Maxwell AFB, Ala.: Air University, April 1986).

54. Futrell, 507; and M. Glenn Abernathy, Dilys M. Hill, and Phil Williams, *The Carter Years: The President and Policy Making* (New York: St. Martin's Press, 1984), 165–91.

55. See Appendix B.

56. See Appendix C.

57. Senate, *Hearing Committee on the Armed Services*, 97th Cong., 2d sess., 19 May 1982, 4.

58. Kotz, 190.

59. Henry Willis Easterling Jr., "Nonmilitary Education in the USAF, 1949–1979" (PhD diss., Indiana University, May 1980), 146; and Kenneth H. Ashworth and William C. Lindley, "The Disgrace of Military Base Programs," *Change*, February 1977, 61.

60. Maj Glen A. Kendrick, "Annotated Bibliography of Research on the USAF Professional Military Education (PME) System" (Maxwell AFB, Ala.: Air University, 1980), 27, 31, 38. Kendrick's research also uncovered several Air University studies during the 1970s that attempted to cut costs and programs.

61. Lt Gen Robert Kelley, interviewed by author, August 1993, and correspondence.

62. Earl H. Tilford Jr., *Setup: What the Air Force Did in Vietnam and Why* (Maxwell AFB, Ala.: Air University Press, 1991), 294–96. Tilford also observes that the Air Force doctrinal manual, AFM 2-1, *Tactical Air Operations—Counter Air, Close Air Support, and Air Interdiction*, was not revised between 1969 and 1989.

63. Ibid.; and Andrew D. Dembosky, "Meeting the Enduring Challenge: United States Air Force Basic Doctrine Through 1992" (master's thesis, North Carolina State University, 1993), 24–33. Dembosky attributes part of the problem to distractions within the Air Staff (AF/XOD), or as one staffer at the time recalled, "Sometimes we feel we are so busy stamping ants [that] we let the elephants come thundering over us." See also Dennis Drew, "Two Decades in the Air Power Wilderness: Do We Know Where We Are?" *Air University Review* 37, no. 6 (September–October 1986): 12; Williamson Murray, "A Tale of Two Doctrines," *Journal of Strategic Studies*, September 1983, passim; and Futrell, 736.

64. The legacy of this influence is plentiful. TAC commander, fighter general Robert D. Russ, in the July–August 1988 *Defense* magazine stated, "Everything that tactical air does directly supports Army operations." Fighter general John T. Chain, SAC commander, in an August 1988 *Air Force* magazine article, offered 66 B-52s for conventional use within a theater; see also Gen John T. Chain, "Strategic Bombers in Conventional Warfare," *Strategic Review*, Spring 1988, 23–32; Lt Col Phillip S. Meilinger, "The Problem with Our Air Power Doctrine," *Airpower Journal* 6, no. 1 (Spring 1992): 27. Meilinger cites a TAC commander in 1991 who asserted "the missions of the tactical air forces are the strategic air defense of the United States and support of the Army. It's as simple as that." If SAC assumed any war with the Soviet Union would be nuclear, and the TAF focused on the air war against massed armies, who integrated a holistic view of airpower that included conventional strategic bombing, the integration of airlift, facilitation of surveillance, special operations, and so forth? Air Force doctrinal manuals in the 1980s did not appear to have an answer.

65. Cited in Robert M. Alexander, "World is Rapidly Changing and Air Force Must Keep Up," *Air Force Times*, 11 February 1991, 23; also cited in Mark Clodfelter, "Of Demons, Storms, and Thunder: A Preliminary Look at

Vietnam's Impact on the Persian Gulf Air Campaign," *Airpower Journal* 5, no. 4 (Winter 1991): 28. General Alexander was the Air Force's director of plans, under the deputy chief of Plans and Operations. He added that during Operation Desert Storm "there was a need for an offensive conventional independent air campaign plan against Iraq. However, there was no provision in the paradigm."

Chapter 9

Conclusion

While I can't prove it, I suspect the absence of a clear mission statement contributed to our reluctance to organize ourselves properly. ***People built loyalties around their commands****—intense loyalties in fact—****rather than loyalties to air and space power as a whole****, to a broader, more comprehensive, mission. So the commands enjoyed support that made it difficult for us to think clearly about our purposes and, hence, our organization.* (Emphasis added)

> —Gen Merrill A. McPeak, chief of staff, USAF
> Policy Letter from the Office of the Secretary
> of the Air Force, November 1992

To a very great degree, all of us are products of our experiences. We are products of our own times and our own experiences. We accept as "truth" only those wisdoms that our experience validates as being true. I would encourage you—as you start down this road of putting different people and things together in a new organizational structure—to recognize that you will not have had an opportunity to experience all of those things that your colleagues have. You will not be able to validate, by your own experience, all of the truths that maybe they have validated by theirs.

> —Gen Russell E. Dougherty, USAF, Retired
> Tactical Air Command Commanders'
> Conference, 8 October 1991

Successful top executives supposedly "stand where they sit." They comprehend well the complex nature of diverse internal dynamics which define their organization. From education and breadth of experience, they grasp how external forces influence within the organization. The struggle of and for the leadership of the Air Force described above differs little from that of other large institutions that attempt to cope with change. The study shows that the champions for influence within the Vietnam-era Air Force were those generals, regardless of specialty, who exploited internal institutional dynamics and grasped new external demands on the military profession better and who were influenced by rapid technological, economic, and political change. This development required education, flexibility of mind, and breadth of military and Capitol Hill experience.

The traumatic, formative war-fighting experience in World War II of a young and narrowly educated yet supremely confident generation of future air force generals colored their perspectives on airpower and warfare. It also circumscribed their future ability to adapt to change. World War II shaped the perspectives of an entire generation, not just Air Force officers. Fresh from the cataclysmic experiences of two world wars and thrust upon the scene as a protector of the free world, the United States sought a way to win or deter the next great war at the least cost. After the supreme effort to destroy fascism, America witnessed the transferal of the root of its security problems to fascism's divorced partner—monolithic communism. The idea of a fiscally cheap "atomic airpower" strategy advocated by the absolutists of the victorious air arm seemed to make strategic sense. America found itself responsible for universal freedom in a different world—faced with nuclear weapons which few understood but everyone feared, especially with an enemy that, we believed, was resolved to do us in. The triumph of communism after World War II reinforced the conviction of the air absolutists in the preeminence of SAC and the efficacy of strategic bombing. This belief ran deepest among the World War II bomber generals, where the intense fight for service independence and preeminence by way of strategic bombing had nourished an absolutist faith that promised strategic airpower would be decisive in itself, as they generally believed it had been in the recent total war.

The insularity and narrow doctrinal focus of SAC on its all-important mission, coupled with the rigid discipline and centralized control demanded by that mission, hampered the dominant bomber generals' ability to contend with the realities of limited war in Vietnam. Led by Generals LeMay and Power, the absolutists remained convinced of the efficacy of manned strategic bombers (despite new technologies) and assumed a national willingness to use atomic weapons that exceeded political realities. With sufficient funding (an increasingly unrealistic premise), the absolutists believed they could win a nuclear war and deter or control smaller wars. As involvement in the Vietnam War grew, absolutists remained to a great extent wedded to their beliefs, but they found their conventional experience little help in a revolutionary war.

More pragmatic views that considered airpower a decisive element in joint warfare prevailed more often within the previously subordinated fighter community. While they too believed in the massive use of airpower, they possessed better equipment for the complex challenges of limited war in the Vietnam era. Flexible Response and the Vietnam War offered this more broadly experienced and educated community the budget, force structure, and combat experience to challenge for senior leadership positions. The fighter community also enjoyed an internal climate that encouraged innovation and delegation. It demanded aggressiveness, flexibility, and versatility—cultural characteristics more attuned to Flexible Response and cultivating future leaders. Additionally, technology increased the range, payload, survivability, accuracy, and flexibility of their systems—even granting access to the sacred strategic bombing role.

By contrast, in an era of limited war, the rise of SLBMs and ICBMs and SALT talks that limited strategic systems further diluted the influence of the bomber arm. Slow bomber procurement programs hurt SAC's morale and reduced its size by the 1970s. The mid-1970s also marked the retirement of most World War II generation generals and the assumption of command of the Air Force by the Korean War generation of predominantly fighter generals—experienced only in limited war. By 1982 these fighter generals were running the Air Force, ultimately because of favorable defense policy (which defined the parameters), beneficial technologies, the Vietnam experience, inherent cultural advantages, and the decline of absolutism in an era of limited war.

Nevertheless, by 1982 the dominant fighter generals faced similar dangers of bias and narrowness of perspective when they too consumed themselves with what they perceived as the principal immediate threat—the massed Warsaw Pact armies. The analogue of SAC's SIOP focus became the TAF's obsession with AirLand Battle.

This historical study ends in 1982 and highlights the enduring dangers of parochialism and bias in any organization that is too homogenous in its senior leadership and culture. Homogeneity, as defined by shared experience, limits a total view of the institution's legitimate role. This organizational condition leans towards myopia and monistic thinking, often manifested in a consuming focus on a purpose or mission that favors the dominant culture. When these organizations face inevitable environmental or contextual change that challenges the existing paradigm, they fail to recognize the need for change because of their uniformity of perspective. This perspective also limits alternatives and adaptability to the change.

Additionally, this study suggests that broad education and experience and a diversity of views at the senior executive level are necessary to cultivate visionary leaders. These leaders must appreciate obvious immediate concerns and manage and anticipate change with a view towards a greater, more holistic, and enduring contribution to the future. These concerns include an understanding of how both internal and external forces influence the institution. For the military, battlefield victory embraces only one dimension of its professional requirements. Sociologist Sam Sarkesian concludes that military leaders "must develop political and social insights to function successfully in today's security environment."[1] "In today's time of geostrategic change, as reflected by the end of the cold war, institutions that maintain broad, pluralistic, and pragmatic perspectives can better recognize and adjust to the new paradigm [or realities]."

For the Air Force, a true understanding of its institutional and cultural past and a realistic assessment of the capabilities and limitations of its doctrinal trinity (globalism, indivisibility, and decisiveness) proved a good start. Ironically, the original air absolutist, Giulio Douhet, once said, "Victory smiles upon those who anticipate the changes in the character of war, not on those who wait to adapt themselves after the changes occur."[2]

Notes

1. Sam Sarkesian, "Two Conceptions of the Military Professional," in Morris Janowitz, *The Military, Militarism, and the Polity: Essays in Honor of Morris Janowitz*, ed. Richard H. Kohn and Joseph P. Harahan (New York: Free Press, 1984), 158. Janowitz states that "battlefield victory is only one dimension of professionalism. . . . The political-sociological nature of warfare must be understood [as well as] arms reduction [and] international peacekeeping." See also Morris Janowitz, *On Social Organization and Social Control*, ed. James Burk (Chicago: University of Chicago Press, 1991), 300.

2. Giulio Douhet, *The Command of the Air,* trans. Dino Ferrari (1942; new imprint, Washington, D.C.: Office of Air Force History, 1983), 30.

Appendix A

Backgrounds of Air Force Senior Leaders 1960

Air Staff

Bombers

Chairman of Joint Chiefs of Staff	Nathan F. Twining
Chief of Staff	Gen Thomas D. White
Vice Chief of Staff	Gen Curtis E. LeMay
Assistant Vice Chief of Staff	Maj Gen Richard M. Montgomery
Deputy Chief of Staff, Development	Lt Gen Roscoe C. Wilson
Deputy Chief of Staff, Personnel	Lt Gen Truman H. Landon
Deputy Chief of Staff, Plans and Programs	Lt Gen John K. Gerhart
Assistant Chief of Staff, Intelligence	Maj Gen James H. Walsh
Assistant Chief of Staff, Reserve Forces	Maj Gen Robert E. L. Eaton
Comptroller of the Air Force	Lt Gen William D. Eckert
Office of the Legislative Liaison	Maj Gen Thomas C. Musgrave Jr.

Fighters

Deputy Chief of Staff Materiel	Lt Gen Mark E. Bradley Jr.
Deputy Chief of Staff Operations	Lt Gen Dean C. Strother

Nonrated (nonflyers)

The Inspector General	Lt Gen Joseph F. Carroll
The Judge Advocate General	Maj Gen Albert M. Kuhfeld
The Surgeon General	Maj Gen Oliver K. Niess
Assistant Chief of Staff for Guided Missiles	Brig Gen Milton B. Adams

Commanders

Bombers

North American Air Defense Command CINC	Laurence S. Kuter
Alaskan Air Command CINC	Lt Gen Frank A. Armstrong Jr.
Air Defense Command	Lt Gen Joseph H. Atkinson
Air Training Command	Lt Gen James E. Briggs
Air Research and Development Command	Lt Gen Bernard A. Schriever
Air Material Command	Gen Samuel E. Anderson
Military Air Transport Service	Lt Gen Joe W. Kelly Jr.
Headquarters Command	Maj Gen Brooke E. Allen

Alaskan Air Command	Maj Gen Conrad F. Necrason
Caribbean Air Command	Maj Gen Leland S. Stranathan
Air University	Lt Gen Walter E. Todd
USAF Security Service	Maj Gen Millard Lewis
Strategic Air Command	Gen Thomas S. Power
Pacific Air Forces CINC	Gen Emmett O'Donnell Jr.
Continental Air Command	Lt Gen William E. Hall

Fighters

| US Air Forces in Europe CINC | Gen Frederic H. Smith Jr. |
| Tactical Air Command | Gen Frank F. Everest |

Generalists

| Supreme Allied Commander Europe | Gen Lauris Norstad |

Appendix B

Backgrounds of Air Force Senior Leaders
1975

Staff

Bombers

Vice Chief of Staff	Gen William V. McBride
Assistant Vice Chief of Staff	Lt Gen Marion L. Boswell
Deputy Chief of Staff, Programs and Resources	Lt Gen James A. Hill
Deputy Chief of Staff, Plans and Operations	Lt Gen John W. Pauly
Deputy Chief of Staff, Systems and Logistics	Lt Gen Robert E. Hails
Assistant Chief of Staff, Intelligence	Maj Gen George J. Keegan Jr.
The Judge Advocate General	Maj Gen Harold R. Vague
Comptroller of the Air Force	Lt Gen Charles E. Buckingham

Fighters

Deputy Chief of Staff, Personnel	Lt Gen Kenneth L. Tallman
Deputy Chief of Staff, Research and Development	Lt Gen Alton D. Slay
Office of the Legislative Liaison	Maj Gen Ralph J. Maglione
Office of Information	Maj Gen Guy E. Hairston Jr.

Generalists

Chairman of Joint Chiefs of Staff	George S. Brown
Chief of Staff	Gen David C. Jones
Director of the Air National Guard	Maj Gen John J. Pesch

Airlift

Chief of Air Force Reserve	Maj Gen William Lyon
Chief of Security Police	Maj Gen Thomas M. Sadler

Nonrated (nonflyers)

The Inspector General	Lt Gen Donald G. Nunn
The Chief of Air Force Chaplains	Maj Gen Henry J. Meade
The Surgeon General	Lt Gen George E. Schafer
Assistant Chief of Staff, Studies and Analysis	Brig Gen Jasper A. Welch Jr.

Commanders

Bombers

Military Airlift Command	Gen Paul K. Carlton
Strategic Air Command	Gen Russell E. Dougherty
Air Force Communications Service	Maj Gen Rupert H. Burris
Chief of Staff, SHAPE	Gen Louis T. Seith
Deputy CINC, US European Command	Gen Robert E. Huyser

Fighters

US Air Forces Southern Command	Maj Gen James M. Breedlove
Tactical Air Command	Gen Robert J. Dixon
Aerospace Defense Command	Gen Daniel James Jr.
Air Force Logistics Command	Gen F. Michael Rogers
Air Training Command	Lt Gen John W. Roberts
Alaskan Air Command	Lt Gen James E. Hill
USAF Security Service	Maj Gen Kenneth D. Burns
Air University	Lt Gen Raymond B. Furlong
Headquarters Command, USAF	Brig Gen William C. Norris
USAF Academy	Lt Gen James R. Allen

Generalists

CINC US Air Forces Europe	Gen Richard H. Ellis
Pacific Air Forces	Gen Louis L. Wilson Jr.

Appendix C

Backgrounds of Air Force Senior Leaders
1982

Staff

Bombers (no input)

Fighters

Chief of Staff	Charles A. Gabriel
Assistant Vice Chief of Staff	Lt Gen Hans H. Driessnach
Comptroller of the Air Force	George M. Browning Jr.
Deputy Chief of Staff, Plans and Operations	Lt Gen John T. Chain Jr.
Deputy Chief of Staff, Logistics and Engineering	Lt Gen Richard E. Merkling
Inspector General	Lt Gen Howard W. Leaf
Chief, Air Force Reserve	Maj Gen Sloan R. Gill
Chief, Air National Guard	Maj Gen John B. Conway

Airlift

Deputy Chief of Staff for Manpower and Personnel	Lt Gen Andrew P. Iosue

Generalists

Deputy Chief of Staff, Research, Development, and Acquisition	Lt Gen Kelly H. Burke
Vice Chief of Staff	Gen Jerome F. O'Malley

Nonrated (nonfliers)

Deputy Chief of Staff, Programs and Resources	Lt Gen Charles C. Blanton

Commanders

Bombers

Air Training Command	Gen Thomas M. Ryan Jr.
Air Force Logistics Command	Gen James P. Mullins
Strategic Air Command	Gen Bennie L. Davis
Chief of Staff, SHAPE	General Lawson
Air Force Communications Command	Maj Gen Robert F. McCarthy

Fighters

US Air Forces in Europe	Gen Billy M. Minter
Tactical Air Command	Gen Wilbur L. Creech
Pacific Air Command	Lt Gen Arnold W. Braswell
Air University	Lt Gen Charles G. Cleveland
USAF Academy	Lt Gen Robert E. Kelley
Military Airlift Command	Gen James R. Allen
Air Force Space Command	James V. Hartinger
Deputy Commander in Chief, US European Command	General W. Y. Smith
Electronic Security Command	Maj Gen Doyle E. Larson

Airlift (no input)

Nonrated (nonfliers)

Air Force Systems Command	Gen Robert T. Marsh

Appendix D

Backgrounds of Air Force Senior Leaders
1990

Staff

Bombers

Office of Legislative Liaison — Brig Gen Brett M. Dula
Assistant Vice Chief of Staff — Lt Gen Carl R. Smith

Fighters

Vice Chairman JCS — Gen Robert Herres
Chief of Staff — Michael J. Dugan
Vice Chief of Staff — Gen John Michael Loh
Director of the National Guard — Maj Gen Phillip G. Killey
The Inspector General — Lt Gen Bradley K. Homer
Assistant Chief of Staff, Studies
  and Analyses — Maj Gen George B. Harrison
Chief of the Air Force Reserve — Maj Gen Roger P. Schemer
Deputy Chief of Staff, Programs
  and Resources — Lt Gen Robert L. Rutherford
Deputy Chief of Staff, Personnel — Lt Gen Thomas J. Hickey
Deputy Chief of Staff, Logistics
  and Engineering — Lt Gen Henry Viccellio Jr.
Deputy Assistant to Secretary of
  Air Force for Acquisition — Lt Gen John E. Jaquish
Deputy Chief of Staff, Plans and Operations — Lt Gen Jimmie Adams

Commanders

Bombers

Military Airlift Command — Gen H. T. Johnson
Air Force Logistics Command — Gen Charles C. McDonald
Chief of Staff, SHAPE — Gen John A. Shaud

Fighters

US Air Forces in Europe — Gen Robert C. Oaks
Tactical Air Command — Gen Robert D. Russ
Strategic Air Command — Gen John T. Chain Jr.
Air Training Command — Lt Gen Joseph W. Ashy

Pacific Air Command	Gen Merrill A. McPeak
Air University	Lt Gen Charles G. Boyd
USAF Academy	Lt Gen Charles R. Hamm
Air Force Systems Command	Gen Ronald W. Yates

Airlift

| Air Force Special Operations Command | Maj Gen Thomas E. Eggers |

Generalists

| CINC North American Aerospace
Defense Command | Gen Donald J. Kutyna |
| Deputy Commander in Chief,
US European Command | Gen James P. McCarthy |

Nonrated (nonfliers)

Air Force Communications Command	Maj Gen Robert H. Ludwig
Air Force Space Command	Lt Gen Thomas S. Moorman Jr.
Electronic Security Command	Maj Gen Gary W. O'Shaughnessy

Bibliography

Primary Sources

Air Force Statistics

Air Force Almanac. Annual special May edition of *Air Force Magazine.*

Defense Manpower Data Center. Computer run. Monterey, Calif., 4 March 1992.

Department of Defense Budget Office. Washington, D.C.

Headquarters Army Air Forces. *U.S. Army Air Forces Statistical Digest: World War II.* Washington, D.C.: Office of Statistical Control, December 1945.

Headquarters USAF. *Air Force Almanac, Annual, 1963–1981.* Bolling Air Force Base (AFB), Washington, D.C.: Office of Air Force History (OAFH).

———. Air Force Military Personnel Center, AFMPC/DPMYAF. Randolph AFB, Tex.

———. *U.S. Air Force Statistical Digest FY 1948–1990.* Bolling AFB, Washington, D.C.: Directorate of Data Systems and Statistics. Comptroller of the Air Force, OAFH.

———. *U.S. Air Force Statistical Digest FY 1957–1978.* Bolling AFB, Washington, D.C.: Directorate of Data Systems and Statistics. Comptroller of the Air Force, OAFH.

Narducci, Henry M. (historian). Offutt AFB, Nebr.: Strategic Air Command Office of History.

Office of the Secretary of the Air Force. Air Force Manpower Statistical Analysis. Washington, D.C.: SAF/FMBMP. Computer run, July 1992.

Biographical Information on Air Force Generals

Air Force Almanac. "USAF Leaders Through the Years." *Air Force Magazine,* May 1989.

257

Neufeld, Jacob. *Organizational Charts, Headquarters USAF, 1947–Present: AFP 210-5*. Washington, D.C.: OAFH, May 1989.

Government Manuals

US Army Manuals

Field Manual (FM) 100-5. *Operations,* 1 July 1976.

War Department. FM 100-20. *Command and Employment of Air Power*. Washington, D.C.: Government Printing Office (GPO), 1943.

Air Force Doctrinal Manuals

Air Force Manual (AFM)1-2. *United States Air Force Basic Doctrine*. Washington, D.C.: GPO, 1 April 1953.

AFM 1-2. *United States Air Force Basic Doctrine*. Washington, D.C.: GPO, 1 April 1954.

———. *United States Air Force Basic Doctrine*. Washington, D.C.: GPO, 1 April 1955.

———. *United States Air Force Basic Doctrine*. Washington, D.C.: GPO, 1 December 1959.

AFM 1-1. *United States Air Force Basic Doctrine*. Washington, D.C.: GPO, 14 August 1964.

———. *United States Air Force Basic Doctrine*. Washington, D.C.: GPO, 28 September 1971.

———. *United States Air Force Basic Doctrine*. Washington, D.C.: GPO, 15 January 1975.

———. *United States Air Force Basic Doctrine*. Washington, D.C.: GPO, 14 February 1979.

———. *United States Air Basic Doctrine*. Washington, D.C.: GPO, 16 March 1984.

AFM 2-1. *Tactical Air Operations—Counter Air, Close Air Support, and Air Interdiction*. Washington, D.C.: GPO, 14 June 1965.

Congressional Records

Committee on the Armed Services, Hearing. *Nominations*. 97th Cong., 2d sess., 1982.

House Subcommittee on Appropriations. *Military Establishment Appropriations Bill for 1948*. 80th Cong., 1st sess., 1947.

House Armed Services Committee Report. *Unification and Strategy*. 81st Cong., 2d sess., 1950.

House Committee on Un-American Activities. *Soviet Total War: Historic Mission of Violence and Deceit*. 85th Cong., 2d sess., 1956.

House Appropriations Committee. Department of Defense Appropriations Subcommittee Hearings. *Department of Defense Appropriations for 1960*. 86th Cong., 1st sess., 1959.

————. *Department of Defense Appropriations for Fiscal Year 1961*. 86th Cong., 2d sess., 1960.

————. *Department of Defense Appropriations for Fiscal Year 1964*. 88th Cong., 1st sess., 1963.

————. *Department of Defense Appropriations for Fiscal Year 1965*. 88th Cong., 2d sess., 1964.

————. Department of Defense Appropriations Subcommittee Hearings: *Department of Defense Authorizations for Appropriations, Fiscal Year 1979*. 95th Cong., 2d sess., 1978.

US Senate. *Hearing Committee on the Armed Services*. 97th Cong., 2d sess., 1982.

Official Air Force Histories

Europe

Headquarters, European Theater of Operations. *Survey of Fighter Pilots in the Eighth Air Force, A Comparison with Heavy Bomber Pilots*. 7 August 1944.

Pacific Studies

Headquarters PACAF. Directorate of Tactical Evaluation. CHECO Division. *SAC Operations in Support of SEA: Special Report*, 17 December 1969.

————. Directorate of Tactical Evaluation. CHECO Division. *Arc Light, June 1967–December 1968*, August 1969.

———. *The Effects of U.S. Air Operations in Southeast Asia: 1965–1968*, November 1969.

———. Directorate of Tactical Evaluation. CHECO Division. *USAF Air Operations Against North Vietnam Operations, 1 July 1972 [sic]–30 June 1972*, 8 June 1973.

———. Directorate of Operations Analysis. CHECO Division. *Linebacker: An Overview of the First 120 Days*, 27 September 1973.

End of Tour Reports

Graham, Gordon M. End of Tour Report, August 1966–July 1967.

Meyers, Gilbert L. End of Tour Report, April 1965–August 1966.

Wehrman, Kenneth E. End of Tour Report, 26 March 1968–20 May 1969.

Strategic Air Command

Headquarters SAC. Strategic Air Command Histories, 1948–1990. Offutt AFB, Nebr., 1949–1991.

Tactical Air Command

History. Tactical Air Command, Vol. 1, 1946.

———. Tactical Air Command, 1948.

———. Tactical Air Command, Vol 1, January–June 1954.

———. Tactical Air Command, January–June 1955.

———. Tactical Air Command, July–December 1958.

———. Tactical Air Command, January–June 1959.

———. Tactical Air Command, July–December 1959.

———. Tactical Air Command, January–June 1961.

———. Tactical Air Command, 1 January–30 June 1961, supporting documents.

———. Tactical Air Command, Vol. 1, 1961–1962.

Studies

US Government Studies

Douhet, Giulio. *The Command of the Air.* 1942. Reprint, Washington, D.C.: OAFH, 1983.

Grinker, Roy R., Sr., and John P. Spiegel. *Men Under Stress.* Philadelphia: Blakiston Company, 1945.

Link, Mae Mills, and Hubert A. Coleman. *Medical Support of the Army Air Forces in World War II.* Washington, D.C.: Office of the Surgeon General, 1955.

Perry, Robert L. *The Interaction of Technology and Doctrine in the United States Air Force.* Santa Monica, Calif.: RAND Publication no. 197908-18, 1979.

Quanbeck, Alton H., and Archie L. Wood. *Modernizing the Strategic Bomber Force: Why and How.* Washington, D.C.: Brookings Institute, 1976.

Stouffer, Samuel A., et al. *Studies in Social Psychology in World War II.* Vol. 2, *The American Soldier: Combat and its Aftermath.* Princeton, N.J.: Princeton University Press, 1949.

————. *Studies in Psychology in World War II.* Vol. 1, *The American Soldier: Adjustment During Army Life.* Princeton, N.J.: Princeton University Press.

US Government. *United States Strategic Bombing Survey Summary Report (European War)* no. 1. Washington, D.C.: GPO, 30 September 1945.

————. *United States Strategic Bombing Survey Summary Report (Pacific War)* no. 1. Washington, D.C.: GPO, 1 July 1946.

Air Force Studies

Air University/RSI Study. "The Relationship Between Past and Present Strategic and Tactical Concepts." Air Force Historical Research Agency (AFHRA), Maxwell AFB, Ala., June 1961.

Board of Visitors (1963), Air University. *AU Ten Year Plan.* Maxwell AFB, Ala.: Air University, February 1964.

Fairchild, Muir S. *Report of the USAF Military Education Board on the Professional Education System for USAF Officers (Fairchild Board).* Maxwell AFB, Ala., 24–25 January 1950.

Fine, Paul M., and Bryce O. Hartman. "Psychiatric Strengths and Weaknesses of Typical Air Force Pilots." Brooks AFB, Tex.: USAF School of Aerospace Medicine, 1968.

Grappe, Ludrew B., Ray W. Alvord, and James V. Poland. *Air Force Officer Performance Evaluation: Rating Trends and Relationships from 1954 through 1965*. Lackland AFB, Tex.: Personnel Research Laboratory, October 1967.

Lightner Board. *Review of Air War College and Air Command and Staff College*. Maxwell AFB, Ala.: Air University, March 1973.

Orleans, Jacob S., chairman (Orleans Board). *A Report to the Commanding General, Air University, of an Educational Survey of the Air Command and Staff School, Headquarters Air University*. Maxwell AFB, Ala., September 1949.

Rawlings, Edward W., Gen, USAF, chairman (Rawlings Board). *Report of the USAF Educational Conference of 18–19 October 1956*. Maxwell AFB, Ala., November 1956.

Richardson, Col R. C., III. AFXPD-LR Staff Study. *The Development and Dissemination of Long-Range USAF Organized Changes*. AFHRA, Maxwell AFB, Ala., 23 October 1959.

Tyler, Ralph W. (Tyler Board). *Analysis of the Purpose, Pattern, Scope, and Structure of the Officer Education Program at Air University*. Maxwell AFB, Ala., May 1955.

Westbrook, Sam. "UPT Assignment System." Briefing. Air Training Command, 1991.

Government Documents

Air University Publications

Books

Hansell, Haywood S., Jr. *Strategic Air War Against Japan*. Maxwell AFB, Ala.: Air War College, 1980.

McCarthy, James R., and George B. Allison. *Linebacker II: A View From the Rock*. Maxwell AFB, Ala.: Airpower Research Institute, 1979.

Studies and Research Papers

Bull, Stephen D. "Job Attitudes—How SAC Personnel Compare With the Rest of the Air Force." Maxwell AFB, Ala.: Air University, April 1986.

Chappelle, Robert L. "Replacement Training Within SAC a Result of U.S. Involvement in Southeast Asia." Maxwell AFB, Ala.: Air University, 1971.

Chase, Levi R. "A Global Mission for TAC." Thesis. Maxwell AFB, Ala.: Air University, April 1956.

Dougherty, Gen Russell E., USAF, Retired. Address. Tactical Air Command Commanders' Conference, Tyndall AFB, Fla., 8 October 1991.

Finamore, Ronald P. "Strategic Air Command Aircrew Considerations." Maxwell AFB, Ala., May 1973.

Frederick, John P. "Good Management Can Help to Reduce the Irritants of the SAC Alert." Maxwell AFB, Ala., May 1972.

Funk, Dale R. "Study of the Use of B-52 Bombers in War in Vietnam." Air War College Report no. 3350. Maxwell AFB, Ala., May 1967.

Gray, William R. "The Case for Combining SAC and TAC." Maxwell AFB, Ala.: Air University, March 1957.

Holmes, Mark K. "Potential for Combat Effectiveness of Tactical Air Command Personnel." Maxwell AFB, Ala.: Air University, April 1986.

Karle, D. D., and J. B. Hall. "Integrating Strategic and Tactical Airpower in Conventional Warfare: B-52 Employment." Maxwell AFB, Ala., May 1988.

Kendrick, Maj Glen A. "Annotated Bibliography of Research on the USAF Professional Military Education (PME) System." Maxwell AFB, Ala.: Air University, 1980.

Kennedy, J. K. "Job Attitudes of SAC Pilots Compared." Maxwell AFB, Ala.: Air University, April 1986.

Klocko, Richard P. "Air Power in Limited Military Actions." Graduate study group thesis. Maxwell AFB, Ala.: Air University, 1954.

Madden, Dewan D. "Tactical Fighter Pilot Selection Considerations." Report. Maxwell AFB, Ala.: Air University, 1973.

Shiver, Lt Col Morris E. "Retention of Junior Officers in the Strategic Air Command." Air War College Report no. 3167. Maxwell AFB, Ala., January 1966.

Solis, A. D. "Strategy for Leading." Maxwell AFB, Ala.: Air University, April 1988.

Teixeira, Leonard D. G. "Linebacker II: A Strategic and Tactical Case Study." Maxwell AFB, Ala.: Air University, April 1990.

Turnipseed, J. K. "Analysis of Crystal Shield 86: The First SAC Innovation Task Force." Maxwell AFB, Ala.: Air University, April 1987.

Miscellaneous Government Documents

Kohn, Richard H., and Joseph Harahan, eds. *Strategic Air Warfare: An Interview with Curtis E. LeMay, Leon W. Johnson, David A. Burchinal, and Jack J. Catton.* Washington, D.C.: OAFH, 1988.

———. *Air Interdiction in World War II, Korea, and Vietnam: An Interview with Earle E. Partridge, Jacob E. Smart, and John Vogt, Jr.* Washington, D.C.: OAFH, 1986.

———. *Air Superiority in World War II and Korea: An Interview with Gen James Ferguson, Gen Robert M. Lee, Gen William Momyer, and Lt Gen Elwood R. Quesada.* Washington, D.C.: OAFH, 1983.

Momyer, William W. *Airpower in Three Wars: WWII, Korea, Vietnam.* Washington, D.C.: GPO, 1978.

The Pentagon Papers: The Defense Department History of the United States Decision-making in Vietnam. Gravel edition. 5 vols. Boston: Beacon Press, 1971.

Putney, Diane T., ed. *ULTRA and the Army Air Forces in World War II: An Interview with Associate Justice of the U.S. Supreme Court Lewis F. Powell Jr.* Washington, D.C.: OAFH, 1987.

Rice, Donald E. *Policy Letter from the Office of the Secretary of the Air Force,* November 1992.

Seamans, Dr. Robert C., Jr. "Continuing Cooperation between NASA and DoD." Address. 1969 Air Force Association Convention, Houston, Tex., 16 March 1969.

Talbott, Harold E. "Statement of Policy, Information, and Education of the Armed Forces." *Air Force Letter 34-23.* Washington, D.C.: Department of the Air Force, 24 September 1953.

US Army. "Army Life and United States Army Recruiting News." Governors Island, N.Y.: Recruiting Publicity Bureau, US Army, December 1943.

Personal Papers

Arnold, Gen Henry H., US Army Air Forces. Personal papers. "Report of the Army H. H. Arnold, Commanding General, Army Air Forces, Air Power and the Future, 1945." Copy found in Walter Millis, ed., *American Military Thought.* New York: Bobbs-Merrill Company, 1966.

————. US Army Air Forces. Personal Papers. *Third Report of the Commanding General of the Army Air Forces to the Secretary of War, 12 November 1945.* US Military History Institute, Carlisle Barracks, Pa.

Ryan, Gen John D., USAF. Personal papers. On file at AFHRA, Maxwell AFB, Ala.

Books

Arnold, Henry H., and Ira C. Eaker. *Winged Warfare.* New York: Harper and Brothers, 1941.

Blesse, Frederick C. *Check Six: A Fighter Pilot Looks Back.* New York: Ivy Books, 1987.

Broughton, Jack. *Going Downtown: The War Against Hanoi and Washington.* New York: Orion Books, 1988.

————. *Thud Ridge.* New York: Bantam Books, 1969.

Chennault, Claire Lee. *Way of a Fighter: The Memoirs of Claire Lee Chennault.* Edited by Robert B. Hotz. New York: G. Putnam Sons, 1949.

Ginsburgh, Robert N. *U.S. Military Strategy in the Sixties.* New York: Norton and Company, 1965.

Kennedy, Robert F. *Thirteen Days: A Memoir of the Cuban Missile Crisis.* New York: W. W. Norton and Company, 1969.

Kissinger, Henry A. *The White House Years.* Boston: Little, Brown and Company, 1979.

Komer, Robert W. *Bureaucracy at War: U.S. Performance in the Vietnam Conflict.* Boulder, Colo.: Westview Press, 1986.

LeMay, Curtis E. *America Is in Danger*. New York: Funk & Wagnalls, 1968.

LeMay, Curtis E., and Bill Yenne. *Superfortress: The Story of the B-29 and American Air Power and World War II*. New York: McGraw-Hill, 1988.

LeMay, Curtis E., with MacKinlay Kantor. *Mission with LeMay: My Story*. Garden City, N.Y.: Doubleday, 1965.

Nixon, Richard M. *RN: The Memoirs of Richard Nixon*. 2 vols. New York: Warner Books, 1978.

Palmer, Bruce, Jr. *The 25-Year War: America's Military Role in Vietnam*. Lexington, Ky.: University of Kentucky, 1984.

Power, Thomas S. *Design for Survival*. New York: Coward-McCann, 1965.

Taylor, Maxwell D. *The Uncertain Trumpet*. New York: Harper and Brothers, 1959.

Twining, Nathan F. *Neither Liberty nor Safety: A Hard Look at U.S. Military Policy and Strategy*. New York: Holt, Rinehart and Winston, 1966.

Articles

Allison, George B. "Bombers Go to Bullseye." *Aerospace Historian*, Winter 1982, 227–38.

Chain, Gen John T. "Strategic Bombers in Conventional Warfare." *Strategic Review*, Spring 1988, 23–32.

Drenkowski, Drew. "Operation Linebacker II." *Soldier of Fortune* 2, no. 3 (September 1977): 24.

Hurley, Alfred E., and Robert C. Ehrhart, eds. "The Perceptions of Three Makers of Air Power History." *Air Power and Warfare: Proceedings of the Military History Symposium, United States Air Force Academy*. Washington, D.C.: OAFH, 1979, 186–97.

LeMay, Curtis E. "Future of Manned Bombers." *Ordnance*, September–October 1958, 202–5.

Pegasus (pseud). "The Forty-Year Split. The Second Twenty Years: 1940–1960." *Army*, August 1965, 59.

Power, Thomas S. "How Much Can Missiles Really Do?" *Air Force*, September 1956, 105–6.

———. "Manned Aircraft Requirement in the 1970s." *Air Force*, November 1963, 96.

———. "A Sure Way to Prevent Nuclear War." *U.S. News & World Report*, 25 January 1965, 72–76.

Richardson, Robert C., III. "In the Looking Glass." *Air University Quarterly Review* 9, no. 4 (Winter 1957–1958): 46–54.

Spaatz, Gen Carl A. "Strategic Air Power: Fulfillment of a Concept." *Foreign Affairs*, April 1946, 385–96.

Secondary Sources

Air Force Organizational Histories

General

Berger, Carl, ed. *The United States Air Force in Southeast Asia, 1961–1973: An Illustrated Account.* Washington, D.C.: OAFH, 1984.

Craven, Wesley Frank, and James Lea Cate, eds. *The Army Air Forces in World War II.* Vol. 6, *Men and Planes.* 1955. New imprint, Washington, D.C.: OAFH, 1983.

———. *The Army Air Forces in World War II.* Vol. 1, *Plans and Early Operations.* Washington, D.C.: OAFH, 1955.

Davis, Richard G. *The 31 Initiatives: A Study in Air Force-Army Cooperation.* Washington, D.C.: OAFH, 1987.

Goldberg, Alfred, ed. *A History of the United States Air Force, 1907–1957.* Princeton, N.J.: D. Van Nostrand, 1957.

Greer, Thomas H. *The Development of Air Doctrine in the Army Air Arm, 1917–1941.* Washington, D.C.: OAFH, 1985.

Strategic Air Command

Anderton, David A. *Strategic Air Command: Two Thirds of the Triad.* New York: Scribner, 1976.

Hopkins, Charles K. *The Development of Strategic Air Command: 1946–1981 (40th Anniversary).* Offutt AFB, Nebr.: Office of SAC History, 1986.

Longacre, Edward G. *Strategic Air Command: The Formative Years: 1944–1949.* Offutt AFB, Nebr.: Office of the Historian, 1990.

Yenne, Bill. *SAC: A Primer of Modern Strategic Airpower.* Novato, Calif.: Presidio Press, 1985.

Tactical Air Command

Richards, Leverett G. *TAC: The Story of Tactical Air Command.* New York: John Day Company, 1961.

Government Documents

Air University Publications

Davis, Richard L., and Frank P. Donnini. *Professional Military Education for Air Force Officers: Comments and Criticisms.* Maxwell AFB, Ala.: Air University Press, 1991.

Dorfler, Joseph F. *The Branch Point Study: Specialized Undergraduate Pilot Training.* Research Report no. AU-ARI-86-5. Maxwell AFB, Ala.: Air University Press, 1986.

Drew, Col Dennis M. *Rolling Thunder 1965: Anatomy of a Failure.* Research Report no. AU-ARI-CP-86-3. Maxwell AFB, Ala.: Air University Press, 1986.

Futrell, Robert Frank. *Ideas, Concepts, Doctrine: Basic Thinking in the United States Air Force, 1907–1960.* Vol. 1. Maxwell AFB, Ala.: Air University Press, 1989.

———. *Ideas, Concepts, Doctrine: Basic Thinking in the United States Air Force, 1961–1984.* Vol. 2. Maxwell AFB, Ala.: Air University Press, 1989.

Herrington, Lt Col Clarence O., Jr. *Innovation in the Strategic Air Command.* Maxwell AFB, Ala.: Air University Press, December 1987.

Mrozek, Donald J. *Airpower and the Ground War in Vietnam: Ideas and Actions.* Maxwell AFB, Ala.: Air University Press, 1988.

Stokes, Richard W. *Preserving the Lambent Flame: Traditional Values and the USAF Officer Accession Program.* Maxwell AFB, Ala.: Air University Press, 1984.

Tilford, Earl H., Jr. *Setup: What the Air Force Did in Vietnam and Why.* Maxwell AFB, Ala.: Air University Press, 1991.

Other Government Documents

Frisbee, John L., ed. *Makers of the United States Air Force.* Washington, D.C.: OAFH, 1987.

Herring, George C. "'Cold Blood': LBJ's Conduct of Limited War in Vietnam." The Harmon Memorial Lectures in Military History. Colorado Springs, Colo.: USAF Academy, 1990.

Keaney, Thomas A. *Strategic Bombers and Conventional Weapons: Airpower Options.* Fort Lesley J. McNair, Washington, D.C.: National Defense University Press, 1984.

Knaack, Marcelle. *Encyclopedia of USAF Aircraft and Missile Systems.* Vol. 1, *Post-World War II Fighters.* Washington, D.C.: OAFH, 1978.

———. *Encyclopedia of USAF Aircraft and Missile Systems.* Vol. 2, *Post-World War II Bombers.* Washington, D.C.: OAFH, 1988.

Lavalle, A. J. C., ed. *The Tale of Two Bridges and the Battle for the Skies Over North Vietnam.* Washington, D.C.: GPO, 1976.

Nalty, Bernard C. *Air Power and the Fight for Khe Sanh.* Washington, D.C.: OAFH, 1986.

Neufeld, Jacob. *The Development of Ballistic Missiles in the United States Air Force, 1945–1960.* Washington, D.C.: OAFH, 1990.

Schlight, John. *The War in South Vietnam—The Years of the Offensive, 1965–1968.* Washington, D.C.: OAFH, 1988.

Wolk, Herman S. *Planning and Organizing the Postwar Air Force, 1943–1947.* Washington, D.C.: OAFH, 1984.

Dissertations/Theses

Caddell, Joseph W. "Orphan of Unification: The Development of United States Air Force Tactical Air Power Doctrine, 1945–1950." PhD diss., Duke University, 1984.

Dembosky, Andrew D. "Meeting the Enduring Challenge: United States Air Force Basic Doctrine Through 1992." Master's thesis, North Carolina State University, 1993.

Easterling, Henry Willis, Jr. "Nonmilitary Education in the USAF, 1949–1979." PhD diss., Indiana University, May 1980.

Martin, Jerome V. "Reforging the Sword: United States Tactical Air Forces, Air Power Doctrine, and National Security Policy, 1945–1956." PhD diss., Ohio State University, 1988.

Reed, George. "U.S. Defense Policy, U.S. Air Force Doctrine and Strategic Nuclear Weapon Systems, 1958–1964: The Case of the Minuteman ICBM." PhD diss., Duke University, 1986.

Wells, Mark K. "Aviators and Air Combat." PhD diss., King's College, London, 1992.

Ziemke, Caroline. "In the Shadow of the Giant: USAF Tactical Air Command in the Era of Strategic Bombing, 1945–1955." PhD diss., Ohio State University, 1989.

Unpublished Manuscripts

Biddle, Tami D. "How Much Can an Economy Devote to Defense?" Paper presented at the International Security and Arms Control Program, Yale University, New Haven, Conn., 2 October 1988.

MacIsaac, David. "The Air Force and Strategic Thought, 1945–1951." International Security Studies Program Working Paper no. 8, 21 June 1979.

Mitchell, Vance O. "The First Generation: A Policy History of the Air Force Officer Corps, 1944–1973." Unpublished manuscript, OAFH, May 1991.

Books

Abernathy, M. Glenn, Dilys M. Hill, and Phil Williams. *The Carter Years: The President and Policy Making.* New York: St. Martin's Press, 1984.

Armitage, M. J., and R. A. Mason. *Air Power in the Nuclear Age.* Urbana, Ill.: University of Illinois Press, 1983.

Beard, Edmund. *Developing the ICBM: A Study in Bureaucratic Politics.* New York: Columbia University Press, 1976.

Betts, Richard K. *Soldiers, Statesmen, and Cold War Crises.* Cambridge, Mass.: Harvard University Press, 1977.

Bletz, Donald F. *The Role of the Military Profession in U.S. Foreign Policy.* New York: Praeger Publishers, 1972.

Borowski, Harry R. *A Hollow Threat: Strategic Air Power and Containment Before Korea.* Westport, Conn.: Greenwood Press, 1982.

Braestrup, Peter, ed. *Vietnam as History: Ten Years After the Paris Peace Accords.* Wilson Center Conference Report Series 2108. Washington, D.C.: University Press of America, 1984.

Brodie, Bernard. *War and Politics.* New York: Macmillan, 1973.

———. *Strategy in the Missile Age.* Princeton, N.J.: Princeton University Press, 1959.

Builder, Carl H. *The Masks of War: American Military Styles in Strategy and Analysis.* Baltimore: Johns Hopkins University Press, 1989.

Clarfield, Gerard H., and William M. Wiecek. *Nuclear America: Military and Civilian Nuclear Power in the United States, 1940–1980.* New York: Harper and Row, 1984.

Clodfelter, Mark. *The Limits of Air Power: The American Bombing of North Vietnam.* New York: Free Press, 1989.

Coffey, Thomas M. *Iron Eagle: The Turbulent Life of General Curtis LeMay.* New York: Crown Publishers, 1986.

Dorr, Robert F. *Air War Hanoi.* London: Blandford Press, 1988.

Eschmann, Karl J. *Linebacker: The Untold Story of the Air Raids Over North Vietnam.* New York: Ivy Books, 1989.

Freedman, Lawrence. *The Evolution of Nuclear Strategy.* London: Macmillan Press, 1981.

Gavin, James M. *War and Peace in the Space Age.* New York: Harper, 1958.

Goodwin, Doris Kearns. *Lyndon Johnson and the American Dream.* New York: Harper and Row, 1976.

Hadley, Arthur T. *A Report From the Field: The Straw Giant.* New York: Random House, 1986.

Halberstam, David. *The Best and The Brightest.* New York: Random House, 1969.

Halperin, Morton H. *Bureaucratic Politics and Foreign Policy.* Washington, D.C.: Brookings Institute, 1974.

Hammond, Paul Y. *Super Carriers and B-36 Bombers: Appropriations, Strategy, and Politics.* Interuniversity Case Program no. 97. New York: Bobbs-Merrill Company, 1966.

Huntington, Samuel. *The Common Defense: Strategic Programs in National Politics*. New York: Columbia University Press, 1961.

Janowitz, Morris. *The Professional Soldier: A Social and Political Portrait*. Glencoe, Ill.: Free Press, 1960.

———. *On Social Organization and Social Control*. Edited by James Burk. Chicago: University of Chicago Press, 1991.

Johnson, David T., and Barry R. Schneider. *Current Issues in U.S. Defense Policy*. Washington, D.C.: Center for Defense Information, 1991.

Kaplan, Fred. *The Wizards of Armageddon*. New York: Simon and Schuster, 1983.

Korb, Lawrence J. *The Joint Chiefs of Staff: The First Twenty-five Years*. Bloomington, Ind.: Indiana University Press, 1976.

Kotz, Nick. *Wild Blue Yonder: Money, Politics, and the B-1 Bomber*. New York: Pantheon Books, 1988.

Lowe, George. *The Age of Deterrence*. Boston: Little and Brown, 1964.

MacIsaac, David. *Strategic Bombing in World War II: The Story of the United States Strategic Bombing Survey*. New York: Garland Publishing, 1976.

MacKenzie, Donald A. *Inventing Accuracy: A Historical Sociology of Nuclear Missile Guidance*. Cambridge, Mass.: MIT Press, 1990.

Masland, John W., and Laurence I. Radway. *Soldiers and Scholars: Military Education and National Policy*. Princeton, N.J.: Princeton University Press, 1957.

Millis, Walter. *American Military Thought*. New York: Bobbs-Merrill Company, 1966.

———. *Arms and Men: A Study in American Military History*. New York: Putnam, 1956.

———. *The Forrestal Diaries*. New York: Viking Press, 1951.

Mills, C. Wright. *The Power Elite*. New York: Oxford University Press, 1956.

Newhouse, John. *War and Peace in the Nuclear Age*. New York: Knopf, 1990.

Osgood, Robert Endicott. *Limited War: The Challenge to American Strategy.* Chicago: University of Chicago Press, 1957.

Overy, R. J. *The Air War: 1939–1945.* New York: Stein and Day, 1980.

Perry, Mark. *Four Stars: The Inside Story of the Forty-five Year Battle Between the Joints Chiefs of Staff and America's Civilian Leaders.* Boston: Houghton Mifflin, 1988.

Prados, John. *The Soviet Estimate: U.S. Intelligence Analysis and Soviet Strategic Forces.* Princeton, N.J.: Princeton University Press, 1982.

————. *The Sky Would Fall: Operation Vulture.* New York: Dial Press, 1983.

Puryear, Edgar F., Jr. *George S. Brown, General, USAF: Destined for Stars.* Novato, Calif.: Presidio Press, 1983.

————. *Stars in Flight: A Study in Air Force Character and Leadership.* San Rafael, Calif.: Presidio Press, 1981.

Rostow, Walt W. *The United States in the World Arena: An Essay in Recent History.* New York: Simon and Schuster, 1960.

Sarkesian, Sam C. *The Professional Army Officer in a Changing Society.* Chicago: Nelson-Hall, 1975.

Schelling, Thomas C. *The Strategy of Conflict.* Cambridge, Mass.: Harvard University Press, 1960.

————. *Arms and Influence.* New Haven, Conn.: Yale University Press, 1966.

Schlesinger, Arthur M., Jr. *A Thousand Days: John F. Kennedy in the White House.* Boston: Houghton Mifflin, 1965.

Selznick, Philip. *Leadership in Administration: A Sociological Interpretation.* Evanston, Ill.: Row, Peterson, 1957.

Sherry, Michael S. *The Rise of American Air Power: The Creation of Armageddon.* New Haven, Conn.: Yale University Press, 1987.

Smith, Perry McCoy. *The Air Force Plans for Peace, 1943–1945.* Baltimore: Johns Hopkins University Press, 1970.

Sorensen, Theodore C. *Kennedy.* New York: Harper and Row, 1965.

Steinberg, Alfred. *Sam Johnson's Boy: A Close-up of the President from Texas.* New York: Macmillan, 1968.

Thayer, Thomas C. *War Without Fronts: The American Experience in Vietnam.* Boulder, Colo.: Westview Press, 1985.

Webb, Willard J., and Ronald H. Cole. *The Chairmen of the Joint Chiefs of Staff.* Washington, D.C.: GPO, 1989.

Weigley, Russell Frank. *The American Way of War: A History of United States Military Strategy and Policy.* New York: Macmillan, 1973.

Wise, David, and Thomas B. Ross. *The Invisible Government.* New York: Vintage Books, 1964.

Wolfe, Thomas. *The Right Stuff.* New York: Farrar, Straus, Giroux, 1979.

York, Herbert F. *Race to Oblivion.* New York: Simon and Schuster, 1979.

Articles

Magazine Articles

Ashworth, Kenneth H., and William C. Lindley. "The Disgrace of Military Base Programs." *Change,* February 1977, 61.

Lewis, Flora. "The Education of a Senator." *The Atlantic,* December 1971, 56.

Newspaper Articles

Alexander, Robert M. "World is Rapidly Changing and Air Force Must Keep Up." *Air Force Times,* 11 February 1991.

Bird, Julie. "Fighter Mafia Taking Over." *Air Force Times,* 1 February 1993.

Kraar, L. "Defense Strategy." *Wall Street Journal,* 16 February 1961.

Staff. "Education Level Must be Higher, Air Force Warns Again." *Air Force Times* 10, no. 18, 8 October 1949.

Journal Articles

Brodie, Bernard. "The Heritage of Douhet." *Air University Quarterly Review* 6, no. 2 (Summer 1953): 126–27.

Clodfelter, Mark. "Of Demons, Storms, and Thunder: A Preliminary Look at Vietnam's Impact on the Persian Gulf Air Campaign." *Airpower Journal* 5, no. 4 (Winter 1991): 17–32.

de Seversky, Alexander P. "A Lecture on Air Power." *Air University Quarterly Review* 1, no. 2 (Fall 1947): 25–43.

Dickman, Lt Col Joseph L. "Douhet and the Future." *Air University Quarterly Review* 2, no. 1 (Summer 1948): 3–15.

Drew, Col Dennis M. "Two Decades in the Air Power Wilderness: Do We Know Where We Are?" *Air University Review* 37, no. 6 (September–October 1986): 2–13.

Greenwood, John T. "The Atomic Bomb—Early Air Force Thinking and the Strategic Air Force, August 1945–March 1946." *Aerospace Historian* 34, no. 3 (Fall/September 1987): 158–66.

Healy, Col John P. "Air Power and Foreign Policy." *Air University Quarterly Review* 2, no. 2 (Fall 1948): 15–27.

Hilsman, Roger. "Research in Military Affairs." *World Politics*, no. 7 (1954): 502.

Hopkins, Charles K. "Linebacker II: A Firsthand View." *Aerospace Historian*, Fall 1976, 128–34.

Kanter, Arnold. "Managerial Careers of Air Force Generals: A Test of the Janowitz Convergence Hypothesis." *Journal of Political and Military Sociology*, Spring 1976, 121–33.

———. "The Career Patterns of Air Force Generals." *American Journal of Political Science* 21, no. 2 (May 1977): 353–79.

Keefer, Edward C. "President Dwight D. Eisenhower and the End of the Korean War." *Diplomatic History*, Summer 1986, 267–89.

Margiotta, Franklin D. "A Military Elite in Transition." *Armed Forces and Society* 2, no. 2 (Winter 1976): 155–84.

Meilinger, Phillip S. "The Problem with Our Air Power Doctrine." *Airpower Journal* 6, no. 1 (Spring 1992): 24–31.

Murray, Williamson. "A Tale of Two Doctrines." *Journal of Strategic Studies*, September 1983.

Pancake, Lt Col Frank R. "The Strategic Striking Force." *Air University Quarterly Review* 2, no. 2 (Fall 1948): 48–56.

Parrish, Col Noel F. "New Responsibilities of Air Force Officers." *Air University Quarterly Review* 1, no. 1 (Spring 1947): 29–42.

Parton, James. "The Thirty-One Year Gestation of the Independent USAF." *Aerospace Historian* 34, no. 3 (Fall/September 1987): 150–57.

Rabinowitz, Eugene. "Atomic Weapons and the Korean War." *Bulletin of Atomic Scientists,* no. 6.

Rosenberg, David Alan. "The Origins of Overkill: Nuclear Weapons and American Strategy, 1945–1960." *International Security,* Spring 1983, 3–71.

Slater, Jerome. "Apolitical Warrior or Soldier-Statesman: The Military and the Foreign Policy Process in the Post Vietnam Era." *Armed Forces and Society,* Fall 1977, 103–8.

South, Oron P. "The Door to the Future." *Air University Quarterly Review* 9, no. 4 (Winter 1957–58): 110–26.

Staff. "Missiles Have No Discretion, Reliability Still Low, AFA Told, 'Need Man in Airplane.'" *Army, Navy Air Force Journal* (March 1958): 3.

Stiles, Dennis W. "Air Power: A New Look From an Old Rooftop." *Air University Review* 27, no. 1 (November–December 1975): 49–59.

Stone, Robert C. "Status and Leadership in a Combat Fighter Squadron." *American Journal of Sociology* (March 1946): 388–95.

Wamsley, Gary L. "Contrasting Institutions of Air Force Socialization: Happenstance or Bellwether?" *American Journal of Sociology* 78, no. 2 (September 1972): 399–417.

Watson, George M., Jr. "Man in the Middle: Eugene Zuckert as Secretary of the Air Force." *Air Power History* 36, no. 24 (1989): 20–29.

White, Thomas D. *Army, Navy, Air Force Journal,* 7 May 1955.

Wolk, Herman S. "Planning and Organizing the Air Force." *Aerospace Historian* 34, no. 3 (Fall/September 1987): 167–75.

Articles in Books

Futrell, Robert F. "The Influence of the Air Power Concept on Air Force Planning, 1945–1962." In *Military Planning in the Twentieth Century: Proceedings of the Eleventh Military History Symposium, USAF Academy, 1984.* Washington, D.C.: OAFH, 1986, 253–75.

Greenwood, John T. "The Emergence of the Postwar Strategic Air Force, 1945–1953." In *Air Power and Warfare: The Proceedings of the Eighth Military History Symposium, United States Air Force Academy, 18–20 October 1978.* Edited by Alfred F. Hurley and Robert C. Ehrhart. Washington, D.C.: OAFH, 1979, 215–44.

Huntington, Samuel. "After Containment: The Functions of the Military Establishment." In the *Annals of the American Academy of Political and Social Science: The Military and American Society,* March 1973, 3–15.

Lang, Kurt. "Technology and Career Management in the Military Establishment." In *The New Military: Changing Patterns of Organization.* Edited by Morris Janowitz. New York: Russell Sage Foundation, 1964, 77.

MacIsaac, David. "The Evolution of Air Power Since 1945: The American Experience." In *War in the Third Dimension: Essays in Contemporary Air Power.* Edited by R. A. Mason. Washington, D.C.: Brassey's Defence Publishers, 1986, 11–32.

———. "Voices From the Central Blue: The Air Power Theorists." In *Makers of Modern Strategy From Machiavelli to the Nuclear Age.* Edited by Peter Paret. Princeton, N.J.: Princeton University Press, 1986, 624–47.

Perry, Robert. "The Interaction of Technology and Doctrine in the USAF." In *Air Power and Warfare: The Proceedings of the Eighth Military History Symposium, United States Air Force Academy, 18–20 October 1978.* Edited by Col Alfred F. Hurley and Maj Robert C. Ehrhart. Washington, D.C.: OAFH, 1979, 386–401.

Sarkesian, Sam. "Two Conceptions of the Military Professional." In Morris Janowitz, *The Military, Militarism, and the Polity: Essays in Honor of Morris Janowitz.* Edited by Michael L. Martin and Ellen S. McCrate. New York: Free Press, 1984, 156–65.